Kabul Classroom

Kabul Classroom

Memoir of an American Teacher in Afghanistan

P. B. TRAVIS

McFarland & Company, Inc., Publishers

Jefferson, North Carolina, and London

ACKNOWLEDGMENTS: I would like to give thanks to my friend Joanna; without her gentle nagging this memoir would never have been started. To my "readers," for their thoughtful comments and suggestions. To my sister, Jo, for her encouragement. And to my son, Jason, for being such a good guy.

LIBRARY OF CONGRESS CATALOGUING-IN-PUBLICATION DATA

Travis, P. B. (Penny B.)
    Kabul classroom : memoir of an American teacher in
Afghanistan / P. B. Travis.
      p.   cm.
    Includes bibliographical references and index.

    ISBN 978-0-7864-7637-4 (softcover : acid free paper) ∞
    ISBN 978-1-4766-0623-1 (ebook)

    1. Travis, P. B. (Penny B.) 2. Educators—United States—
Biography. 3. College teaching—Afghanistan. 4. Teachers—
Afghanistan—Kabul. 5. Americans—Afghanistan—Kabul.
6. Afghan War, 2001—Personal narratives, American. I. Title.

LA2317.T724A3 2014
370.92—dc23
[B]   2013041030

BRITISH LIBRARY CATALOGUING DATA ARE AVAILABLE

On the cover: (left to right, top to bottom) AUAF campus; Friday Mosque in Herat; at school, a gate and a greeter, with a gun; sacrificial ram in the Eid Festival; horse and buggy; gardeners; items for sale; hillside homes; schoolgirls; shops (all photographs by the author)

Manufactured in the United States of America

McFarland & Company, Inc., Publishers
  Box 611, Jefferson, North Carolina 28640
   www.mcfarlandpub.com

To the students and faculty of the American University of Afghanistan. There is great hope for the future because of their dedication.

The words of St. Paul's First Letter to the Corinthians floated into my consciousness. They are about the longing to be seen fully for who one is:

> For now we see through a glass, darkly; but then face to face: now I know in part; then shall I know, even as also I am known [Corinthians 13:12].
>
> That is what feels missing in a veiled world, or at least for someone who comes to it unveiled.
>
> —Alissa J. Rubin, Kabul bureau chief, *New York Times;*
> "My First Afghan Burka," May 5, 2011

Table of Contents

Preface

In the spring of 2009, at the grand age of 60-something, I realized I was not going to live forever. If I wanted to do great things, I had better get started.

I was thinking about saving the world. I could see myself tramping through the wilds, passing out books to the literature-starved populace, dispensing wisdom and demonstrating the American way as I went. And I wanted somewhere rugged and fierce: Somewhere different.

I had lived in England and Australia for several years, but they hardly counted as being particularly rugged or fierce. And they weren't particularly different. English (more or less) was the spoken language in both those countries, and alcohol, while not encouraged, perhaps, was not banned.

Afghanistan was always on the list of places to visit and high on the list for being rugged and fierce. After 9/11, I read more and more about the country and the problems it was having — particularly the problems of its women and their children.

The tipping point was a rug show I visited in May of 2009, where rugs made by Afghan women were sold, and I heard the stories of the women and their lives. I was hooked. I wanted to go.

That week I went online, found a job in Kabul, applied and was hired. (I suspect my application was the only one received.)

After rearranging my life and questioning my sanity, I was on my way to a rugged and fierce country to teach science at the American University of Afghanistan. And I was going to a war zone. I knew that before I went. I was advised of safety issues and of the security that the university provided for its staff of internationals. But I, in my delirium on the edge of a dream, paid no attention.

I was to find out that life with the threat of kidnapping and bombings was not so easy. "No mingling," I was told; no wandering around the market or stopping by a café for a cup of coffee. Travel to and from the city of Kabul was in a security van and my photographs of the streets were taken through the windows of that van. Many of those pictures were posted on my blog (http://adventureinadfghanistan.blogspot.com).

I didn't make much progress saving the world in Kabul but I did have a chance to live in a country and meet a people who really deserve better.

1

On My Way

Next time you hear from me.... (Email to a friend, August 22, 2009)

My son Jason drove me to the airport, helped with my bags and sat with me in the bar while I waited for the plane. Then we hugged and he left. I sat there fiddling with my new laptop and tried to remain calm.

Omigod.

I'm going to Afghanistan.

Omigod.

My rising panic was interrupted, however, when Jason reappeared. He loved me, he said, and he was proud of me, and then he added, "I just wanted to give you a chance to change your mind."

Perfect. I have a great son.

"No, dear, I'm good. I'm going, and thanks."

So we sat together again and played with my laptop. Eventually he left for home and I was truly on my own. My adventure had begun.

I was contemplating retirement a few years earlier and thinking about what I was going to do next. I wanted to go somewhere remote and exotic. Do something important. Make a difference.

Then came 9/11 and Afghanistan was in the news. Afghanistan had been in my folder of "remote exotic places" for a long time. And from what I had read and seen of the country, it was certainly rugged. Kipling wrote in "The Young British Soldier,"

> When you're wounded and left on Afghanistan's plains
> And the women come out to cut up what remains
> Jest roll on your rifle an' blow out your brains
> An' go to your Gawd like a soldier.

That's fierce, I thought.

A plan was being birthed.

3

While not committing to anything yet — still not retired — I decided to at least learn the language of Afghanistan, just in case. My first move was to find out what language that was.

Much to my chagrin, I learned there is no one language spoken in Afghanistan. In fact, according to the CIA World Factbook,[1] there are more than thirty languages spoken there and none of those languages is called "Afghanistani."

Most Afghans speak Dari (50 percent) or Pashto (35 percent) and I read that a small (very small) group speaks Arabic, which happened to be taught in my hometown of Charleston, South Carolina.

So for two years I studied Arabic and I semi-retired. Then in April of 2009 I read about an upcoming rug show by Arzu Rugs — a "not-for-profit organization whose mission is to provide sustainable income to Afghan women by sourcing and selling the rugs they weave."[2] Education of the women and their children is part of the program.

I went to the show.

The rugs were gorgeous, of course, but also displayed were pictures of the women weavers and their children and the countryside. And then there were the stories.

One woman finally earned enough to buy a veil; in her village, without a veil, she could not leave the house. I asked about the men. How supportive were they? What did they think about their wives and children attending school? The response was one I heard over and over again. The men (as well as the women) wanted better lives for their children and they realized it was only possible through education. The name Arzu means "hope" in Dari.

It was a sales pitch. I knew Arzu was trying to sell rugs, but it sold me on Afghanistan.

That night I went to my regularly-scheduled poker game, but the "hook" was in and I started thinking. If I wanted to go, so went the internal dialogue, just when was that going to happen? (I'd had this sort of conversation with myself more than once in my life the last time being when I started thinking seriously about getting a Ph.D. — if I wanted the degree, just when was I going to get started? That's when I filled out the graduate school application.)

"Now" was my answer and the next day I wrote to Arzu Rugs and enthused about wanting to go and help and blah blah blah. I may have gone a bit overboard in my presentation. In any case, I didn't hear back. I didn't really expect to as it had been my experience that only a small percentage of job applications brought even an acknowledgment.

But it was a start; I was moving down a road. I knew there was an American university in Afghanistan so I went online and found its web-site and learned it needed someone to teach physical science. I had earned degrees in the sciences and had taught chemistry for several years. It looked like a fit so I sent off my résumé with a cover letter that burbled on about how I was passionate about working in Afghanistan and wanting to do whatever I could to help the people there. And, to top it off, my subject line was "Appliation." I didn't spot the misspelling until much later ... after I came to realize I could probably have written gibberish and the result would have been the same.

Again, I did not expect a reply.

But a week later, sitting at my desk reading email, I saw this:

Thank you for sending your résumé. I would like to set up a time to talk to you over the phone.
Jane Holmes,[3] Professor, American University of Afghanistan

I couldn't believe it; I couldn't stop saying, "Oh, wow." My office mate thought I was having a heart attack or a seizure. I had actually heard back — from Afghanistan. Now what?

At that point I was reminded of the joke about what the dog plans to do with the car once he catches it.

I replied, of course, and we made arrangements and I got a call from Kabul, Afghanistan, shortly thereafter.

I was hired a few weeks later. Although no one would ever confirm it for me, I suspect I was the only person who applied to work in a war zone. A subject line of "Appliation"— my misspelling of "Application"— made no difference! The semester was to start August 30 and I was expected to be there a week early, which meant I had almost three months to get ready — and to worry.

I started the first of many lists of things to do before I jumped off the world: passport, shots, insurance and power of attorney. And then what was I to do about the house, the car, the furniture, the plants and the cats, Mojo and Slick ... and all my stuff. And then the "what to take" list.

Meanwhile I was enjoying the mini-notoriety attached to going on my trip. I liked saying, "I'm going to Afghanistan." It made me feel special and a little adventurous. One of my friends enjoyed telling people about my upcoming trip even more than I did — some kind of shared glory, perhaps. Before I could even open my mouth I would hear, "That's Penny. She's going to Afghanistan, you know." "Why?" was the universal question.

So the word went out and the local newspaper called me and there was a story in the paper and another one in the local weekly tabloid; I was enjoying the "fame."

Some people did not know where Afghanistan was. But they knew it was far away and foreign and maybe dangerous. Wasn't there a war going on over there? And, again, "Why are you going?"

I didn't have an answer. I tried "I've always wanted to" and "to save the world." The truth was a bit of both, I guess. My son and my sister simply went along with the plan. Or at least they pretended to. People started sharing stories and contacts with me. One had a friend in the State Department who took up the "harbinger of doom" role. "Make sure that woman lets the American Embassy know where she is so, God forbid, they know where to ship her remains" and stuff like that.

My son tried to look up the American University of Afghanistan on Google Earth, but, not surprisingly, couldn't find any close-up pictures. We thought it might be due to security issues — the war zone scenario, again. We never considered that no pictures on the ground in Kabul, Afghanistan, simply meant there were no cameras on the ground in Kabul, Afghanistan.

I was in touch with Dr. Holmes at the university several times that summer, by email and by phone. She answered many of my questions, both those that I thought to ask as well as others that hadn't crossed my mind. One of her first communiqués was "Make sure your clothes hide your crotch." That meant I would be looking for tunic tops and long skirts or pants. New list: "things to buy."

She told me once that one of the secrets to surviving in Kabul was actually "living" there rather than camping out. In an effort to do that, I decided to take several of my favorite things: a teddy bear, a stuffed frog and a comforter (gifts from my son), some books, a mobile and some plants. (More about the plants later.)

I found out I'd be able to get beer (alcohol was tolerated for foreigners)[4] and I would have my own room in the university-maintained guesthouse and share a bathroom. A generator would provide back-up heat and the classrooms had PowerPoint capability. I found out everything was available in Kabul, just not all the time.

And I received this from the university on July 1:

Internationals do not, of course, wear burkas. However, everyone I know buys one to have in their room "just in case." If you wear eyeglasses like I do, the fit can be a problem. There are shops where you can try one on to make sure that it is not too long and that you can see (a bit).

"Just in case" caught my attention. In case of what?

No burka, but a head scarf was suggested for public appearances. I was warned to pack warm clothes. And from the library at the university: bring Scotch tape.

The lists got shorter and then new ones were made. I was in the process of finding a text for the course I would be teaching. I was looking at laptops.

The wheels were turning and I was getting closer to August and a departure date. Anxiety was building.

The University was arranging and paying for transport. But I still had no word on when I'd be going. Since school started on the 30th of August, I guessed I would be heading out around the 22nd, giving me plenty of time to get my head around the idea of going to Afghanistan. But then Dr. Holmes wrote to say I should plan to leave on the 9th. I panicked. Wait a minute. Wait a minute. I wasn't ready. I needed more time to think about it. I felt like a freight train was bearing down on me and I had no way of stopping it.

As it turned out I didn't leave until the 24th of August. A presidential election in Afghanistan was scheduled for the 20th, and in July I was introduced to "security concerns" when I received the following from Human Resources at the university:

> We also strongly urge all international faculty members (current and newly hired) that they schedule their arrival to Kabul after Aug 22nd. It is difficult to predict how the security situation will be (hopefully it will be peaceful) but apart from that, there may be problems with road closures in Kabul city that could be inconvenient and uncomfortable.

"Hopefully it will be peaceful" and "inconvenient and uncomfortable"? Was he talking about gunfire and death, for heaven's sake?

This "alert" was one of the first reminders of exactly where I was going — to a war zone. Another reminder was an ad in an online newsletter about what was going on in Kabul. It advertised a hotel which boasted "security bunkers" and "armored" cars. Oh dear.

And then when I talked with the acting president of the university about the job and the safety issues in Kabul, he said I wasn't to worry. It wasn't Mogadishu or Baghdad. So I guess that meant it was safe in Kabul?

To be honest, the safety issue didn't really concern me. Too naive to be scared, I jokingly remarked when asked if I was worried. I really did not have a clue about what I was getting into. I am not sure anyone from a relatively peaceful country understands what it means to worry about personal security and armored vehicles. In my mind, I had heard enough to believe I would be at least semi-protected and safe.

In any case, I wasn't going to change my mind — that's not my way —

but it didn't stop the night musings. In my big bed in my nice safe house of many years surrounded by both kitties and two stuffed animals, I had terrible misgivings and certainly questioned the sanity of my decision. What the hell was I doing? This was not just a trip to San Francisco or even to Mexico. Or London where I'd lived for years. It was Afghanistan, a Muslim country, somewhere on the edge of the Himalayas!

Afghanistan. I would try to imagine what the place was like. I knew Kabul was a city. I wouldn't be living in a thatched hut. I would have a room of my own with a queen-sized bed. But that's all I knew. I couldn't get my head around what it would be like, except it would be very little like my life in Charleston. Did Afghans[5] speak English? Would my students like me? I wasn't coming back in a couple of weeks. I was going to be gone for a whole school year and I was going to Afghanistan. What was I thinking?

My life in Charleston, while perhaps boring and not quite fulfilling, was very safe in many ways. Here's when I understood the concept of "comfort zone": a familiar place with familiar people and familiar stuff—a place where one feels at ease, comfortable. That was my life in my little house in a little town in a southern state in the United States in the Western world. I was leaving all that.

But I just couldn't change my mind. I had made a commitment. Not just by signing a contract, but I had told people: my family, my friends, everyone who came within earshot. I had to go.

Years ago, when I was in my 20s I had reached an impasse in my life: not married, not in school, boring job. What to do? I decided to go around the world, to start in England and then proceed from there. I began telling people my plan and soon those people wanted to know when I was leaving and then a friend wanted to go with me and we made plans and somehow I ended up in England. Sometimes it takes the push of other people to get one moving along the way. Anyway, it worked for me.

The last thing on my list of things to do was "yard sale"—get rid of the detritus that had gathered in my house over the years. I fretted about it and dreaded it and finally decided it wasn't worth the aggravation. Instead, I sold what I could to a dealer and donated the rest—one less thing to worry about that last week.

By the 22nd of August, I had done it all: rented my house, sold much of my furniture, packed my books, made the arrangements and completed the lists.

I walked around my house one last time and said bye to my kitty kitties. I emailed a friend:

I'm off shortly to Jason's and then on to the airport. I can hardly wait to get on that plane — these last few days have been worrying and exhausting. Next time you hear from me I'll be in Kabul Afghanistan. How about that!

After my son left me at the airport that day in August, I began talking with a fellow who was also waiting for a flight. I told him where I was going; he thought it was pretty exciting. So did I.

And I was on my way.

2

Arrival, Security and the Afghan Way

Hi, sweetie. I'm still in Dubai — it's 7:30 A.M. here — we're headed out to Kabul this morning. I have lots to tell, but I'm still wired — and jet-lagged — and tired ... so stay tuned. Love, from your Mom (Email to my son, August 24, 2009)

Arrival

My flight to Kabul went first to Washington, D.C., then to London, and on to Dubai. On the plane from London I met Dee, another new university hire. We were both scheduled to spend a night in Dubai and then fly to Kabul the following day. We had assumed our luggage would be accompanying us. We were wrong.

When we arrived in Dubai our luggage did not.

We used this unfortunate occurrence as an excuse to stay a second night. Dubai, in the United Arab Emirates, while not quite "like home," was not Kabul, and I think we felt the need for another night away from whatever awaited us. We had already flown hours and hours and miles and miles from our comfort zones and were headed into who knows what, so another day of near normalcy seemed not too much to ask.

We finally got hold of the university by email — phoning Kabul was problematic. We explained that our luggage had not arrived so we needed to stay and wait for it. This clearly leaky reasoning somehow made sense to the university. After all, we had moved into the world of never-on-time flights and never-to-be-seen-again luggage.[1]

As it turned out, Dee's luggage appeared the next day; mine was still missing when we left for Afghanistan.

Memories of my arrival in Kabul are hazy at best, and I'm still missing

10

large pieces of it. Contributing factors were jet lag and the "I'm not terrified of flying" pills I had taken. Images and sounds came at me, but I did not seem to be able to focus on where I was or what was going on.

Kabul from the air was a gray-brown flat plain with mountains off in the distance. The airport was a building or two surrounded by a parking area and lots of dirt. And it was hot and dusty. We were shuffled across an expanse of broken concrete to a waiting van, and I seem to have heard, "We can all fit," and "Where's...." "Wait a...." Somehow I was delivered to the Peach House, a guesthouse run by the university, and to a pleasant single room with "Dr. Penelope Tarvis" on the door and a welcome basket of toilet paper, crackers and boxed milk.

I remember being at a restaurant that evening; we were outside at a table and I was eating my first Afghan meal. No alcohol. I remember trying to figure out who the people were at the table; my boss was there but I still don't know who else was present. I could have used a drink.

My second day in Kabul and I was nearly back to earth; start of school was still a week away and I had time to worry about reassembling my life. First step was to find my missing luggage, which contained mostly clothes but also some other small items from home. I had listened when someone in the States suggested I pack a change of clothes in my hand luggage. So I did have a another set of clothes, but the second tunic top, while covering my crotch, as I had been warned it should, was particularly ugly and wildly inappropriate in Afghanistan, having been bought in a maternity shop. I needed some other clothes.

In addition to my luggage I had also shipped books and other personal items, like my stuffed teddy bear and a green frog with a bright red tongue. Those boxes were also among the missing.

That second day I was also to get an introduction to life in a war zone.

Security

As security concerns permeated the lives of internationals in Kabul, it seems appropriate to at least introduce the issue at this point and provide some background.

The Soviet Union's "deployment" in Afghanistan ended in 1989 and civil war broke out shortly thereafter. Warring Afghan factions fought each other for control of the country and they fought in Kabul. The city still has many scars from that fighting.

The Taliban, an extremist group that had originated in Afghanistan and Pakistan in the 1990s, finally took over Kabul in 1996. They brought an end to the fighting and a measure of peace. They also brought a social order that imposed severe restrictions on the populace, particularly on the women.

The Taliban were still in control in 2001 when the U.S. was attacked on September 11. Responsibility for the attack was claimed by Osama bin Laden, the leader of the terrorist Al Qaeda organization reportedly headquartered in Afghanistan. NATO forces, including the U.S., attacked Afghanistan in October of that year when the Taliban refused to turn over bin Laden to the international authorities. By December the fighting was over and the Bonn agreement was signed.

One provision of the agreement was for an International Security Assistance Force (ISAF) to provide security for Kabul to allow an interim government the opportunity to become established.[2] (This area of protection was extended in 2003 to include all of Afghanistan.[3])

Because of this arrangement, fighting in the streets of Kabul was kept to a minimum and the capital city was relatively safe, at least from stray bullets. But it is hard for any security force to stop the random car bombings or other acts of violence that were part of life in Kabul.

During my discussions with the university while I was still in the U.S., I was told that there were some security concerns, but I did not get a lot of details. Or I was not paying attention. I was told that we had transport to and from school, with a driver and an escort. I thought of it as a service: "How nice we get rides to school." The reality was that "transport" was not truly optional.

Actually the worst concern was not the bombings but kidnappings — kidnappings by the Taliban and also by the criminal element in Kabul trying to make a buck.

My life in Kabul was defined by efforts to keep me and the rest of the international faculty and staff safe. This issue determined how and where we lived, where we could go and how we moved from place to place.

The Afghan Way

That second day I was off to school to sign papers and look around and see about my things. I was still in enough of a daze that it did not register that our guesthouse had razor wire on top of its walls or that there were two fierce-looking young men in uniforms standing around and one was holding a gun. It was a rifle and it looked real.

A school van with two more fierce-looking young men drove me to the university. The roads were pitted and strewn with rocks. There were no sidewalks: people and animals walked in the streets. Hills were all around and everything was brown and dusty. One piece at a time, Kabul was slowly becoming real.

The American University of Afghanistan (AUAF), located a few miles from our guesthouse and about ten miles outside of Kabul proper, did not fit my picture of a typical university. There were no signs to the site, and no tree-lined drive — just an armed guard waiting for us on an unnamed side street next to a gated entrance.

The security gate opened, and we drove into the walled property where a guard checked the underside of the van for bombs. Nope, we weren't in Kansas anymore.

The small campus, about five acres, consisted of a grassy area in the middle of several buildings: offices and classrooms, a cafeteria and a new gym.

Some of the buildings looked like abandoned army barracks, which they may well have been. The website mentions that "two buildings, heavily damaged in clashes between Afghan and Soviet forces in the 1980s and the factional war that followed, were repaired for office and classroom use."[4]

The walkways were lined with rosebushes which were gloriously in bloom. In the far distance were mountains; in the near distance were walls and guard towers.

And men with guns.

My first stop was to the office of the university's liaison, whose sole job was to work with internationals: finding and sorting out their paperwork and tickets and, if need be, lost luggage. The office was on the third floor of the Administration Building. Here's where I found out that I would be climbing stairs a lot in the near future — there didn't seem to be any elevators available.

The administrative offices were stark: desks, but no file cabinets. A few three-ring binders were perched on a shelf. Computers were everywhere, but no telephones. Everyone used a cell phone. I had already been issued mine and told to keep it with me at all times — just in case. ("In case" of what? again crossed my mind.)

I soon realized that rectifying my luggage problem was not going to be easy. For one thing, just as it was difficult to call Kabul from Dubai, we could not call Dubai from Kabul using the phone system available at the university. There were no land lines on campus, only mobile phones. And the liaison officer did not have a phone with the capability to call out of the country. We had to resort to emailing the airlines. I was assured everything would be fine. The luggage might possibly be in Dubai and once it was found it would be shipped to Kabul. Okay then.

Next stop was to Morad, a clerk in Procurement. He was in charge of

Walls adorned with razor wire and the winter remains of a grape arbor were part of our guesthouse environment.

shipping and receiving and perhaps could help find my boxes. And maybe even my luggage, should it ever appear in Kabul. Getting shipments into the country was one thing: getting shipments from the airport to the university was another problem altogether.

Morad was extremely good-looking, as are so many Afghan men. He smiled a lot and we always seemed to be in quasi-flirt mode in our subsequent interactions. That day he was quite solicitous when I explained about my luggage. While not agonizing over my loss, he seemed to be sorry I was inconvenienced and willing to help.

"So what's to be done?" I asked.
"I'm looking into it," said he.
"When?"
"Today."
"Will you call me when you know?"
"I will call."
"When?"
"Soon."

Looking south from my balcony I could see the rooftops of Kabul with the mountains in the background.

I walked away realizing that my luggage would arrive when it arrived.

Thus began my first experience with Afghan hospitality: everything you read about the people in Afghanistan always mentions their hospitality. And the hospitality is extended to guests in their home and guests in their country — like me.

What better way to make sure your guests are happy than to tell them what they want to hear. Why worry them with details or the irritating truth?

I would ask my class, "Where's Mustafa?"
"He's coming," was invariably the reply.
"When?" I would ask.
"Soon."

Which was, of course, what I wanted to hear. But was it true? Maybe, maybe not.

In any case, no one really knew where my luggage was and no one really cared but me. But everyone knew that it would show up — eventually.[5]

And that's what it did — the following week.

As it turned out, the luggage had been at the Kabul airport the whole time, just waiting for me. No one thought to call there and no one from the airport got in touch with the school and and and. Morad had no explanation. By that time, what mattered was that I had some of my stuff. My hand lotion had sprung a leak and a messy, gooey glop was in one of the suitcases.

The boxes that I shipped arrived that first week as well. Now I had my clothes and books and stuffed animals and comforter and pictures and mementos. I was moving in and life was cranking up again.

3

The Guesthouse

I'm the "warden" of this guesthouse—whatever that means—and have a meeting with the Security Chief today re: the safe room—which is kinda non-existent in this house—unless you consider the basement which has small windows that can easily be broken and provide entry for bombs.... Stay tuned. (Email to friend, November 19, 2009)

I lived in a guesthouse operated by the university. It was a three-story peach-colored building, appropriately called "Peach House," in what was probably an upper-middle-class neighborhood.

All the houses in the neighborhood were surrounded by walls. Our wall had extensions to make it higher — more difficult to climb. On top of the wall extensions was razor wire — more protection, but it was never absolutely clear whom we were being protected from. When security issues were mentioned in my pre-hire conversations, I was never quite sure of the source of the problems. Perhaps, as internationals, we were just an all-around target for trouble.

Anyway, we had high walls topped with razor wire — which kept the bad guys out. (As I was to realize quite soon, it also kept us in.)

I often wondered what the neighbors thought of our presence on the street. We couldn't have been much of a secret. We were the only house in the neighborhood with coils of wire adorning the walls. We were the only house where armed guards appeared in the street when a car drove up. In any case, we rarely saw anyone on the street but children. They always waved and we waved back.

The guesthouse had seven bedrooms, four baths, two kitchens and two sitting rooms. Five of the seven people in the house when I moved in were women. There were five Americans, one Canadian and one Afghan. The two men had the first floor to themselves.

The demographics changed regularly as turnover was high. Some people had only a two- or three-month contract and others left to live on their own or moved to another guesthouse.

Initially I lived on the second floor in the midst of everything. My room faced east and I could see the sun struggle up past the mountains in the morning. Then a temporary employee left and I took over her room on the third floor. There was only one other person on the floor and we shared a bathroom and a refrigerator. It was heaven. She and I had access to a full balcony and stairs to the roof. From the balcony we could look down onto the rooftops of the houses around us and onto the street.

A desk with my computer faced the balcony and a grand view of the hills surrounding Kabul. I had a loveseat, a queen-sized bed and a bookshelf with books and memories from home. My son's picture as a child was on the wall and a more recent one was on the shelf. I had also brought a mobile with a Vote Obama button hanging from it.

During the course of my stay I hung maps of Kabul, postcards of famous Afghans and a picture of a Buzkashi game. (Buzkashi is the goat-grabbing/tossing game played on horses primarily in northern Afghanistan — an extreme form of polo with a dead animal. Another fierce aspect of Afghanistan.)

On my bed were the stuffed frog that my son had won for me at a local fair and a teddy bear he had given me for Christmas.

It was home.

I welcomed the privacy this third floor perch allowed me, because guesthouse living soon became a challenge.

When I first arrived, guesthouse living was, dare I say, fun. Most of us got together on the weekends with other internationals and went shopping or sightseeing — such as it was in Kabul. And all of the women shared a fondness for alcohol. As a matter of fact, one of our first outings was to obtain large quantities of adult beverages.

After a few months, the situation changed. Two of the original women left for home, and another got sick and never fully recovered. The reality of living with other people was not so much fun anymore. I didn't go to college in my twenties, never lived in a dorm and always regretted that I had not had that experience. Maybe it would have been fun as a young person, but as an aging adult it wore thin fast.

It seemed that each new person moving in had a greater set of problems than the person who left. And, of course, my delight in the situation had waned considerably. One newcomer was convinced the Taliban could climb the walls into her window at night. She kept her shoes outside her room so the bacteria on her shoes could not get in. We suggested that the bacteria would simply open the door if they wanted to invade her room. She didn't think that was funny.

A really young woman moved in, one who apparently never had to pick up after herself, and she didn't. And so it went.

Coping with the confined quarters was another problem. For instance, the kitchen on the second floor was used by as many as six women. We mostly had different schedules, but sometimes at night it got chaotic, particularly if there was a power failure and we were all trying to cook.

Power did not so much "fail" as "fade." Brownouts were almost nightly events and happened, of course, when everyone in Kabul, including us, was trying to cook dinner. (On the few occasions when power was totally lost, we had a generator, which the guards would turn on in short order. We did not suffer, but others in the city were not so lucky.) There might be just enough light to see to cook, but not enough to see the colors of what we were eating. Fortunately, we had a supply of alcohol by this time.

We all had candles and other light-emitting devices and generally power "downs" were not considered a problem. More like "Uh-oh"—find the flashlight/candles/lantern and carry on, all in a night's entertainment. I considered my camping days and my years in late 60s London (coin-driven hot water and heat, for instance) as training grounds for my stay in Kabul.

Even when the power was working, the kitchen presented other challenges. The stove was gas and the oven was either on, really on, or off. Sometimes lighting the stove produced a scary whooshing sound; other times nothing happened. Which meant the gas was gone and we had to wait for our houseman to replace the cylinder.

Using the microwave was a learning experience for some. One person was obviously not aware of how food could spray the insides of the oven if it was not covered. One of my housemates reminded me about this regularly.

We were all territorial about our food supply. Everyone had her own cupboard and generally left everyone else's food alone. We had a common shelf for condiments, herbs, spices and sauces which mostly worked well. One housemate, however, never bought sugar; she counted on us to provide it for her. That got annoying. There were two refrigerators, again more or less divvied up among us. The same annoying housemate used all my black olives one night, pissing me off.

The house had plenty of bathrooms but only one bathtub, probably not a standard feature in Afghan homes. Ours had no plug for the drain. When I asked the facilities manager about getting one, he had no idea what I was talking about. "You know ... something to keep the water from running out." We used a washcloth which was not 100 percent efficient.

I found drain plugs in Dubai on my next trip; I bought two and kept one in my room.

We had Internet access at the guesthouse — most days. During the time I was in Kabul, service was changed more than once. First we had our own server and then we were connected to the server at school and then we went back to having our own server. If that doesn't make sense, well, that's the way it was. At least twice a week, someone would yell out, "Internet's down!" and then finally "Internet's back!"

We all had cell phones, but most didn't have international service and we had no land lines. (There were land lines in Kabul, but I understood they were used mainly by the ministries and other organizations that need more secure means of communication.) We had a TV, but news stations were not in English so we were left with the Internet for news of the world as well as communication with our family and friends. It was our lifeline to reality. I went online for news, email, Skype calls and to play bridge. When the Internet was down there was a lot of moaning and groaning and excessive drinking. To the school's credit, they understood the importance of Internet access and tried hard to maintain the service.

One of the only great things about guesthouse living is that we did not have to clean the bathrooms or wash dishes or mop floors. We had a house-man — Jawid. He was a thirtyish young man who came to the house every morning on his bicycle in his motorcycle jacket and "did" for us. He washed the dishes and swept the floors and fixed things: the drawers, the oven, the drain, the washer, the refrigerator, the gas, the heaters and the shower.

The shower was particularly problematic. The curtain hung on a U-shaped piece screwed into the wall. However, the U-shaped piece kept coming detached from the wall and the shower curtain would droop and finally fall — not a serious problem, but an irritating one, particularly if you were in the shower when the curtain fell. Jawid finally fixed a chain to the ceiling to hold the damn thing up. Thank God for ingenuity.

The tap water in Kabul was undrinkable. We had two clean-water carboys in the guesthouse which we used for most water needs. Jawid used hot tap water and soap to wash the dishes. He then let them air dry. They were probably bacteria-free — bacteria needing a watery environment to survive. I used the "clean" water to wash fruits and vegetables and for my coffee. Some of the other houseguests soaked fruits and vegetables in a salt solution to kill bacteria. I took my chances. As it turned out, we all got sick at least once.

Jawid was pleasant to have around. His English wasn't great, but he always smiled. When I started my Dari lessons, I would practice on him and he'd correct my pronunciation. I had a Dari dictionary/phrasebook when all else failed. As time went on we found out bits and pieces about his life. We found out he was married, but he didn't have a picture of his wife on his phone — he had some pictures of Indian-style movie stars, however. One morning he announced that his wife just had a baby, which was the first we knew that she was even pregnant. Afghan men do not discuss their wives with strangers, or perhaps with anyone. When I asked, he told me she wore a burka.

Thus I was introduced to the reality of the three sexes in Afghanistan: men, women and foreign women. His wife wore a burka and yet he was exposed every day to women who did not. In fact, he saw all of us in far less clothing than most Afghan women wore.

He told me one day that he wanted a motorcycle (to go with the jacket he already wore). We also talked about his cell phone, which was much more elaborate than the ones we had been issued by the school. He told me it cost him $20 a month. In the first of many fairly insensitive remarks I made during my stay, I said, "Oh, $20 a month, that's not bad." He just looked at me. Twenty dollars was almost two days' pay for him.

As I mentioned, our house was surrounded by walls and razor wire. Within the walls in front of our guesthouse was a guard shack, a diesel generator and a garden.

All of the guesthouses had gardens; ours was small and basic. Rose bushes edged a minuscule, barely green patch of grass. There was a grape arbor and a separate area that sported a watermelon vine and some gourd-type vegetables. In the morning huge bunches of red grapes were seen dripping from the arbor. By the afternoon and our return to the guesthouse, they would be gone. The watermelons and vegetables similarly disappeared. Perks of the job, perhaps?

"The roses are all in bloom" was one of the selling points when I was interviewed by the acting president of the university. He seemed to be saying, "How bad could it be, if the roses one in bloom?" And when I arrived, so they were and they seemed to bloom forever. Then came winter and then spring and the roses were blooming again. They were breathtaking — one in particular was mauve, but with a bluish tint. And then there were the yellow ones and the yellow ones with touches of pink in their blossoms.

Afghanistan may be green in parts, but Kabul was not. There were lots of trees at one time, perhaps, but not when I was there. What trees there were had leaves of a grayish green, thanks to Kabul's pervasive airborne dust problem. The city is brown and gray and tan, spotted with the dusty blue of burkas. The roses were a startling sight in that monochromatic setting.

Jawid did not work in the garden. We had a gardener. It seemed that all households had gardeners; gardening was not a leisure-time activity in Kabul.

Our gardener was a Hazara, an ethnic minority in Afghanistan. They are a mixed race and some have Mongolian features. Unlike most Afghans who are Sunni Muslims, the Hazaras are Shias. Many servants are Hazaras, including our own houseman.

The gardener and I communicated by smiling and pointing: I would smile and point at his roses and say "beautiful" and he would smile and bow. I lent him a picture book of plants that I had brought with me from the States.

Besides a houseman and a gardener, we also had two uniformed guards who shared a gun and worked twelve-hour shifts within the walls of the compound. During cold weather they stayed in the guard shack, which had cots and a bathroom. In the warm months they would sit under the grape arbor out of the sun. When it was time to pray they would spread their prayer rugs, kneel facing Mecca, and begin their prayers.

I committed several social gaffes, as it were, in Afghanistan. An early one was when I saw a guard who had taken off his shoes and socks and was washing his feet with the garden hose. I jokingly said, "You taking a shower? Ha, ha." "I'm doing my ablutions," was his reply in English. Oops. Then I learned that the Qur'an instructs Muslims to clean themselves before prayer.[1]

Many Afghan homes hire someone to open their gates for visitors; our guards fulfilled that role. When someone knocked on the door or shouted through the peephole, the two guards would race to the door, one of them getting the gun in position. Fortunately, it was always transport coming to pick us up or the gardener or a delivery, but nary a dangerous (or armed) visitor.

I practiced my rudimentary Dari on the guards and they pretended to understand me. They also asked me regularly how old I was. Again, foreign women are different from what most Afghan men are used to and our age was a point of curiosity and generated a fair amount of discussion. I never told.

The guards treated us well and we tried to reciprocate. We always said good morning and asked how they were. They always said good morning and asked how we were. We said *tashakoor* (thanks) a lot. Some of us brought them treats from the store.

But they were also our benevolent jailers. The "company line" was that the guards and the guns (well, the one gun) and the precautions were to protect us from the bad guys — the Taliban, the street hoods, whomever. But sometimes it wasn't quite like that. One housemate tried to leave in a taxi one day and the guards told her she couldn't go. It was in the middle of a heightened security event (a.k.a., a bomb incident), and all movement was halted: no travel into the city and, in this case, no leaving the guesthouse.

She wanted to go shopping and was told she was being reckless. She decided to follow their instructions, but I wonder if they would have physically kept her from leaving if she had insisted. I think she stood a chance of getting in serious trouble with the university if she left when advised not to, since she was not only putting herself at risk, but others as well.

But most of the time the guards sat around and talked and waited for the next "call to arms." It was a long, long day (or night) for them.

Besides the guards and the generator, we were also supposed to have room for an emergency vehicle inside the walls, in case we had to evacuate the area. The door in our wall, however, was too narrow to easily accommodate a vehicle. If an attack was imminent or likely, a vehicle was brought from school, which happened during the bombing on Darulaman Road in May, right before I left for the States. A van showed up in our yard and stayed all day.

One other security measure for all the guesthouses was a "safe" room, where one was to go if under attack and, I guess, wait for rescue. It was the bathroom in most guesthouses. Our "safe" room was the basement, which was a large concrete-floored room, with no bathroom and with glass windows. Fortunately we never had to use the safe room.

In August, when most of us arrived, we decided in order to create a "normal life" in Kabul we should adopt one (or two) of the neighborhood cats. There were lots of them. They were feral and roamed the area, climbed the walls, wended their way through the razor wire and strolled through our yard. Their meows were pitiful.

Of course, we wanted to invite them all into the house for lunch. "Not going to happen," said Jawid. As he was "in charge" of the house and, more importantly, washed our dishes, we went along with his dictum. One or the other of us would sometimes leave food for the most persistent cutie. She was an unusual multicolored cat (with almost a pink hue) and seemed friendly enough. She purred a lot and I thought she liked me. One day she scratched me, however, and that was the end of our relationship.

Dee, in another guesthouse, adopted a family of cats. She even bought cat food for them. Personally I didn't think that was necessary. When she moved to another guesthouse, she worried about the cats and who would take care of them. The cats, on the other hand, went back to their scavenging ways.

A young boy lived next door and he and a friend would fly kites from their roof. Sometimes his sister would join them and watch, but I never saw her fly a kite. When I was on the second floor I could chat with them from the balcony. Kambiz was the boy's name and he was learning English. I was learning Dari and so we tried to talk. His kites kept ending up in our yard, but the guards could be pressed into returning them.

I bought a kite finally for myself—which I could never get aloft. I also bought two kites for Kambiz and his friend. They ended up in our yard as well.

Everyone was moved into a guesthouse when they first arrived; guesthouse living, while irritating at times, provided a transition between life in the West and life in Kabul. No one knew exactly how the initial assignment of a guesthouse was made, and if it turned out to be a bad choice, changes could be made.

I got a chance to change guesthouses at one point—to a brand new house. I turned down the opportunity, even though my room would have been much larger, and had its own bath. However, it was cheek-to-jowl with the building next door. That and its balcony overhang would have kept natural light to a minimum. But the real reason I turned it down was that there was a squatter camp right next door. Unlike Peach House, which was in an established neighborhood, this guesthouse was in an area of new growth and empty lots. Homeless families would move in and set up tents: the children and mothers would beg and the fathers might look for work. I didn't want to live in a brand-spanking-new building next door to such misery.

Guesthouse living was not a requirement of my contract, but the university recommended that an employee spend a few months in a guesthouse before moving out; at that point they would provide a monthly stipend for rent. Living on one's own in Kabul, however, is problematic.

The main difficulty with living "off campus," as it were, was the inconvenience of getting things fixed. Stuff broke—a lot—in Afghanistan. At the guesthouse, things were fixed and problems taken care of. It would be a chore to find someone (or "someones") to fill the shoes of the staff. And then there was the language issue. Although many people spoke at least some English in Kabul, I didn't speak sufficient Dari to make myself understood. I would have considered moving out on my own if I had stayed longer, and some at school did just that.

Transport was also a problem. The school would not pick us up and take us home if we didn't live in a guesthouse. Cabs, however, could be hired to get to school and out and about.

Walking in downtown Kabul could be done, but walking alone, particularly at night, did not seem to be the best of ideas.

I met an international who was a lawyer and had lived in Kabul for some years. We had dinner a couple of times. She lived near the restaurant and would walk home by herself. I saw her walking down the street one night — she walked fast and kept her head down.

Our neighborhood was on the outskirts of Kabul and consisted of houses like our guesthouse with surrounding walls. The walls abutted the street so there were no sidewalks or curbs. Cars were parked inside the walls.

The roads in the neighborhood were largely unpaved and dusty with crater-sized potholes, and strewn with boulder-sized rocks. The roads looked as if they had taken several direct hits during the civil war and had never been fixed. There was little traffic and no speeders as it was difficult to build up speed weaving around holes and dodging rocks. In the winter, snow melted in the potholes and in the ruts left by tires and the dusty street turned to mud. (Oddly enough, no one wore boots in the winter. Even though it was only a short distance to walk in the mud — van to gate — it was slippery and wet and hard on both shoes and nerves.)

Now and then a new rock would be found in the roadway. It was often large enough that we had to drive around it rather than over it. The story was that having large rocks on neighborhood roads restricted high-speed chases by the Taliban. Faulty logic or wacky reasoning? Didn't the boulders also slow down the good guys trying to get away?

The state of the roads in Kabul was one of everyone's favorite laments. How could the roads be in such terrible shape considering the millions and millions of dollars that had been spent in Afghanistan to help rebuild the country?

We all agreed that with a couple pieces of modern road equipment, the leveling and paving of our road could be done in a weekend. But nothing improved while I was there and there seemed to be little hope of change in the future.

Around the corner from our guesthouse was a mean little park called Needle Park, presumably indicating the type of activity that took place there. Usually only men were seen in the park, and sometimes children — mostly boys — would run around. The park had large patches of dirt and barren trees — not much seemed to bloom there, even in the spring. Some benches were scattered around but it was still a mean-looking park.

We couldn't walk in that park. We couldn't walk alone out of the guesthouse. When we visited the guesthouse around the corner, we were accompanied by an escort. Mostly when we left home, we left in a security vehicle.

A pretty French restaurant was within walking distance, but we couldn't walk there either. A couple of Wednesdays at the end of my week, I would get transport to drop me off there for lunch. I would have an omelet and read my book and pretend that I was free to wander a city enjoying a meal and a read. But then I had to call Transport to come and pick me up and take me home.

At night our street was dark and perilous; there were no street lights and any illumination from the houses was hidden behind walls. Hungry and barking dogs skulked about in the shadows.

But inside the guesthouse walls, it was bright and safe. Guards were at the gate with their gun. Pizza was available from a local restaurant. And they delivered.

4

Morning in Kabul

The rooster is crowing again. It apparently doesn't get it that it's supposed to crow only ONCE — at daybreak. (Email to my son, March 8, 2010)

Morning came early in Kabul[1] and it arrived with a racket.

The Muslim call to prayer is at dawn, which is variously defined, but definitely before the sun rises. The muezzin no longer has to climb the minaret to sing out the call; he generally stays on the ground and uses a loudspeaker. The local mosque sometimes broadcasts not just the call to prayer but a complete "sermon," which was not only loud but long.

Then the rooster started — the rooster that never once got the time right. And then the boys' voices were heard from the orphanage next door. Apparently they had some early morning routine that involved shouted responses.

There was a barking dog in the house behind us. Generally Afghans do not have pets, but we lived next door to the one Afghan family in Kabul with a pet dog and it barked and barked and barked.

The first time I heard the dog bark for what seemed forever, I considered calling Animal Control. (Animal Control? In Kabul? What was I thinking?)

When I first arrived, the dog was a puppy, and we made excuses for his barking because he was a puppy and didn't know any better. But then, he grew up and it became apparent that he barked because he was kept outside and tied to a doghouse and was largely ignored by the children in the house. We figured he just wanted to play.

One of my housemates thought about giving the family $100 to "lose" the dog. I think she was also considering funding a hit man. I, on the other hand, was working on a plan to rig up the garden hose to the faucet in the sink, intending to spray the dog when he started barking.

The dog was joined in the spring by a pair of peacocks — all living in the same household.

The male peacock is stunningly beautiful and excessively vain, strutting about with his plumage spread. But then in some weird Darwinian accident he calls to his mate: SCREEECH, SCREEECH. She runs. He chases. And the game begins. The peacock is a lonely beast, forever trying to plead with his drab mate for his conjugal rights, but with such a squawky unpleasant call, it's surprising that the peacock gene pool has not long since been wiped out

The dog continued its barking. The rooster crowed. It was a zoo.

And then there were the street vendors. I never knew what they were selling, but they sang of their wares in a peculiar harmony that was one more sound of the early morning.

I was wide awake by this time.

I set my alarm for six, but I was always up before it buzzed, and the sun would be rising then too. Before the sun was truly up, Kabul was a gray-blue monochrome — the hills visible against the lightening sky. Often I would see a yellow balloon heading skyward or a red kite soaring on the wind.

After the morning wake-up calls, the workday began with a clanging and banging on our gate. The guards would "gun up" and then peek through the peephole. It was the gardener. He would wrestle his wheelbarrow through

Darulaman Road was always under construction. A ditch separates much of the main road from the frontage road.

the gate and then just stand there, surveying his domain: the rosebushes — assuring himself, perhaps, that every one was in its place. Satisfied, he'd start watering or weeding or pruning. No dead or even dying flowers remained for long. And no mowing debris, either. After he was finished mowing the small center quadrangle of grass, he gathered up the clippings into a bag and took them away when he left.

Breakfast was coffee and usually a hard-boiled egg and some cheese, crackers and vitamins. I'd load everything up and trundle upstairs to my laptop and, hopefully, to messages from the States.

Most of us read email and Skyped first thing in the morning. 7:00 A.M. in Kabul was 10:30 P.M. the night before in Charleston, South Carolina.

After breakfast, the hardest part of the day — shower time.

I remembered summer camp and how taking a shower was a fearsome experience. It was like that but worse in Afghanistan. This is a country where everything works except when it doesn't, and that was so true of the shower.

Water for the showers was pumped (from somewhere); the noise of the water pump was a constant, except when it wasn't and that meant there was a problem.

It could be that the guards had forgotten to turn the pump on, or something worse — no water. And then there was the issue of hot water. Not hot water by itself, but the delicate mix of hot and cold that makes a shower delightful — or not. In Kabul it was problematic. Turn the knob a little this way ... ah, just right. Eek ... no, turn it slightly the other way ... aargh ... the other. And so it went every morning. Some mornings the water would slow to a trickle, mid-shower and pre-rinse. Nevertheless, I would eventually emerge somewhat cleaner, and triumphant.

And, of course, I had to remember — keep my mouth shut while in the shower. The bacteria were always looking for a way in.

A van or an SUV picked us up from the guesthouse every morning, arriving every half hour from 8 until 11 A.M. Each week the exact time would vary: first fifteen minutes before the hour and fifteen minutes after, then on the hour and half hour. We were also transported back to the guesthouse at night, 5:00 until 8:00. The times were again varied. The "reason" being that it wasn't wise to do anything at the same time every day or the Taliban would figure out the routine and attack. The Taliban were not considered to be very smart.

Each morning I'd be ready — early. Head scarf covering my hair, tunic and trousers covering my butt, carrying my bag with books, lunch and cell phone. I'd hear the crackle/garble of the radio: the school's transport office letting the guards know they were turning the corner into our street and the muttering of a guard's reply. One guard opened the gate, the other moved into the street with rifle a-ready. I stayed within the wall's perimeter until the van had pulled up in front and then climbed aboard, with a

"*Salaam! Sobh ba khayr.*" (More or less.)

"Hello! Good morning."

I could manage some rudimentary greetings. I think I was understood. In any case, the drivers and escorts always smiled.

And we were off.

5

School

...the 50th reunion weekend coming up. We will be toasting you ... and I just must say, you have chosen the most creative way to avoid a high school reunion that I have ever heard of! (Email from a friend, September 13, 2009)

Transport took a different route to and from our neighborhood on a daily basis — another part of the security scheme meant to confuse the Taliban. It looked good on paper, but in reality it was a pain in the ass. Literally. Every road in the neighborhood had its own set of holes and rocks and debris, some worse than others. It was only thanks to the skill of our drivers that none of us suffered permanent injury.

The main drag from the guesthouse to school was Darulaman Road. It ran alongside the university, passed the Parliament buildings and ended at the hill where sat the ruined Darulaman Palace. The palace was the vantage point from which the road and the rest of Kabul were bombed when Afghans fought Afghans in the early 90s. In the other direction, Darulaman Road was the main artery into Kabul proper, approximately ten miles away.

The road was constantly under construction. Once one section of the road was finished, it was time to repave a previously paved section. The story goes that the international money given to build the road was so diluted by the time it got to the contractors actually doing the work that only cheap material was used, which led to the pave/repave cycle.

The road was wide; it had no lane markings, but then Afghan drivers don't abide by "stay in your own lane" rules anyway so it didn't matter. Frontage roads ran along each side for most of its length. With the proposed trees and walkways and new surface it was to be a beautiful boulevard leading to Parliament and the palace. But not any time soon. Vehicles moved on either of the access roads or the main road, or alternated between the two, depending on the state of road construction. Trucks zipped around, kicking up sand and

31

Top: This young man seems befuddled by his choices: a restaurant, a fishmonger and a butcher vie for his business. *Bottom:* A blue-shrouded woman negotiates with a street vendor at the early morning market on Darulaman Road.

dirt and pebbles; pedestrians dodged cars and cars dodged each other. There were no sidewalks and the trees were yet to be planted.

Sometimes a sand-colored armored vehicle — NATO variety — would lumber down the road. Sometimes traffic would pull over. I thought initially it was for the same reason that one pulled over for fire trucks in the States — getting out of their way. More likely traffic pulled over, when it did, out of fear — fear that a trigger-happy youngster riding in the turret seat would take offense at some perceived disrespect and start shooting. I always resisted the temptation to duck as we passed. (Once again Kabul was a war zone and we were reminded of that fact daily.)

Generally, though, it was a pleasant drive in the mornings before the dust was airborne. Shopkeepers opened their shuttered doors or tarps were unrolled from what looked like shipping containers rusting along the road. A market area sat at an intersection near our turnoff and the vendors would already be out with their tents or tables, having claimed their "spot" at first light. Everything was sold on the street, including shoes and tires and fuel, but the busiest stalls in the early morning were the ones selling fruits and vegetables.

Most of the customers at the stalls in the early morning were women — burka-clad women. And here's where I saw the reality of life in Afghanistan for many women. I knew about burkas, of course. I had read about them and seen pictures, but here they were in real life. Women covered head to toe, front to back in a dusty blue shroud. The mesh that covers the face actually restricts air flow and vision and it is made of strong cloth that is not easily torn. That first look at these "hidden" women cinched it for me: I had left my world and was in an alternative universe.

Many mornings a horse and carriage were stationed at the turnoff to school; rides were presumably for sale. It was an old-fashioned carriage with a fringed top and big wheels, and it was decorated with plastic flowers. The horse, too, was decorated with flowers, and he sported a plume-like affair on his head — which was always hung low with shame at the indignity foisted upon him.

Across from the horse and carriage was a butcher's stall; skinned, headless and fly-ridden animal carcasses were ever on display.

Every morning guards and gates welcomed us to school and checked for hidden explosive devices, and the day began.

We were supposed to flash our ID badge at an electronic device when we arrived. I rarely bothered; no one seemed to care and I think it was broken in any case.

I was one of the early ones to arrive at school, preferring to be there rather than hang out at the guesthouse. There were no early morning classes (my classes that first semester started at 3:00 P.M.) so school was quiet and fairly empty when I arrived. Few students and only one or two of the regular faculty were on campus.

My office was one of four in what I called a "pod," a separate office section with its own door into the main hallway. Each pod had only one air unit for both heating and cooling; it was located in one of the offices. So if the owner of that office was not in, and the office was locked, there was no access to the controls on the heating/air unit. Ongoing and mostly unsuccessful attempts were made to remind the office owner to leave the remote control on the ledge of her doorway. Sometimes she did; sometimes not. Climate in the "pod" was a problem. When it got very cold, the boiler would kick in and then two of the offices would have heat — those with the pipes. The rest of us stole space heaters from the supply office.

In the warm weather, flies visited our offices. Many, many flies. Luckily we all were issued fly swatters and knew how to use them.

As many as three of the five daily calls to prayer fell within school hours.

Every morning a horse and buggy waited for customers who never seemed to come.

At school, a gate and a greeter with a gun met us every morning.

The mosque was just down the street and we could hear the muezzin sing out "Al-laaaaaaah Ak-baaaaar." That particular muezzin had a mournful, drawn-out call. "Al-laaaaaaah Ak-baaaaar." I still hear that mournful cadence in my head.

The school was only four years old and was still smoothing out several wrinkles. For instance, not everything worked — all the time. Internet service usually worked and the power was generally consistent. But sometimes during my night classes, the lights would go off. Emergency lights would eventually flicker on and everyone would wait to see what happened next. Sometimes normal power resumed; other times an emergency generator would start up and classes would continue.

Another concern that bothered me and some others: not everything was up to western standards of sanitation. The women's bathrooms, for instance, were a problem. They included hoses and faucets for the women's pre-prayer ablutions. The drains were always clogged and the floors were always wet. I suspect the men's bathrooms were much the same, and there were no separate bathrooms for the faculty.

The school had a cafeteria where all of the students and most of the fac-

The AUAF campus on a winter's day with the administration building in the background.

ulty and staff ate lunch and dinner on a daily basis. (Breakfast wasn't served.) A chicken or a meat dish was always on the menu. The only difference between the two, as far as I could see, was the color of the meat, which was always thoroughly cooked and absolutely without any flavor. Slaughtering practices in Muslim countries entail bleeding the animals out,[1] and therefore they have no "juice" when they are cooked, which means there is no gravy and to me, no taste.

The kitchen was open to view and filled with cooks and helpers chopping and stirring and wiping and washing, amidst ovens and pots and pans. Dishwashing was in large sinks in a separate room which was also visible from the seating area. Not a pretty sight. Meals were assembled as we watched: a piece of chicken or meat from one pot, a dollop of rice from another. "May I have a knife, please?" I always had to ask. And one of the cooks would grab a paring knife and wipe it off for me on his apron.

Rice was always available and it was good. Now and then French fries were on the menu. Despite our pleas to cook them longer, however, they were always disappointingly limp.

Fresh vegetables were offered every day, usually tomatoes and cucumbers. I ate them when I first arrived in Kabul, until someone suggested that they were being washed in the bacteria-ridden local water supply. I stopped eating anything raw at that point. It was probably too late; I am sure that I was probably already infected. (Infection with at least one of the bacteria found in the water is asymptomatic and I wasn't to find out about its presence until much later in my stay.)

The food was plentiful, however, and nourishing (except for the bacteria) and other than the tasteless meat not bad at all.

In the warmer weather, bees joined us for lunch. They didn't sting; they just wanted our food. They were a distraction.

The administrator in charge of the cafeteria, in response to our complaints and concerns about menu selection and sanitation practices, asked for volunteers for a cafeteria committee. I raised my hand. This turned out to be another instance of Afghans doing whatever possible to meet the needs of their guests. (In this instance, the international faculty and staff.) We had meetings, we came up with ideas and we suggested hand-washing routines.

We even had a party one night to see if the students would be interested in some American-style food.

The event was held at the men's dorm, and the women's dorm was also invited. We brought Cokes and pizza. Someone made macaroni and cheese and a chili dish. Pizza won hands down.

We also asked if a vegetarian meal could be offered a couple of times a week. In our minds that might be a tomato sauce with veggies and rice. It was suggested, instead, that we simply not ask for meat on the lunch plate — *voila*, a vegetarian meal.

The outcome of these meetings was that a cook was hired who could make cheeseburgers (more or less) and pizza (Afghan style) and they were subsequently offered for dinner. (I usually ate dinner at the guesthouse, however.) Luncheon selections remained chicken or meat with rice and fresh vegetables. Vegetarian meal were available consisting of rice and fresh vegetables. Hand washing and dishwashing practices improved somewhat for a while. I was bringing my own lunch by that time: canned sardines and canned soup.

It was in the cafeteria at lunch one day that I was introduced to a version of the "Ugly American" found in Afghanistan. The students, faculty and staff all lined up around noon at the counter to order a meal, pay and then move along to the "plate assembly" area. Afghans are not big on forming lines and I had to remind a student now and then that he couldn't just jump in ahead of me. On the other hand, one American faculty member made it a practice to go to the head of the line. She told me that it was OK — we were faculty, and we could go first. I think she meant that we were Americans and we could go first. Anyway, I didn't want to use up any "passes" I might be entitled to by barging ahead of my students in a food line.

Probably the best part of the university was its small but well-used library. It had a limited holding, but it was growing. Many of us brought books with us when we arrived and donated them to the library when we left. I was part of a book campaign that resulted in the addition of a few dozen Newbery Medal books, shipped from the States. At that time, the library staff was going through the steps of including its holdings in an international database.

Computers and computer hookups were available in the main room and in three glassed-in quiet areas where the students could study or surf the Internet or hang out. Cozy sitting areas were also scattered about. The university did not have a student center as such, so many of the students congregated in the library. I always enjoyed stopping by, for it was vibrant with youthful energy and dedication.

The library clerk was an Afghan. Fahran was a young man with a bruised look about him. It seemed as if Afghan men were either relentlessly cheerful or disturbingly sad. Fahran always tried a smile, which made it to his lips, but not to his sad eyes. His English was not good and neither was my Dari, but we managed to communicate. He helped me find my way about and I tried to thank him. It was to him that I would bring my almost daily lament: "Fahran, the copier doesn't work." And he'd smile his shy smile and come and clear it up or unplug something — whatever made the pesky machine begin chugging along again. He was accepted into the school's undergraduate program the second semester I was there; then he started smiling more often.

Construction of some sort was always going on at school. The cafeteria porch was enclosed. A door was fixed. A wall was built. Outside the library there was an enclosed patio that would be pretty one day, but wasn't yet.

The gardeners always seemed to be out and about: digging holes, planting trees and flowers, turning the soil and pruning and nurturing the rosebushes. The grass that peeked up between the rose beds and the sidewalk was clipped by hand; the clippings were put in a flat bowl and then removed. Old dead grass was never seen littering the sidewalks.

What was seen littering the sidewalks and the grassy areas was litter — particularly cigarette butts and empty cigarette packs. ("No smoking" was not a campaign that had reached Afghanistan.) The grounds were swept clean daily, making room for new litter. The use of trash receptacles was encouraged, but that seemed to be a new concept for many of the students.

The cigarette pack litter turned out to be a bonanza for me at one point.

One of the lab experiments called for a flask to be covered with tinfoil. A hole was then poked through the foil, allowing a heated gas to escape. Just as the lab period started, I realized that I had no foil, which meant no experiment. Yikes, what to do? And then I remembered the litter outside and the tinfoil that was usually part of the cigarette packs. After corralling several students to help in my search, we found enough discarded cigarette packs with enough foil to save the day.

For a while, through some fluke of misunderstanding there was a newspaper waiting for me each morning when I went to the administration building. The guard at the door would smile and nod and I would ask — in Dari — "Is my paper here?" "Soon," he would reply.

It was the *Afghanistan Times* and it was written in English, but English as written by an Afghan and unedited by a native English speaker, which meant the language was fractured. I wondered who read the paper. Certainly not Afghans: if they were literate they would probably read an Afghan paper in Dari. Certainly not internationals: they would read an English-language paper — if one could be found.

Near as I could figure it, the paper was for the internationals who were used to reading a daily and local paper (like me). Apart from the garbled syntax and misuse of words there was little real news. There were editorials, which seemed to be unbiased, and there were reports of President Karzai's latest maneuvers. There was never any "what's happening" kind of story: an art show coming to town, a play, a festival. And, of course, there was no news of women's events. Mostly for security reasons, I was told. Crowd management, perhaps. For one reason or another, a gathering of internationals or women in one place was not publicized.

Staff

Our involvement as internationals in the Afghan community in Kabul was severely limited; the only opportunity that most of us had to meet and interact with Afghans on a daily basis was at school. Apart from the triumvirate of white guys who were the top management, Afghans filled most of the middle management, clerical, janitorial and gardening roles. And the students were all Afghans.

When I arrived at school, an older gentleman on the cleaning staff (I never knew his name) would be mopping the hall or dumping trash. We would go through the morning greeting: how are you, good morning, fine, thank you, good morning — in a pidgin English/Dari exchange. He would always stop and bow his head and touch his chest (heart) and we'd both smile.

I always thought he looked at me with wonder: "So that's what an American looks like." But he made me feel welcome.

Each morning he would ask with gestures if I wanted my office dusted. (Kabul air is filled with dust that creeps inside at night and covers desks and computers. Dusting every day was a good idea.) My answer depended on how many papers and files on my desk needed to be moved.

There was a faculty lounge down the hall from my office which had a table and some comfortable chairs, a microwave and a disappearing refrigerator. One day it would be there, and then the next it might be *gharob* (broken)—which happened a lot. And then the next day it would not be there. Apparently it could not be fixed in situ. Some days the cleaner and I would have a nodding and gesturing conversation about where the refrigerator (and my food supply) might be.

On the mornings when the refrigerator was *gharob,* but still in residence, I would have curdled milk for my coffee. The cleaner would nod and smile and nod. And try to look sad about the mess in my cup. He was only being polite. Warm or curdled milk was not on his "worry" list. He would say in English. "It is Afghanistan."[2] And that explained the problem to him, and finally to me.

There was a mouse in my office one day. The crisis started with a rustling in my wastebasket. I imposed on a male colleague to help; he moved the basket and a mouse jumped out and hid behind the bookcase. At that point I called for reinforcements: the cleaner. He arrived to move the bookcase; other men arrived to stand around. One of my pod mates stood on her chair. No one knew what to do about finding the mouse.

After more standing around and thinking the cleaner decided the mouse was not in my office. How did he know? To ensure that it would not return, he tucked folded papers into the gap between the bottom of the door and the floor. Presumably mice can't climb cubicle walls. I did not know this. It struck me that mice could probably chew through paper if needed, but I didn't bring this up. The cleaner was happy having solved the problem. I certainly hoped he had.

During the day I would run into several of the cleaning women on the staff. They were dressed in what looked like an old-fashioned nun's outfit with only their faces uncovered. One woman in particular wore brown a lot and stopped when she saw me and touched her chest and always smiled. She made me feel like royalty when I greeted her.

Several Afghan women worked in the offices. Badria knew all there was to know about the admission records. She was a beautiful young woman in her early 30s who had helped teach girls in secret when the Taliban were in power. And there was Hasti, in the IT department, who left because she found a better-paying job. I would call her regularly when there was a computer glitch — which was often. Her English was as bad as my Dari, but she understood "Please come," and soon she appeared in my office to fix whatever I had screwed up.

And then there was Habib, in the cafeteria. He meticulously wrote down everything that was sold and its price. He was a living cash register. He always smiled at me and tried to explain the finer points of that day's meal.

All of the Afghan staff— the drivers and escorts, gardeners and maintenance people and administrative personnel — went out of their way to be friendly and helpful. In many cases we were deferred to as teachers and older women. In some cases we were looked upon as favored children: amusing and hard to understand, but relatively harmless. As I was to appreciate later, as long as I wasn't being pushed around, that was fine with me.

Faculty

All faculty members had to have a degree from a Western school, which meant that if you had a degree from India or Pakistan or any African nation you could not teach at the university. Exceptions were made, but generally Afghans were not on the faculty unless they had been educated in the West. Several Afghans (men and women) were on the faculty. They had left the country during the Taliban times and were educated in Europe or in the States. Once the Taliban were ousted from power in 2001, these expatriates returned. They had strong familial and political ties to the country and some came back to make a difference. I was impressed.

The International faculty was an oddball group. I guess you have to be something of an oddball to choose to go to a war zone. I mean we were not shanghaied; we were not dragged there in chains. And the salary was not so great. We made a (presumably) conscious decision to go there. Once again — why?

There were several couples among the faculty. I envied them for all the sexual reasons, but I thought having a constant companion in a guesthouse would be tedious. Two rooms of your own — maybe. But most of the rest of the facilities would be shared with housemates. Living conditions for couples were anything but private. An option was to move into an apartment, but again, that option had its own set of problems: getting broken stuff fixed, for one, as noted earlier.

Most of us were single. Several had lived and worked abroad, some for many years, and some had no U.S. home to return to. A few 20-something-year-olds were looking for adventure. One or two internationals wanted to help and others were simply keeping their heads down and hoping to survive until their contract was over. One group "needed" to go home: they did not like being in Kabul and had nothing but contempt for Afghans and Afghanistan. At least two men had issues at home and were, I suspect, "on the run." One older woman needed a job; one staff member saw this experience as his last chance to have a meaningful life. And then there was me.

One thing I noted about some of the internationals on the faculty and staff—their memory loss about how to behave in public, particularly with regard to littering. Littering is not a punishable offense in Afghanistan; in fact, nobody cares. And neither did some of the internationals, who probably did not throw stuff on the ground in their home country, but in Afghanistan — well, everybody does it and so did they. It pissed me off.

Students

The students were Afghans. Afghanistan is still a tribal society and students in large part recognized themselves and their classmates as a member of a tribe first: as Pashtuns from the South, or Tajiks or Uzbeks from the North and West, or as Hazaras from central Afghanistan.

Anger and hatred still existed between the various tribes and those same feelings were just under the surface at school. Generally, however, sticky situations were avoided and an uneasy peace reigned. There was one fellow who was outspoken and ranted loudly and constantly against a unified Afghanistan. Although what he was preaching was a hot-button item for some, the students chose to laugh at him or discount him rather than engage him in an argument.

Taliban or Taliban sympathizers were certainly present on campus. It's not as though the Taliban are distinguishable from other Afghans. They are Afghans after all, and blend in just fine. This was not an issue that I discussed with my students. At least we were not blown up.

We were, however, a target for attack. Even though the university was an Afghan NGO (nongovernmental organization), it was called the American University of Afghanistan. "American" in the title elicited strong and negative feelings in some quarters. There was a part of the Afghan population that thought America was an immoral society and that Americans promoted unhealthy thought and libidinous behavior. Attacking the "American" school would be a good way for extremists to make an antiwestern statement. Our gated entrance would not deter a determined terrorist.

The theory was that what saved us from the wrath of the extremist element, including the Taliban, were the parents of the students. The university was expensive and many of the students had wealthy parents with possible warlord connections. Perhaps those powerful connections protected the school. It was one thing, perhaps, to bomb innocent people, but another thing if one of those innocent people was your daughter.

I'm sure everyone at school — students and faculty and staff— realized how vulnerable the school was to attack, but there was nothing to be done, and life went on.

The students all spoke and understood English. However, writing and reading English well was another matter, as I was to find out.

Many of the students had had a splintered early education; their families had left Afghanistan when the Taliban were in power. Now they were back and trying to continue their schooling.

One Afghan student, who had received a medical degree in Pakistan, was not allowed to practice in Afghanistan so he was currently seeking another degree.

One group of young men was raised in Iran where, I was told, since they were not Iranian citizens they were discriminated against and had a hard time getting into an Iranian university. I thought of them as the "Young Turks." They were slightly wild and bursting with testosterone, and they were the dancers, the athletes, and the bad boys.

Some students lived with their parents or other family members in Kabul. Others lived in the dorms, which were within walking distance of school. The men and women's dorms were separated by a wall and I heard that there was no sneaking back and forth. I wondered if that could possibly be true.

The young men dressed in Western clothes, jeans and tee-shirts, often with a *shemagh* (striped scarf) around their necks, or they wore the traditional *shalwar kameez* (tunic top with loose pants).

In Afghanistan men are physically close — to a degree that is unusual and would be questioned in the West. We saw this behavior at school, as well. When Afghan men greet each other they shake hands and draw together and nudge each other's face. Often they will continue to hold hands as they talk. It is not unusual to see two men walking down the street holding hands and it is not assumed that these men are gay. Women, too, are physically close to one another, holding hands and hugging, even more so than in the West.

The women students did not wear burkas. While burkas were seen on the streets and in the shops, they were not seen at school. Our drivers and escorts led us to believe that it was generally lower-class women who wore the traditional blue burkas. It seemed that if higher-class women or working women chose to be totally covered in a burka, they wore a modification of it.

For instance, at school, a few of the women wore what looked to me like a nun's habit, leaving only the face visible.

Most of the women students dressed as I did, in tunic tops and pants or skirts and they covered their hair. A few students, however, stretched the limits of what was probably considered appropriate attire. For instance, the female version of the *shalwar kameez* was brightly colored and glittery and was often worn with high (and sexy) heels. These women were not bold in demeanor, by any means, but certainly bold in manner of dress.

And the young men were delighted.

The sexes do not mix in Afghanistan. Even in Kabul, which is more liberal than the rest of the country, men and women live largely separate lives. Some women are out in the workforce, but it is usually with the approval of their fathers, their brothers or their husbands. Marriages are generally arranged and there is little social interaction between the couple before marriage. Dating is rare. Now and then I would see a young man and woman walking down the street together, maybe even holding hands. But it was not a common sight. Husbands and wives could be seen walking together, but again not often.

It was different at school. Women made up twenty percent of the student population, and just as in Afghan society, changes were happening. The student government's charter guaranteed several seats to the women students,[3] which meant that an opportunity existed for women to take over student government by claiming their seats and then winning a majority of the rest of the open seats. This did not happen, however, while I was there.

Cultural boundaries still existed, but they were looser and the sexes pretty much mingled freely. A large part of the student population came from the city and from wealthy parents who were most probably not as conservative as their provincial countrymen. Many of the students had been exposed to Western ideas of dating and other male/female interactions. Some had spent time in the West or gone to school in the States.

One group of students had attended a high school in Kabul — the International School — that catered to wealthy children. They had learned English and spoke it with an American accent. These students, both males and females, tended to hang together and isolated themselves from the rest of the students. It may have been due to their wealth, their education, their westernization, or a combination, but these were the socially elite. They generally lived with their families in Kabul rather than in the dorm.

There were several other cliques at school that consisted of both genders. Several female students had spent time in the West. They were called back to Afghanistan by their families, mostly their fathers, to ensure that they were not affected by "loose" Western ways. These young women were used to having young men around and were often part of a mixed crowd that hung out together. One student told me that she and the male students were "just friends." This group would roughhouse on the lawn and smoke cigarettes together. Since smoking is another example of "inappropriate" behavior for women, they usually smoked behind one office building — which turned out to be outside my window.

For these young people, the university was the only place where they could spend time together and many came to school to be with their friends, even when school was not in session.

Even though at school there was much freedom between the sexes, it was cautious, and traditional separation still remained in many instances.

At the party we held to try to interest the students in cafeteria meals other than meat and rice, we laid out the food and sodas on several picnic tables and then stood back as the males attacked the food. The women sat off by themselves and would not join the crowd even with our annoying urging. They only helped themselves once the men left the tables, and then they sat elsewhere to eat.

The separate-eating routine seemed to be standard operating procedure. In the spring we held a staff appreciation lunch and had it catered. The men were everywhere; the women were seated together in a corner. Food was Afghanistan buffet style with sloppy queuing. The men filled their plates. I suggested that maybe some could come back for a second helping rather than risk collapsing the plate under the weight of multiple servings. No, the Afghan way was to go through the line once and pile the plate high. I did not know if this was a result of their tottering economy — grab what you can when you can — or not. After the men had helped themselves, it was the women's turn to come to the tables and take what was left.

One of my students was a heavily cloaked, stocky woman. A fellow always seemed to be waiting for her after class and I would see them together on campus now and then. I asked her once if he was her boyfriend. (It was none of my business, of course, but that had not stopped me from asking impertinent questions in my prior life.) "My cousin," she said. I wasn't sure if she had answered my question.

The two of them were also in one of my labs. He was always quite solicitous of her: leaning over her constantly, seemingly protective, and he often spoke up for her in class. I had a chance to talk with her on her own once or twice. She seemed to have direction and drive and substance. But then when he was around, she was different ... shrunken, somehow. I felt that she was pleading with me, albeit silently, to understand that her behavior around him was expected in their culture and in their family. And perhaps the only way she was allowed to attend the American school was if she was accompanied and protected by this male relative.

There were some "liaisons" at the university between the men and women, but they were extremely covert. It was one thing to hang around with a group of mixed-gender friends, quite another to go off as a couple.

Some hanky-panky was going on as well. Or so I was told. The faculty generally turned a blind eye to what was not too obvious. One teacher caught a couple in the midst of a sexual encounter. She spoke to them about it, not so much about the morality of the action but to point out how any hint of impropriety that was seen to be allowed or encouraged by the American University could bring harm to the school and to faculty, staff and students.

In general, I got the sense that the students at school realized what an anomaly their "mixed" society was in ultraconservative Afghanistan — and how fragile. The students were careful to maintain the look of tradition even if not its letter. I helped one female student celebrate her birthday. Ordinarily she either wore her head scarf or not, depending on how she felt at the time. When a picture was taken of her with her birthday cake however, she put her scarf on. She said it would not be a good idea if the picture found its way to Facebook and she was seen without a covering for her hair.

Now and then a student would push the limits. One of my students sent me a desperate text message one day. She wanted to spend time with her boyfriend on his birthday and school was the only place they could go. The student had no reason to be on campus that particular day and so she asked me to lie for her and say we were meeting. Her parents would "kill her," she said, if they knew she was meeting a boyfriend. "It's Afghanistan, after all," she explained. I told her I'd back her up if needed, but as it turned out nothing happened.

Some of the young women were standoffish with the young men. One told me that they were scared of the men. Someone could take a picture of one of them and post it online and her family in the provinces would hear about it and she might be pulled out of school and brought home and left to an arranged marriage — or worse. They had to constantly be on guard of their reputations. Flirting and dressing provocatively could be misinterpreted and the consequences could be severe.

Some of the young men had never been around a woman who was not a relative — had never talked with any woman other than their mother or sister or aunt or grandmother. These students had never been exposed to a society where men and women were viewed as more or less equal. Many simply did not know how to behave. They ogled the women and trailed them, tripping over themselves to get their attention. Some of the "oglers" gathered at the entrance to the library building and made it difficult for the young women to pass without being harassed. Some of the women used another entrance to avoid having to walk through the gauntlet of aggressive males.

But generally everyone got along or at least gave the appearance of getting along. I got the feeling that the students liked their life at school and most seemed willing to accept and even embrace a society where men and women talked with one another and listened to one another and were friends. It seemed to work — at least at school.

6

Teaching

I meet the two lecture classes for the second time today—I sure hope I can be interesting and cool! (Email to my sister, September 1, 2009)

The American University of Afghanistan (AUAF) is a liberal arts school. When I was there it offered degrees in business as well as in computer science.

All the classes at the university were taught in English. The students had to achieve a certain level of competence in the language before they were admitted to the undergraduate program. Those not qualifying were enrolled in a series of English courses on reading, writing, speaking and understanding the language, designed to improve their proficiency to the point where they could make a 500 on the TOEFL (Test of English as a Foreign Language). At that point they could apply for entrance into the university.

For many of the students, however, additional courses in English were not necessary; some had lived in the States or abroad, and others had attended the International School in Kabul.

AUAF was expensive compared to the other main university in town, Kabul University, but scholarships were available. The classes at Kabul University, however, were taught in Dari and the selling point for the American University was the emphasis on English. Attending the American University implied that you were capable of studying and performing in English; being competent in English was necessary for any possibility of emigration to the West and also increasingly important for success in the business/finance community in Kabul.

I was hired to teach chemistry, or so I thought. However, to be fair, I'm not sure I was paying close attention to some of the details of my contract. I knew I was going to Afghanistan to teach and would get paid. The rest, I confess, may have been tucked into a safe place for later review.

I was hired in May of 2009 and the contract was for ten months starting in August. When I signed the contract, I had at least three months to pack, to worry and to wonder how scared I should be.

I would also have time to choose a book, write a syllabus and plan some lectures for a new course — Introduction to Science. Not chemistry, but close, I guessed. (As it turned out, I did teach Chemistry during the second semester in Kabul.)

And then began the first of many problems associated with teaching in Afghanistan: textbooks and how to get them there. A postal service exists, but not many use this service. I'm not sure how packages got to Afghanistan, but I doubt it was by mail. I never found a post office, a mailbox or a postman. Instead goods (including books) were shipped through an independent carrier which avoided not only Customs but also the "Ministry of Censorship." (It's not actually called that, but that's what it does.)

One group of friends in the States did try to mail a box of goodies to me. It took four months to arrive. Customs, as I found out from this personal experience, apparently opens several packages at one time, inspects their contents and then repacks the boxes, but not necessarily with the original items. I ended up with a bottle of Prosamax along with the books my friends had sent. I feel sure that the prostate cancer medicine was not meant for me. I wondered what the intended recipient had found in its place when he opened his box!

Getting review copies of texts was complicated. Few companies published general science books at the university level, and those few had difficulty with the concept that I could be reviewing a book in the U.S., but would need it in Afghanistan. The other problem was that representatives of U.S. publishers abroad wanted to send review copies to Kabul where the book was to be used and not to the U.S. where I would be reviewing it.

I was told by the librarian at AUAF to keep an eye out for books with minimum text as the students' command of English, so he said, was marginal. College-level science books have pictures, yes, but also whole paragraphs of the written word. Finding "picture" books for college students was not going to be easy. I tried to minimize the amount of reading required by allotting twenty pages (of text and pictures) per assignment. I also decided to prepare my classroom presentations using PowerPoint. I figured if the students were struggling with English they might find it difficult to follow a lecture in English; maybe cartoon pictures and brief text on slides would work better.

As it turned out, I gave only one lecture with the PowerPoint slides. The students wanted copies of the slides as study guides, which I wasn't willing to do. Some students tried to take pictures of each slide with their cell phones; some students chit-chatted to their neighbors and ignored me and my slides altogether. So much for my PowerPoint presentation.

I had assumed that my students would need snappy pictures and mono-syllabic text to understand the basic science I was to be teaching. In fact, I had infantilized my students. When I was growing up my mother was called "Penny's mom." I suppose saying "Mrs. Burnett" was considered beyond the capability of a child. In the same way, some of the teachers at school gave their name to students as Dr. Jane or Dr. Dana. I cringed when I first heard "Dr. Penny" and, subsequently, insisted on Dr. Travis from my students. Amazingly, they handled it just fine.

I decided to start lecturing as I had in the U.S., using a marker and a whiteboard. My students soon learned to cope not only with new English words (scientific terms) but also with my incredibly bad handwriting.

The course itself— Introduction to Science — was also an infantile course as it turned out. Imagine teaching an intro course to physics, chemistry and biology — in one semester. Most of the students, contrary to some beliefs, were already aware of the basic tenets of all three disciplines. Many had attended schools elsewhere and some already had degrees. These students did not need to be introduced to science; most were way ahead of where they were assumed to be. But the course served as a good way to introduce me to the students (and them to me) and I was happy with our interactions, if not with the course content.

The class roll came with pictures of the students — a huge help since pronunciation of many of the students' names did not come easily. Calling the roll that first day of class was a disaster for me, but the students had a great time listening to me mangling their names. Some were impossible for me to even guess at the pronunciation: Yetylbayeva, for a start. But even the more common names like Jafar and Fawad did not come trippingly off my tongue. And it was hard to tell from the class roll I was given which was a last name and which was a first name. (The distinction is fuzzy in Afghani-stan.)

So ... the next day I handed out 3 x 5 cards with their enrollment names and asked them to write down what they wanted me to call them and return the cards to me. This exercise was only somewhat successful. One young man wrote, "You can call me Attaey," and then I was left with the problem of pro-nouncing "Attaey."

I also asked the students to write anything else on the card they thought I would like to hear. Here's where I learned from some of them that much was expected of me. For instance, one student wrote, "Let's see how this class is, I hope it is interesting and cool." This particular student also informed me that he learned "much better when the subject is taught in an interesting way."

I found that brown-nosing crosses international lines with this comment: "Science is my favorite subject." And "Happy to be in this class."

One student "loves science, but not complexity in science." I enjoyed the complexity of that thought.

Quite a few liked soccer and many were business majors.

Several had been in the States: "I like DC, because it is the capital and also green."

One young woman wanted to be a doctor.

It was Ramadan,[1] so I got, "We're fasting; let us go a bit earlier."

There was a Nirvana fan and one who was planning on an MBA at Stanford.

And, my favorite one: "I'm so excited."

Perfect.

I was also introduced to the chasm between the genders in that first week of classes. The students were filing in looking for seats at the two-chaired tables that served as desks. One young man, Fawad, tried to sit with two of his male classmates. Seeing the "crowd," I gestured for him to move to the next table which had a vacant seat. He froze. A head-scarved woman was sitting at that table, with her head down trying for invisibility. It was obvious that sitting next to this woman was a big problem for the fellow and perhaps for her as well. I decided not to confront this "issue" and bowed out with "Just sit somewhere else" to him.

Gender issues, while present, were not generally a problem because they were ignored by everyone, including me. Time, however, was another issue.

Time in Afghanistan is loosely woven and is reflected in the casualness with which my students showed up for class, sometimes as much as ten minutes late. One lab day students were dribbling in at a slower pace than usual. I had a "meltdown" (not the last one I was to have in Afghanistan). I picked up my papers and books and announced that I was going back to my office and they could come and get me when everybody was in class.

Once in my office, I felt beyond foolish and wondered how I was going to emerge from the situation with my pride intact. It wasn't long before two students showed up and sheepishly asked if I would come back as everyone was present. I had some terrific students.

I taught chemistry the second semester. The subject had been taught the previous spring, but it was called Chemistry and Man or something equally lightweight and it didn't have a lab period to go with the lecture. This time the course was to be more chemistry and less biology and would have a two-hour lab co-requisite.

The chemistry lab, which also doubled as a physics and a biology lab, had running water, lab tables and a board. It had no gas line and no chemicals. My job was not just to pull together some lab exercises but also to arrange for the purchase of chemicals and glassware for the experiments.

Here's where I ran into another gender issue at the university. It turned out that the lab assistant's husband also worked at the university. They had an office together and he walked her to the classroom. On our first trip to buy lab supplies, he came with us. He apparently did not think it was appropriate for his wife, even in the company of another woman, to be out and about on the streets of Kabul. I put a stop to that particular "custom." When the two of us went out the next time, without him, he called her several times to find out where she was and when she would be back at school. It was an impossible situation; she was an educated woman and loved her husband, but that's the way things were.

I had planned for the first experiment to be one in which the students would gather data about each other — in this case ages, gender, and class (freshman, sophomore, etc.). Their job was to organize the data and present the results graphically using Microsoft Excel. The students knew how to use the software, so I thought this would be a nifty exercise in analyzing and graphing data.

The results ranged from excellent to awful.

This was my first experience with plagiarism among the students. Of the twenty or so reports I received, eight included exactly the same graph — same font, same titles, and same errors. This led to one of my several rants with this class. How disappointed I was in them and how they should know better. I also commented on what bad "cheaters" they were since they had all made the same dumb mistake. I can't remember how I graded the papers, but I remember many of the students were not pleased.

The next day my student buddy Aziz showed up in my office and plopped down in the other chair. After a certain amount of hemming and hawing, he admitted that it had been his paper that everyone copied. When I reminded him that this was not appropriate behavior, he said he couldn't say no to his friends. I went through the spiel about his role as the start of the next generation in Afghanistan of presumably educated people and how the future of the country was in his hands and and and. He said he knew, but he couldn't refuse to help.

We worked it out that he would turn his lab reports in before the deadline so that when his friends asked to see them, he could honestly say that he had turned them in. Afghanistan is a country of hospitable people — not only to guests but to one another. Helping friends trumps concerns about plagiarizing and, as I found out later, cheating.

Anyone who's ever been a teacher (and can admit mistakes) knows the feeling of standing in front of a class, lecturing, drawing on the board, pointing and suddenly realizing that what was being said made absolutely no sense. Often you just carry on and hope that no one is paying attention, which is often the case, or you stop and try to get back on track. There's also the time when what you're saying is not correct; the facts don't back up your assertions. Such was the case one afternoon, early in my first semester.

That afternoon I was talking about density, the measurement of mass per unit volume. I drew a glass on the board and a line in the glass and labeled the bottom half of the glass "oil" and the top half of the glass "water." One female student who was sitting in the front row questioned my drawing and suggested that oil would really float on water since it is less dense. Well, of course, she was right, but I had a senior moment and blanked, mumbled a bit and said I would check it out. I'm sure that impressed them with my knowledge of the scientific world. One student even remarked, "I guess things are different in America."

Anyway, I fretted over my mistake and kicked myself thoroughly overnight. The next day at the beginning of class I drew two glasses on the board with a line on each separating the oil and water. On the first, I wrote "water" on the top and "oil" on the bottom as I had the day before. And then I drew a big "X" through my drawing. On the second, I labeled the two liquids in their proper place — oil floats on water — and put a big check on that drawing. Before I could turn around, the class started cheering. It was wonderful. I don't know what that meant, but it made me feel good. I did a "ta da" and apologized. What an experience.

I tried to think before speaking after that and kept mistakes to a minimum. The class cheered other times as well; they thought it cheer-worthy if I managed to express a complete thought in Dari, for instance.

I had great students and generally felt accepted (and appreciated) by them, and we had some interesting exchanges. In our classroom discussions we did not discuss certain topics — politics being one. Actually we discussed little of life outside the classroom.

I did tell them, however, that I had a son and two cats. In fact, a picture of one of the cats, Mojo by name, was the last slide of my abortive PowerPoint presentation. One day when several students were exceptionally late, I told the rest of the class the name of my other cat — Slick — and that his name would be a bonus question on the next test which they would know and the late students wouldn't.

I told them that I supported Obama for president and that I was from Charleston, South Carolina. One test problem was whether or not water boiled at a higher temperature in Charleston than in Kabul, based on the difference in their heights above sea level. (It boils at a lower temperature in Afghanistan.)

They also knew I was restricted in my movements around Kabul and they knew how crazy that made me.

My students had their own restrictions as I was to find out when I told them about my plans to go to India for a week over spring break. The students were generally responsive in class but were somewhat less so when I made that particular announcement. I asked Aziz what the problem was. He said, "We can't go."

That's when I found out that if you're an Afghan, you are stuck. You cannot leave the country. Well, you can if you find a country willing to give you a visa, but not many countries will.[2]

The travel restrictions imposed on Afghans also affect their ability to exit airports between flights. For instance, I could take a flight from London to Kabul via Dubai and leave the Dubai airport on the layover. Afghans could not; they were not allowed in the country without a visa and, thus, could not leave the airport.

Many Afghans would like to leave their country and some would not go back. From another country's perspective, that's the problem. Countries are loath to give student visas or tourist visas for fear that the Afghan travelers will disappear and ultimately become a burden on that country because they cannot legally hold a job. An Afghan can travel outside of Afghanistan if he has a job and/or a sponsor.

So what this meant to my students was that they were trapped.

However, Afghans could go freely to Pakistan to the East. I worked with a woman from Pakistan and she still had family there; she had no problem visiting them whenever she liked. Internationals, that I knew, did not visit Pakistan; it is not on the list of places to go. Afghans did not want to go there either. Why? I asked one student whose family had moved to Pakistan during the troubles why she didn't stay there to complete her education. She said Pakistan was even worse than Afghanistan for educational opportunities.

Even traveling west to Iran was problematic for an Afghan. One of my students whose family had fled there during the Taliban era had a difficult time visiting relatives who were still there. The Iranian government was afraid that this young man, who was an Afghan, would not leave Iran once admitted. Whether they thought he would become an unemployed burden on the state or whether they simply didn't like Afghans can't be answered. Most internationals didn't visit Iran either. It was also missing from the list of preferred places to go.

But other than Pakistan and Iran, the places that Afghans could visit were limited. Here was a new concept for me: the idea that people couldn't simply leave a place whenever they chose, even with a moderate amount of paperwork.

So when I told my students about my plans to go to India and how I'd never been and wasn't that exciting, their rather desultory reaction was due to envy. We can't go, they said. Did they wonder if I was really so stupid that I didn't realize that they were stuck; that I had freedoms they could only dream about? It was not my finest moment.

But, in a sense, my traveling about Kabul was also restricted. I couldn't just leave the guesthouse anytime I wanted. I had to arrange transport, or a guard. Oh yes, I could call a cab. In fact I could have moved out of the guesthouse and lived in an apartment on my own. But as mentioned earlier, there were problems attendant to that move: language problems, handyman problems, security problems. Essentially, I could not move around freely.

I had several favorite students. High on that list was Aziz. He was the student who admitted to being the originator of the copied lab reports. The first time he dropped by after that encounter I greeted him with "Now what?" I said it with a measure of annoyance: sometimes the demands of school and the classes and the students were overwhelming. What did this one want now? Needless to say he was nonplussed by my response — at least initially. But then we settled into a routine. He'd come by regularly, whether a class or lab was scheduled or not, plop down in my visitor's chair, spread his legs and look at me. I'd say, "Now what?" and we'd both laugh.

Sometimes he had a question about the lab or a question about an impending test and sometimes we just chatted. He was one of my best students, but his true love was sociology. I found it fascinating that he found sociology (of all things) fascinating. He was not a reader and spent most of his off-campus time watching movies, as did most of the students. In fact, he provided me with copies of all the Oscar winners that spring. I don't know how he got them and I didn't ask.

Three of my young women students were Ara, Marwa and Mina. They were smart, best friends and always together. Once when I saw them sitting on a bench, I told them they reminded me of the three monkeys, "See No Evil, Hear No Evil and Speak No Evil ... all sitting in a row."

Another time I sat with them and watched a cricket game being played in the grassy area between buildings. I told them I knew what they were doing: that I had been young once and had enjoyed watching young men at play. (Actually still do.) "Oh, no," they said. "We're not doing that." Afghan young women do not admit to "eyeing" young men — simply not done. And the young men — well, they, like young men everywhere, were showing off for the women, and perhaps doing a bit of their own "eyeing." The music between the sexes, while muted in Afghanistan, is still there!

Marwa was the "intellectual" of the group — diagnosing a problem, probing for reasonable solutions, always with a serious expression on her face. Because of her good grades she was invited to the U.S. one summer as part of a student delegation. (I found out later that she was too homesick to enjoy herself on the trip.) It was Marwa who was elected to come by my office after one of my hissy fits to ask me to please come back to class.

Mina was a reader and a writer and the most sociable of the three. She talked with me a lot about her childhood in Iran during the Taliban times and her commitment to her studies. She wanted to be a writer and submitted her stories to an online zine.

And then there was Ara — a shy, introspective and self-effacing young woman who did not think she could do as well as her friends. "Oh, I can't do that," she would tell me with her head tucked down into her shoulders. She earned good grades, however, and I particularly enjoyed awarding them; she always looked so pleased with herself.

These three women (and there were others as well) were super students. They seemed to enjoy the classwork; they spoke up regularly (unusual for Afghan women) and they generally just "got it" — understood what being a student was all about. In the lab, for instance, I had told all the students that I expected them to collaborate and work with each other on their reports, but that when it came time to actually write up their reports, it should be their own work. Not many listened and I had to have several more meltdowns in order to get their attention. With these three, however, even though they always worked as partners, their reports were their own — their own mistakes and their own triumphs. They just got it.

Generally the women did better overall than the men. The women were not as loud as the men and they never asked the irritating and waste-your-time questions that some of the young men enjoyed throwing out. One young student called me on a mistake (the density error mentioned previously) and she would not back down. She knew she was right — and so she was.

I think the women had to be exceptional in order to convince their fathers (or their brothers) to allow them to attend school. Most of these women would not have been there if not for the active support of their families — particularly the male members of their families. Even though the genders are equal under the Constitution of Afghanistan, in reality, women generally followed the dictates of their male relatives.[3]

Another of my favorite students was Kareem. He was tall and shy and excelled in my classes. He came by my office one day to tell me he was going to have to miss lab that afternoon. When I asked why, he said that his family was having work done on their house and his father was away. He had to go home to deal with the workers because his mother was not allowed to talk to the men. He looked shamefaced as he told me this. I thought this young man realized how bizarre this sounded to me since I came from a country where I could talk to whomever I chose. I just nodded. Many of the young people at school realized the need for change, particularly in their social contacts. This was another subject, however, that I rarely discussed with my students.

I saw a couple of women students, ones who were not in my classes, every day. They knew who I was and what I taught and they would always greet me with my name and a smile. I am sorry I did not have the opportunity to teach these young women. One was taking advanced mathematics and from what her professor told me, she was a whiz and far outpaced the men in the class.

One young woman came to talk to me about taking my course. She had plans. She was engaged to marry someone in the States. But first she was going to finish up at the university, go to the States and get her doctorate and then come back to Afghanistan and be the finance minister. Wow. I was so impressed with how she had her life mapped out. This young woman wore clothes that completely covered her body and her hair; only her face was visible. She had made the choice, she said, to dress conservatively rather than in the jeans, tunic top and scarf that many of the other young women wore. Her mother was conservative and her father liberal and they apparently encouraged her to think for herself, which she did.

Another student wanted to go to Australia and study to be a doctor. But her father did not want her to go, which meant she would not be going to Australia.

I shared books with another student — a young woman who was a voracious reader. I gave her several collections of short stories and she lent me action novels. One book I shared was *Earth and Ashes* by Atiq Rahimi, a story of devastating loss in Afghanistan. It probably was not a good decision. She didn't need to be reminded of the sadness in her country and, of course, did not enjoy the detachment from the sadness as I did. Once again, not my finest moment.

One young woman sent me text messages regularly with "How are you today?" and "Are we having a quiz?" Several students would text me to make sure I was OK after one or two of the bombings that occurred while I was in Kabul, and particularly after the incident of the car bomb in May.

In nice weather the students sat on the grass or on the benches. Some of the young men would hang out by the door to the library building, smoking and talking and ogling the young women. A cricket pitch was available and the men would play soccer and sometimes fly kites or throw a Frisbee.

I enjoyed being at school. I felt respected and needed and mostly liked. The students smiled and said, "Hi, Dr. Travis"; my colleagues said, "Hey"; and in the distance were the wonderful mountains of Kabul. Life was good.

7

Extracurricular School

Dari lessons start this week ... wanted to get started earlier, but nothing much gets done here during Ramadan: everyone too hungry or too thirsty. Or during Eid: party time. (Email to my sister, September 26, 2009)

English Problems and Dari Lessons

The Afghanistan Constitution specifies that the state shall "foster and develop all languages of Afghanistan." It also states that Pashto and Dari shall be the official languages of the state, but in areas where Uzbeki, Turkmani, Pachiaie, Nuristani, Baluchi or Pamiri were spoken, that any of those languages "in addition to Pashto and Dari, shall be the third official language." Afghanistan is a tribal society and the placation of the tribes and the recognition of the various languages were important issues in the formulation of its constitution.[1]

Many Afghans, including most of my students, could speak or at least understand several languages, including some of the above, as well as Urdu and Hindi, spoken in Pakistan and India. (I felt woefully inadequate, language-wise, with only English and a smattering of high school Spanish and French in my repertoire plus a couple of years of college Russian — none of which did I remember with any clarity.)

Dari is essentially the lingua franca of Kabul. It is actually Farsi (Persian), the language of Iran. It was explained to me that the relationship between the two is similar to the relationship between British English and American English.

Dari is written in Arabic script. I had taken two years of Arabic and unfortunately, or fortunately, as it turned out — the only thing I learned in the class was how to sound out some simple words. In Kabul when signs were written in Dari, they were often transliterations of English words — so I could tortuously work my way through a sign that read "Ch Ken" or "Ch z Brgr" and figure out what was being sold. I was quite pleased with myself when I was able to do this; nobody else was impressed.

My students generally spoke decent English and were able to understand most of what I said. I think. In any case, they rarely asked for a translation.

It may be that they did not understand as much as I assumed they did. For instance, I used the words "digit" and "decimal" frequently in my discussion of precision and accuracy in science. I finally realized that some students did not hear the difference between the two words; to a non-native English speaker, they sound somewhat alike. Since the students didn't realize that they were hearing two different words, they didn't ask for clarification, and I continued merrily on my way — thinking I was making sense.

Despite the language problems, however, my students generally did well in my classes, at least if they studied. The cheaters and those students who were relying on end-of-the-semester grade negotiation did not do well.

Although the students could understand and speak English, their reading and writing skills were generally poor. They were mostly nonreaders; their knowledge of the world came from their own experience (and from videos) rather than through the window of books. I asked a question about an igloo on one test (with reference to the heat capacity of water) and someone asked what an igloo was.

Reading English was a chore for many and I doubt some of them read the textbook — ever. But then I am not sure if my students in the States ever bothered to read the textbook either.

Most of the students struggled with writing in English. I was eternally grateful that I did not teach any of the writing classes or classes that required reports. From what I heard, they were excruciating. A modicum of writing was necessary to complete some lab reports and for short answer questions on the tests. To say the students' written English was inadequate is being kind.

I, of course, knew no Dari when I first arrived and there really was no pressure on me to learn the language. In class everyone spoke English, at least to me. All of the Afghans at school, including the escorts and drivers, spoke at least some English, enough to make themselves understood. Since we had so little contact with Afghans other than at school, it was not absolutely essential to know Dari to get along. Very few of my colleagues were able to speak more than rudimentary Dari.

I soon realized that hearing a language spoken regularly that I couldn't understand was increasing the societal isolation that I was beginning to feel. We did learn to say *tashakoor* in the first week. And *salaam* (hello). So when the university offered Dari lessons to those of us interested (and paid some of the cost), I signed up eagerly.

The lessons went well; Dari is a relatively easy language.

I learned to say *Man yak ostad hastam.* (I am a professor.)

Emrose juma hast. (Today is Friday.)

Kabul yak keshwar na hast; ein yak shaher hast. (Kabul is not a country; it is a city.)

And in response to the mouse threat — see earlier discussion — I learned to say: *Derose yak mooshdar daftar-e man bud.* (Yesterday a mouse was in my office.)

At least once a week in class I would write a new phrase I had learned on the board. And try to say it. My students would laugh.

I had problems with pronunciation. I would say *Kahoob astom* (I'm fine). Someone would say, "No, *Khub,*" giving it the back of the throat effort that can only be mimicked in English with "kh" (not an easy sound). And I'd reply "Right, *kahoob,* that's what I'm saying." And we'd all laugh.

Unfortunately life in Kabul started to interfere with the Dari lessons. School was closed for three weeks in November and Dari classes were cancelled; then came the holidays and the new semester. Administrative problems arose at school and resuming Dari lessons was not on the agenda of important items. Plans were made to start lessons again, but they never came to fruition. If I had stayed longer, I would have pursued language classes.

One thing I learned: not everyone at school felt it was important to learn the local language. The other thing I learned: although the Dari grammar was relatively simple, pronunciation was difficult: *Khub/Khahoob* being a case in point.

Rock Concert

In the fall the school's Music Club held a rock concert. Proceeds were to go to one of the refugee camps, specifically to buy blankets for the coming winter. The event was not advertised because of security concerns — it was unwise to encourage the gathering of crowds of people that no one knew. It was one of the many frustrating problems in Kabul. Word of mouth was how the word got out. The English-language newspaper reported only events in the past, never upcoming events, and flyers were never posted nor were ads run on the TV or on the radio.

Despite the lack of advertising, there were some guests at the concert, but almost all the attendees were associated with the university. The students were there en masse and some of the faculty and staff showed up as well. I wouldn't have missed it for the world.

Kabul Dreams, a local band that was beginning to generate interest in the rock world, was scheduled to perform, as was a group of Afghan musicians playing traditional instruments and Afghan folk music.

The musicians set up on the stage of the gym. Some chairs were set on the floor, but not many. Certainly not enough for everyone they expected to attend. In fact, the chairs were for the female students. I'm not sure why — perhaps as a way to isolate them from the rest of the crowd. If they were standing, they would be able to mingle and I don't think that would have been culturally acceptable.

The Afghan musicians played first. It is very difficult way to describe the sounds of Afghan music. Usually in concerts (and that night as well), the musicians start with slow and soulful laments of the "lost loves" variety. To my ear the music at first sounded twangy, like bluegrass instruments in need of tuning. But the ear adapts and I learned to appreciate the music, particularly when the beat picked up and the rhythm turned lively. Really lively. As it did that evening.

An area was soon cleared and the dancing began, but for only men. One young man started by moving towards the center, swaying to the music. I particularly remember the way his upper body undulated and his arms and hands beckoned. I was standing with a woman colleague and we were both absolutely transfixed by this young man and his moves. Then we realized it was one of our students. What a transformation!

Afghan society provides little opportunity for the release of the raging hormones of the young students. Some of the men played cricket and some of the women did aerobics. Release also came, at least for the men, when there would be a chance to dance. As a group.

It is called Attan dancing and it is the national Afghan dance. My first experience with it was at a music festival I went to one night at the German Embassy. That night as an Afghan band played Afghan music, several young men got up, formed a loose circle and began to move about, weaving and bobbing and waving their arms faster and faster to the drum beat.

It was a sight to behold. I had seen men dance before. Every now and then at the local pub a few men with a lot of booze in them would get up and dance together. And I had seen *Zorba the Greek*, of course, and admired the moves of Anthony Quinn as he moved faster and faster to the compelling sounds of the Greek bouzouki. I thought at the time how sexy it was to see men dance. That night in Kabul I was happy to admit that men dancing still made this old heart sing.

That evening, once one man started to dance, others quickly joined in and they danced in a circle, more or less. There seemed to be specific steps but very little rigor in the dance. Just down, up, wave, turn, down up, wave and turn. And only the men danced.

Afghan women dance too, but not with the men. I was told that a curtain could be hung between the sexes and then they could both dance. At weddings, the sexes danced together but only if they were closely related. At this concert the women sat in the chairs with bitter faces — hiding their tapping feet, I suspect.

I suggested that maybe the next time a concert was held that the chairs could be removed and then everyone, including the women, would be forced to stand, getting people up and moving around. And then I thought, the women might sway a bit with the music and then might sway a bit with each other and then maybe everyone (men and women) would sway as a group and then they would be dancing. I was not thinking straight. That wasn't going to happen. Not even at the school, in its fairly liberal setting. Cultural strictures still ruled.

At this concert a "fog" generator was brought in. The idea was, as silly as it might sound, that the fog might help "hide" who was dancing and maybe the sexes would mix. It didn't work. The idea of a curtain was not considered, I think probably because it encouraged even more separateness of the sexes.

The second performance that night was rock music and then the dancing morphed into jumping up and down and waving one's arms. A student told me they didn't know the steps to rock music. "Could I teach them?" Oh how I would have liked to have said, "Yes, I can do that."

But I don't really know how to dance. An old magazine ad featured the caption, "They laughed when I sat down at the piano," showing a pianist who had obviously wowed his friends with his newly learned skill. I always wanted to be that person. I wanted people to say to me, "I didn't know you could (dance, sing, draw) like that!" It never happened.

In any case, I couldn't teach the students a rock step. Actually, I don't think there are any. So they jumped up and down. One student asked me to dance and I jumped up and down too.

The girls all sat on chairs off to the sidelines and watched.

I asked one of the young female students who appeared to have both male and female friends why she didn't dance. "You hang with the guys and study with them and they're your friends. Why don't you dance with them?"

"The boys would think differently of me," was her response. Dancing is sexy; even bad dancing is an exhibition of sorts. And I knew that some of those women were excellent dancers when separated from the men. So dancing was crossing that line between friendship and a possible liaison that would not be allowed in most of Afghan society. Also, people talked, and some of the students could not afford to have word of any unacceptable behavior get back to their parents. Immorality or perceived immorality was vastly inappropriate and could have had them removed summarily from the university.

I asked my buddy Aziz, who was an enthusiastic and tireless dancer, about the dancing situation. He said he wished that when they had dancing opportunities at school everyone would just set aside the traditions for that time. Everyone would dance — males and females — and have a great time. Then the next day, he said, everything would go back to usual. Didn't happen while I was there. Probably won't for some time.

It made me sad to think of the innocent encounters these young people were missing — particularly dancing with one another. I think it made many of the students sad as well.

Club Adviser

Mina asked me to be the advisor for the Arabic Club. It was to be a club for all girls and I was honored to be asked. I told her how I had studied Arabic for two years (for all the good it did me in Afghanistan). I burbled on to her about how important it was for them to learn the language since the Qur'an is written in Arabic and if you can't read the language you have to trust the mullahs to tell you what is in the Holy Book and how that might not be a good idea — mullahs being men and all that. So on and on I chattered and Mina just nodded and smiled. Here was another instance of Afghans letting you believe what made you happy: It was obvious to Mina that I was willing to help and apparently whatever else I had to say was fine with her.

When I signed up as the official advisor I found out that the Arabic Club was in fact the Aerobic Club. I wonder now what on earth Mina thought I was talking about — the Qur'an and mullahs and women's rights. Gad. Just for the record: "Arabic" and "aerobic" can sound quite similar coming from a non-native English speaker.

The only function of the club, apparently, was to do aerobic exercises in the gym a couple of times a week. In order to use the gym they needed an advisor, a.k.a. chaperone. That was me. I think I was also to serve as protector.

A guard sat at the door to the gym, but now and then a male student would sneak in, whereupon the girls would run shrieking into the bathroom. On campus these women were never without their head scarves, and they wore body-disguising tunics and loose trousers as well. For the aerobics sessions they dressed in jeans and brief tops and no scarves. But it wasn't appropriate for a male to see them dressed in that manner; their fathers and their brothers would not have approved. (And it would have been viewed by the extremist element as another instance of Western decadence taking over the school.) So there I was guarding their privacy and their honor.

Since there were limited opportunities for exercising in Kabul I decided to join the class. It wasn't really an exercise class that most Western women would recognize, but was instead more like a dance routine. The teacher tried to get us to step, slide, step, slide, kick, in unison; which most everyone could do, more or less — all to the rhythm of what to my ears sounded like pots and pans clanging together. Sometimes, however, the music was heavy metal rock — and loud. The teacher did not speak English and I did not speak Dari, but I got the message that I was an underperformer. She would even step next to me and patiently try to help me get my feet going in the right way at the right time. It was a challenge for both of us.

I don't know what the girls thought of my efforts: I did manage to stay upright and keep moving. I would have done better in an Arabic Club, but no matter.

8

Issues at School

I asked one of the better students why people were cheating. "They want a better grade." Well duh. Passing isn't what it's about for many of these students—getting A's is. They want not just an education, but A's. (Email to friend, October 20, 2009)

Cheating

I had taught for more than fifteen years in the U.S. before teaching in Afghanistan. I never had any issues with cheating on tests. I always said that if my students were cheating, they weren't very good at it, as no one was getting grades that were not justified by other classwork.

I was warned, however, that cheating in Afghanistan was a problem. Cheating for many students, as I was to find out, was not considered a dishonest act, but rather an acceptable way of achieving success. And they were helped in this endeavor by their family, their friends and their classmates.

I was told, for instance, to have at least two versions of each test since the students sat at small tables for two and it was easy to glance at their tablemate's paper. I followed that advice when I gave my first quiz; I had two different tests for each table. In one case a student had an answer wrong, but it turned out that it actually was the right answer for the question on his tablemate's test. So, it was obvious (and slightly surprising) that the student had merely copied the answer and not bothered to check if the answer fit the question. A lazy cheater, that one.

At the time I didn't think about the fact that there is generally a cheater and a "cheatee," as it were — not only someone who copies, but someone who allows the copying. When I graded the cheater's paper, I wrote on it that he had copied the answer from someone else's paper, which I found unacceptable. I marked his quiz with a big fat zero. The student never said anything to me about this quiz and he subsequently dropped the class. I feel remorse now that I didn't know enough to also punish the "cheatee."

I don't think the issue of the "cheatee" is so important in the U.S. I'm guessing that cheating there is not quite the group activity that it turned out to be in Afghanistan. In my classes at the university, for instance, there always seemed to be a willing supplier of answers. Cheating was definitely a two-person operation.

In any case, after this quiz and my reaction, which I shared with the class, I thought I had solved the problem. Little did I know.

The first big test rolled around after a month or so. I had two versions of the test and made sure that tablemates got different ones. I brought a book to read (which I had always done in the States) while I waited for the students to finish their tests.

Problems started almost immediately. A student had a question. I got up and walked over and tried to answer the question, which was of the "I don't know exactly what you mean here" variety. Students think this type of question will elicit a hint to the answer. "Can't help you," was my universal response.

Then another student raised his hand and another. And each time I'd walk over to the student and try to help. (It was obvious that I was not going to be reading my book.) More than once it was the same student, a certain Cal who had spent some time in the States, spoke English perfectly and with an American accent and always was just on the edge of being obnoxious and/or disrespectful. The other frequent questioner was the big man in the class, the star that everyone wanted to hang with and emulate — Mustafa.

Finally I figured out what was going on. When the next student had a question I told him to come up to the front to talk with me. The first time I did this another student sitting close to the front, looked up and gave me a look that said, "About time you figured it out."

The scheme: When I bent down to talk to a student and had my back to the rest of the class, some of the students signaled one another, passing on information. I suspect there was a certain amount of cell phone use in play as well. I did catch one student reaching down to open up his book bag to reveal his class notes. What a mess!

We all survived that test — barely, but I was in a snit afterwards. I was mad and hurt and totally amazed at the cheating attempts. I talked with Habib, who had tried to look at his notes. I spoke with Mustafa about cheating. He told me he didn't cheat. I said, "I know you didn't cheat, but I think you allowed others to do so." And I warned him that I would be keeping an eye on him. I yelled at Cal. It was awful.

At the time I didn't realize how universal the cheating seemed to be. Not everyone was cheating, but everyone seemed to know what was going on. I felt betrayed.

After that incident I scheduled tests in a large conference room so that each student could have his own desk. I made them put their packs and cell phones against the wall and out of their reach. And the coup de grace was that I scheduled a security guard to proctor the test with me. He didn't carry a gun, but he looked just mean enough that he could have been.

In the second semester I had two students who were friends and who probably helped one another out in other classes. They tried to do so in my class, but I got in the habit of watching them. One would sit looking at his test for most of the period, not writing anything, perhaps thinking, but plotting is more like it. I asked the guard to keep an eye on him because I suspected he was waiting for an opportunity to look at his friend's paper, one seat over from him. It would not have helped much since his friend had a different version of the test and had not studied anyway.

I gave a written test in the lab during my last semester at the university. Everyone had finished the exam except for two students who, I was pretty sure, were working out some scheme to cheat. Neither of them was writing on their paper; both apparently were waiting. Waiting, I think for me to turn my back. I finally ended up standing by one student so I could watch both him and his friend across the room. It was a true waiting game and a test of wills that I was determined to win. At one point they tried to speak in Dari to one another. I had a meltdown. "How dare you speak to one another during a test in a language that I don't understand?" They handed their tests in shortly thereafter. The one student (the cheater, I think) received an F for the lab that he so richly deserved. The cheatee received a B, not the A that he so erroneously thought he deserved.

In some cases the cheating was blatant. I think the most egregious case I had was during a final exam. A young man, Samad, was tired of being badgered by his friend Mehrab to help and just gave in. When Samad finished his test, he slung the scrap paper he had used for doodling and problem solving onto the desk of his friend. I saw it and grabbed the worksheet, telling Samad that I would talk with him later. Unfortunately, Mehrab didn't get a chance to look at the sheet and so I couldn't accuse him of cheating as well, and he was probably the initiator. I gave Samad a zero for the exam, which assured his failing grade for the course. He and several of his friends came to my office to plead for another chance. He "didn't mean it, he was upset, he was tired...." Whatever. I did not back down. At this point in the school year it should have been no surprise about my policy on cheating.

I was not aware of any cheating going on among my women students. I'm not sure, but perhaps it was because women were not familiar with the way the world worked outside the home. Also, I was not aware of cheating among the students who had attended the International School, maybe because they had been inculcated with the anti-cheating message from an early age. I don't know.

Recognizing that cheating was a problem, the school had held several seminars on what cheating was, the university's policy prohibiting it and the punishment for getting caught, and so on. Some students paid attention; most did not.

I ended up reporting several students to the Academic Affairs Department. One of the main problems with the system was that many of the faculty chose not to report cheaters, but to deal with them in their own way. Therefore no record existed of perennial cheating behavior when this behavior continued in subsequent years. Efforts were being made to rectify the situation; I served on a committee to set guidelines for how to report and how to punish cheaters. We never got far in this regard. By the time I left, the committee was bogged down in a bureaucratic quagmire.

Cheating was an ongoing problem at the school. I barely managed to control it in my classes.

Grades

Again, AUAF was only four years old and was still learning how to be a decent University. One problem that had not been fixed was the inflation of grades — the giving of grades that were not based on performance in the classroom.

Some faculty simply did not bother to evaluate the students and gave everyone an A or B, based on who-knows-what criteria. They were not the good teachers and they were slowly being removed.

Some faculty, while employing various methods of assessment, still felt that Afghans should be given a break. After all, they had suffered hardships in their young life and a grade nudge was somehow deserved. These "nudges" (as well as the outright grade handouts) resulted in a history of classes where no one received a grade lower than a B, including science classes. I know in my science classes in the States that never happened.

A grade spread was not evident for many of the classes at AUAF. Grade inflation was a reality.

I did not operate that way. In fact, most of the newer faculty members didn't either.

And then there was the negotiation for grades. Some students (certainly not all) viewed grades as not being related to performance on their part, but rather to be "discussed" at the end of the semester and an amicable "deal" made for a better grade. This attitude was not too surprising since the students, of course, had been in classes where their final grade appeared out of nowhere and didn't seem to be based on anything other than the teacher's whim. Negotiation, which is closely related to bargaining, is part of the Afghan culture; the price for almost anything is negotiable. Grades, too, apparently fell in that category.

The later hires, me included, felt that giving unearned grades was not a good idea because ultimately it made the whole concept of studying and test-taking and actually learning a subject a moot point. Times were changing. However, some of the students had not realized this.

I had my first experience with grade negotiation when a young woman came to my office to pick up an exam. She insisted on a "discussion" of every point I had taken off. The "discussion" went far beyond simply wanting to know what she had done wrong; she was, in fact, negotiating at every question for more points.

That same semester I left the final exams outside my door for the students to pick up. (They were coded by ID numbers so the grades were confidential.) Unfortunately, as each student picked up his test, he dropped in to discuss it with me, point by excruciating point, bargaining at every opportunity for a better grade. After that I gave the tests back en masse with the warning that I would not discuss each individual test question by question, but that if anyone felt that I had committed a gross miscarriage of justice, they could come see me. That cut down on the negotiations.

And then there were the "gifts." Or, bribes, more accurately. I had one student who was smart, spoke good English but simply did not perform on the tests. I think now he really didn't understand that the test was just that — an indication of how much he knew — and he could increase that amount of knowledge by opening his notes or his book and studying. But he didn't and he consistently failed all tests. We had a nice talk one day and he showed me pictures of his home in the mountains and he gave me a necklace of lapis lazuli. I assumed the gift, which did not cost more than appropriate, was not a bribe. But of course it was. Ultimately I still had to fail him. I did not return the gift since by considering it a gift, returning it may have offended him. I don't know whether or not I did the right thing.

One student brought me a much-beaded hat from the provinces, assuring me that it was not expensive and he thought I would like it. Here's what he sent me after he received his final lab grade, but had not yet received the grade for the lecture.

...don't know what would be the outcome of my final exam and am worried very much for receiving a failing grade.... Today, you posted the grades for Chemistry Lab and I had received B. As a compromise I would even suggest to grade me down to D in order to not receive an F in Chemistry lecture.

Now, that's negotiating: trading a worse grade in lab for a better grade in lecture.

He received the failing grade in lab that he deserved. I kept the hat.

And then there were the pitiful pleas:

...I got an F. It is very disappointing because I spent 3 months and I studied more for this course than any other course I had taken, at least I should have gotten a "D."

And as a final resort, some of my students felt that if they discussed their grade with the department chair they would get a "deal." That didn't happen.

School was a learning experience for all of us.

Censorship

I served on several committees at school; one was the library committee, which had occasion to consider the issue of censorship.

The university seemed to have a good reputation and was welcomed by many, but the connection of the school with the U.S. was problematic. It did have "American" in its name. And American troops, along with other NATO forces were stationed in the country. Feelings were mixed about our continued presence — were we benefactors or malefactors?

And then there was the issue of the connection of the university with the U.S.'s perceived immoral lifestyle.

Parents sent their children to the university primarily because classes were taught in English, and the ability to communicate in English was seen to be a necessity for the future leaders of Afghanistan.

Even though the school was started with USAID seed money, it was in fact an Afghan nongovernmental organization (NGO) and had to obey Afghan rules. And not just obey the law, but be aware of and respect the Muslim culture; which leads me to the topic of censorship.

The library had a collection of popular movies on DVD that the students could check out. Until the inception of the censorship committee, there were no rules in place regarding the checking out of these films.

Then we heard of an incident that had occurred in a province some miles out of Kabul. It was at a *jirga*, or a meeting of tribal elders. Before the *jirga* began, everyone was discussing the American University in Kabul that was "inculcating" American cultural values into the minds of Afghan students and was showing sexually explicit movies in the classroom.

One of our students happened to be at the *jirga* and told the assembled elders that the reports were an exaggeration and that AUAF was a good school and doing good things for Afghanistan. This student had actually been in attendance in the class in which the movie in question was shown and was one of those who had walked out at a particular point in the film. Rumor was that the movie in question was Million Dollar Baby and the "sexually explicit" part was a shot of a woman's bare midriff.

The student in question attended one of our meetings and warned us that news travels fast in Afghanistan, even to remote places, and that AUAF needed to be careful about what went on at school because reports "soon soar beyond the walls" in exaggerated form. He wanted the elimination of immoral movies that violated Islamic mores. Apparently it was not controversial ideas, speech or even violence that was in question: only the public showing of sexual images, in particular women in the nude or partially nude.[1]

The two Afghans on the committee pointed out that an incident like the one described could result in AUAF being placed on a target list and that it was best for us to develop a conservative policy with respect to students' access to controversial films. It was further explained that in a sense the school existed through the largesse of the Afghan government, which, of course, was supported by wealthy Afghans who were the fathers of many of the school's students — in particular, the fathers of many women students. Those women were enrolled because of the support of their fathers, but if there was any hint of impropriety at school, including impropriety in the classes or in the subject matter, those women might be immediately withdrawn.

Additionally, it was suggested that faculty members should think twice before showing any movie that might be offensive to the local culture.

When the subject was brought in front of the entire faculty, many had severe reservations about any kind of censorship. This was a university, so the argument went, and the students' exposure to new ideas (and pictures) should not be restricted in any way. Additionally, many felt that interfering with a teacher's right to teach her course as she saw fit, including showing perhaps questionable films, was a violation of academic freedom.

And then there was the point that the students could get any film they wanted from the DVD stores and from black market sources like the one that had supplied Oscar-nominated films to my student friend. But the counter-argument here was, of course, that the school should not be the one supplying these films.

And so the battle raged. I tended to side with the conservative viewpoint, feeling that we were guests in a foreign country and perhaps we should be sensitive to their culture in our classes. But I was conflicted.

This was a touchy subject and was not resolved in the time that I was there ... and may never be.

Sexism

Generally I was not personally a target of sexism. When I first started, a few of my students had an attitude problem — as if what could I possibly have to teach them and how dare I act so boldly. They got over it, mostly.

But then towards the end of my stay some problems arose. Several events were planned at the university where more "outsiders" were present — more young people than I was used to seeing in one place and most of them were not my students.

It was obvious that many of the young men were new to the school environment, perhaps enrolled in the English prep program necessary for some before admittance to the undergraduate program. These students were not just perfecting their English but also learning what it was like to be at an "American-style" university, and particularly how to cope with women — foreign women — who did not cover themselves up and who were in charge.

Some of the young people on those occasions may possibly have been guests of other students — there for a concert or a craft show. I was conscious on those days of being jostled: of walking through a doorway and someone knocking into me or passing someone and having them brush my shoulder.

It took me a while but on one occasion I finally felt the extra contacts and started feeling pushed around. The next time some young man knocked into me as he was coming out of the gym, I jabbed my arm at him. He looked, startled, and I said, "Oh, I'm sorry, was I in your way?" He glared, but stopped himself from doing more and moved off.

It was not an accident when I was bumped into, and I found it denigrating. I was invisible or too tiny to be seen, not worth the trouble to go around. The men just kept walking and I was expected to move aside. That was a brief glimpse of what it meant to be less than human in the eyes of another person. Not a good feeling.

9

Elections, Earthquakes and More Security Issues

Looks like we dodged the bullet here yesterday — no bad stuff even with Clinton being here and Karzai getting inaugurated. I'm still keeping my head down. (Email to friend, November 19, 2009)

Sometimes Afghanistan didn't feel like a collapsing third world country, and other times it did. Afghanistan's second national election was held on August 20, 2009, which was four days before I arrived in Kabul. Hamid Karzai, the U.S.-backed president since 2001, was running for reelection against 40 opponents.[1] Hard to know what to say about a presidential election with 41 candidates.

After the election, the Election Complaints Commission threw out over a million fraudulent votes and, as a result, Karzai did not have the 50 percent majority he needed to win outright.[2] A runoff election (against second place Dr. Abdullah Abdullah) was scheduled for November 7.

Everyone in the international community was involved one way or another in the politics of Afghanistan at the time, primarily because of security issues. Westerners are often targeted when problematic situations arise, and the run-off promised to be problematic, to say the least. Here's what our head of security had to say:

Pre-election: During the build up to Election Day the aim of insurgent/anti-government forces is to disrupt the election process and dissuade the population from voting. This will increase pressure on the government and demonstrate to the wider world that the Afghan security forces are unable to maintain security and conduct a free election.

Election Day: On Election Day a spectacular high profile may be conducted against government, military targets or polling stations in order to draw attention away from the voting and demonstrate the government's inability to secure the capital against attack.

Post Election: Insurgent groups will want to disrupt the collection of ballot boxes and the general election process.

Nothing had been decided as to what the university was going to do, but the people who were present for the first election on August 20 told tales of a five-day lockdown when no one could go anywhere and everyone watched movies and drank.

Days before the rumblings in the political arena became deafening and deadly the earth did some rumbling of its own.

Early in the morning of October 23, I woke up feeling that the earth was being stretched beneath my bed. It was an earthquake and I knew that it was not just my imagination or a dream remnant: the mobile hanging from the light fixture was swaying and there was no wind in my room. An earthquake registering 6.2 on the Richter scale occurred 125 miles away and underground in the Hindu Kush mountains of Badakhshan province in the far northeast of Afghanistan, but the tremors reached Kabul.

An earthquake seemed to be exactly what we were missing to complete the picture of life in Afghanistan: security issues, lack of privacy, restriction on movement, unsafe water, erratic wireless connection, head scarves, and now an earthquake. In fact, that wasn't all that was "missing," as it turned out.

Two days later there was a demonstration down the road from us, centered closer to Kabul University. Demonstrators were reportedly students and it was supposedly set off by a rumor that NATO forces had burned a Qur'an in Wardak province. (The allegation was later denounced by both Afghan and Western officials.)

The demonstration started in the morning and led to a stopping of all transportation between the university and the guesthouses. If you were at school, you stayed there; at home, that's where you remained. People in one guesthouse reported hearing gunfire and a stray bullet found its way onto the campus.

There was also a demonstration at the Serena Hotel (a popular international hotel in town) protesting a banking issue. Another demonstration occurred near a Kabul park. All demonstrators dispersed in the afternoon and the ban on travel was lifted.

The story was that the Taliban, who make up a large percentage of the student population at the other universities in town, were responsible for encouraging these demonstrations, again to disrupt the election process and to discourage voting. (There may have been Taliban, or certainly Taliban sympathizers, who were members of our student population. They kept a low profile, however, and did not take part in demonstrations, as far as anyone could tell.)

Another demonstration erupted on the following day, Monday the 26th; no word on what was the spark. And officials set another ban on travel to and fro. The election was still twelve days off and I, for one, was getting nervous.

Also that day, fourteen Americans died in two helicopter crashes in Afghanistan.

Tuesday the 27th, another demonstration and another ban on travel. It was getting old.

We were then advised that we would, in fact, be locked down for three days around the election (Friday, Saturday and Sunday).

And then on Wednesday the 28th, a UN guesthouse was attacked and five of the UN staff killed along with three Afghan guards. The Taliban claimed credit for the attack, and they announced that they were targeting those who were working on the election. The same day several rockets were fired at the Serena Hotel, but no one was injured.

A Western journalist staying at the hotel was interviewed on National Public Radio and stated that foreigners were "leaving in droves" from Kabul. I'm not sure about the "droves" part; no one from the American University of Afghanistan left.

And here's part of what we got from our head of security:

> As you are aware, fighting erupted in Kabul this morning as Taliban gunmen stormed a UN guest house close to the diplomatic district of the capital. In the run-up to the election it is possible that there will be similar attacks. I do not want to alarm anyone, but....

He had my attention!

> ...I am recommending all residents be prepared for lockdown or short-notice relocation to a safe haven, if required. The advice on "go bags" sent by email yesterday should be adhered to.

My "go" bag consisted of two toy animals, a favorite mobile, a change of clothes and hygiene stuff. We all stocked up on food. And booze.

I asked one of my students what the dorm residents thought of what was going on vis-à-vis the UN bombing. She looked a bit shamefaced when she said that they were largely hoping that the midterm exams would be cancelled. Inured to violence or just students being students?

So three days' worth of demonstrations and an attack on the UN and, of course, more restrictions on travel.

The next night: another earthquake. It was a 6.0 on the Richter scale and from the same area, and again we felt the tremors. We were having a going-away party for a colleague heading back to the States at my guesthouse. Maybe ten people were sitting around a couple of tables, drinking, eating pizza, being silly, and the room started shaking. We assured each other that it was not alcohol-related shakes, but in fact another ... earthquake. Ha, ha! Drinks all around!

On Thursday November 5, five British soldiers were killed by an Afghan policeman who had been working with them.

On the same day the UN decided to pull out some 600 of its 1100 staff members in Kabul: moving them, temporarily, to a safer locale either in Afghanistan or out of the country. This was not good news.

The run-off election was scheduled for Saturday, but Abdullah decided to boycott; the run-off was cancelled and Karzai declared the winner.

The situation calmed down after the non-election, for a while, and security restrictions were lifted. The promised lockdown did not materialize and we were free to travel, more or less. At least two restaurants catering to drinkers of adult beverages were closed on Friday night. Word was that this might be a move towards a more rigid non-alcohol-serving Islamic state — arising perhaps from a promise or two made during the presidential campaign. The other word, and better one from my standpoint, was that it was a temporary situation and could well change as the election receded further into the past. Apart from having our in-town drinking restricted, I did not like the juxtaposition of events: a demonstration with gunfire over an unproven allegation of NATO burning the Qur'an and the deaths of at least fourteen Americans and five British in service in Afghanistan. It just didn't make sense: NATO forces in the country to help, NATO forces falsely accused and NATO forces being killed. And then the bombing in Kabul. The random earthquakes rounded out the picture of life in a war zone. It was not so much fun.

10

Swine Flu

*Can't get out of Dodge. Classes are cancelled, but the school's still open.
And we have to show up.* (Email home, November 2, 2009)
Could you organize faculty seminars? Teach each other stuff? (Friend's
reply)

One fall night on the ride back to the guesthouse, a colleague who was
an Afghan (and knew all the good gossip) told us he'd had the word that
Afghan President Karzai was going to close the schools for three weeks in
response to the global swine flu scare. The next day we found out that the
"word" was true.

The minister of education announced that classes at all public and private
(that was us) schools in Afghanistan would be cancelled for three weeks to
prevent the spread of the disease.

Afghanistan declared a health emergency on Monday to help the government prevent the rapid spread of H1N1 and ordered schools closed for
three weeks as part of measures against the deadly virus.[1]

That was the official story. In some quarters it was felt to be a knee-jerk
and extreme response to the swine flu pandemic. But it was effective. What
better way to instill fear in a population of Muslims than to say "pig"[2] and
"disease" in the same breath?

The unofficial and widely accepted story was that Karzai was concerned
about groups of young people gathering and discussing the recent and
extremely flawed national election results. Closing the schools, not just AUAF
but also Kabul University, would presumably cut down on face time for dis-
sidents. Kabul University, in fact, was a hotbed of political thought and unrest
and generated many of the demonstrations that occurred in the city. I was
not aware of any "unrest" at AUAF, but I'm sure it was there, albeit quiet.

The swine flu closing issue was a textbook example of a politician speaking out of both sides of his mouth. From one side, Karzai says he is a big sup-

porter of education for young Afghans, and then from the other side comes the decision to close the schools in the middle of the year for three weeks and for spurious reasons.

My students were mostly unimpressed with these antics.

Here's a discarded note I found at the library Xerox machine.

Political swine flu disordered all my studying plans.... I was really shocked what to do. I decided to study with my self but it was boring. Then I planned to go Ghazni for some days, I went there and I stayed for three days than I came back. Most of the time I was in dorm. Every moment I took decision to study hard but I couldn't use make the best use of my time. I say applause for the government because of it's prudently decision. Our governors really know how to cheat the people, but in fact it was a deniable treachery for all the students. That is why I complain of my government because I couldn't make best use of my time and all my studying plans disordered.

The faculty's lives were disordered as well. Most of us were just as bored and anxious to start moving again as were the students. Even though the school was technically "closed" and there were no classes, it was still open. The staff came to school; they still had work to do even without students. The faculty was supposed to remain in country and available in case the order was rescinded. Some faculty, however, decided to take a vacation. Some faculty called it a "desertion." I stayed.

To make up for the lost time, plans were to continue the fall semester in January when we came back from our winter break and final exams would be in February. The spring semester would be extended two weeks, to the end of May, and classes would be 10 minutes longer — 85 minutes. Faculty members were not pleased.

So even though school was closed, we had to be there anyway and many students came to campus as well. They used the library's Internet services, they played games and the men watched the women. The students who lived in the dorms came to school because they told me it was more fun than staying in the dorm all day. My student buddy said he was tired of watching movies in his room.

I talked to some of the students who hung around campus during those long weeks. All of them said they were bored!

One student said, "We're wasting time being off in the middle of the semester."

No one mentioned the "threat" of swine flu; in fact the joke among the students was for someone to cough and then everyone would laugh.

11

The New Campus

*Look forward to seeing you on Tuesday. I think we'll just do the salad
thing. I'll provide the salad greens, dressing, bread and dessert. Everyone
else bring salad ingredients and whatever you care to drink. We'll meet at
6:30 as usual. I hope the weather will be nice, so we can sit on the porch.
Bring a sweater, cause it gets cool after the sun goes down. Let me know....*
(Email from Charleston Book Club member, May 18, 2010)

*A suicide bomber detonated himself and others this morning. Blew a big
hole in the wall of the new campus property where I was walking yesterday. The Taliban took credit. I won't be coming to the book club meeting—we can't go anywhere right now. See you soon.* (My reply)

The simple act of walking around by myself was not a possibility in
Kabul—not necessarily exercising, just being able to move about freely and
alone. We walked from building to building at school, of course, but it was
a small and confined area. It was a great deal larger, however, than the garden
at our guesthouse—the "garden" that housed the generator, the guard shack
and two men with a gun. I never thought I would miss simply being able to
get out and walk—alone.

One day some of us heard about a 45-acre plot of land not far from
school where a new campus was being planned. It was suggested that we could
walk or run around the property if we chose. When I first learned about the
land and the possibility of walking there, I was still new in Kabul and still
thinking in U.S. mode. I envisioned a park with paths and trees and maybe
benches scattered about. Then I was told the area was being opened because
all the land mines had finally been cleared out.

The property was not only now mine-free, it was surrounded by a wall
and guards. It was protected and deemed safe for us to visit.

The land was in a barren part of Kabul. Across the road and up on the
hill was Darulaman Palace and behind that the Queen's Palace. All around
us were the mountains of Kabul.

The land still bore the scars from the civil war in the 1900s; one Afghan faction bombed Kabul from the palace, and the campus site caught the stray bomb. The remains of several buildings sat off in a far corner. One had no windows and no interior walls. The roof was only partially intact. In what may have been a courtyard, the remains of a garden still grew. It was covered in sunflowers in deep autumn.

Leftovers from the Soviet occupation in the 1980s were also lying about. A Soviet tank was on site — upside down and rusting into the sand. Shell casings were here and there and in one area rocks had been placed to spell out CCCR — Russian letters for United Soviet Socialist Republic.

It was a rough piece of plowed-up land; excavations were visible, perhaps where a backhoe had worked removing the mines. Some sections were marked off with bricks, which we were told marked off mine areas. But then we were also told that the area was mine-free. I tried not to be confused. Then there were piles of white stones and posts with red flags. Who knew what they meant.

The land had been used by Kabul University and several intact buildings still sheltered animals which were part of their veterinary program.

A half-hearted attempt at a road crawled through part of the property, but it was rut-pitted and covered with fly-away dust in the summer and snowy mud in the winter. Some trees had been planted, but their shade-giving capacities were far in the future.

A soccer field had been marked out and fitted with goalposts, but nothing else. A guard shack or two also sat on the property.

Three of us visited the area two or three times a week. I walked; the two men ran. Sometimes another colleague would come along, but mainly it was just three of us.

The first time I went I remember how free I felt. A great big expanse of land that I could just walk all around, any ol' way I wanted. It was heaven.

One of my exercising colleagues didn't understand my delight in being alone: "We're alone at the guesthouse," said he. But this was different. Here it was alone and outside and just somehow better. Yeah, we were alone in the guesthouse or at school, but we were confined, so it was much like being in prison. The new campus property, with the enclosing walls out in the distance and the mountains as a backdrop, gave the appearance of wide open space.

There were guards, of course. We usually picked up an additional guard on the way and two guards always stayed in a guard shack on the property. The shack was a couple of hundred feet from the locked entrance gate. When we drove up, the driver called the inside guards and eventually one of them

The property for the new campus was a wasteland, but the beauteous, but bombed, Darulaman Palace was always in the background.

would get on a bicycle and ride down the dirt track to the gate and let us in. Then he would get back on his bicycle and ride back to the shack and we would follow him in the van.

I think the guards were there to protect us from snipers. I'm not sure how close to his target a sniper needs to be, but there seemed to be relatively few sniper-hiding places, discounting the buildings of Parliament down the road. There was, however, an abandoned guard tower outside the wall that could have been used as a hiding place. The guards discouraged us from investigating the bombed-out buildings; they said they wanted to be able to see us at all times. I tried not to be nervous.

Several wild dogs were usually lying about the property or prowling for small animals. Food was scarce, however, and the weaker ones did not last long. Periodically, dead dogs would appear; the story was that the mayor of Kabul was having the dogs poisoned.

Mostly the dogs stayed away from us, but now and then one would be brave and approach. At least one of the armed guards always walked around the property, keeping an eye on the dogs, and I guess, us.

The new campus property still contained remnants of the Soviet occupation including this overturned tank.

We went out two or three times a week. It rarely rained in Kabul so that was not a deterrent. One Saturday it was snowing, but we went out anyway. We usually stayed about 45 minutes, which I spent walking around and around the property. I inspected the excavations where presumably mines had been found. I tried to identify some of the wildflowers when spring came — poppies, for one, but not the opium-producing variety. I reveled in the solitude and the physical exercise.

During the swine flu "vacation" when we had more free time, we exercised every day. I came down with a bad lung infection at that time, maybe due to the increased exposure to Kabul's polluted air.

When I was tired of tripping over the rugged terrain that was in some places beaten into a "road," I would walk around the soccer field. They had "planted" a concrete boundary line that encircled the field. The surface was flat, albeit narrow, and I could walk round and round without concentrating on where my feet were falling. When it snowed, I followed my footsteps around and around the field.

Here was where I got my introduction to kite flying. Downed kites were

Neither rain nor snow nor blustery days deterred my exercise companions and I from our chosen mission: get outside and move about.

always lying about. One day one of the guards brought one back to life. I took a turn trying to get the kite aloft. It was not easy. I ran and tried tossing it skyward. And it crashed. I swung it around and it crashed. Finally, one guard took pity on me and showed me how easy it was. But it wasn't. The kite never soared for me. One of my housemates took pictures of our attempts that day. She also caught another guard in the background, watching the fun, seemingly upset because he couldn't join in. But he was in charge of the gun.

Some of the animals from the Kabul University vet school were still in residence. On one of my first trips to the area I noticed an older man seemingly caring for these animals. When I approached him he immediately put out his hand for me to shake. I was surprised since I had been told that men and women didn't shake hands (or touch much at all) in Afghanistan and here was an older and, by the look of him, traditional Afghan reaching for my hand. It was a "write it down" moment.

I was able to greet him in Dari, "Good morning," "How are you," "I'm fine," sort of thing and tell him that I was a teacher at the American University. I think I made myself understood. At least he nodded and smiled. He had several goats with him and there was a cow in the yard and several staked sheep. He told me the words for the animals: *boz, gospan* and *gaw*. He and his goat (the *boz)* posed for a picture — one of my favorites from Afghanistan.

In the spring I noticed that the goats were no longer around, and I asked him, *Koja boz?* (Where's the goat?) He smiled and made a slicing gesture across his throat — gone.

This gentleman was one of the few Afghans I had contact with and he made me feel welcome. I usually stopped to chat (as it were) with him when I first started coming out to the property. Then I stopped. I think it was because of the dog.

A dog hung out around the farm animals and was usually tied to the fence. At first, it seemed friendly enough. It barked and wagged its tail and the caretaker would grab it or tell it to shut up. Then either they got another dog or the puppy grew up — in any case, while the barking continued, the tail wagging didn't; and it was no longer tied to the fence. When I walked too close to the compound, it barked and moved towards me and I got nervous. So I would just wave and keep walking. It still bothers me that I did not keep up the relationship with the caretaker; I hate to think fear of dogs kept me away. But maybe I just wanted this time away from school and the guesthouse to be only for me.

The guards and our driver and escort never really understood why we were out there: why we walked and ran around an empty field for close to an hour — and seemed to enjoy it. But they never said anything and if they smiled, they did it in private. Once again, I can only put their reaction down to Afghan hospitality. We were their guests and if we wanted to walk in the cold or the heat or the snow, then we were welcome to it.

While we exercised they would sit around and drink tea. I was invited to join them one day.

Generally I walked around the property, but in the spring I tried bike riding. Several bikes, in various states of deterioration, were parked at the guard shack. I finally worked up my nerve to ask if I could borrow one.

Once again, Afghans are incredibly hospitable. If an old woman wanted to ride a bike around the dusty, pitted road, well, OK. So on several days I borrowed a bike and rode it up and down the one stretch of "road" that was relatively flat and rock free. Once I skidded and fell. But no one saw me. Or if they did, no one said anything. Overall bike riding was not so much fun, but I did it anyway just to show that I could.

Walking was the pleasure. When I first came back after a short illness and had little energy for walking, just sitting outside and reading was a joy. For some reason there was always at least one school desk on the sidelines of the soccer field. That's where I would sit.

The property also held a small vegetable garden, which I was told was used by some of the Afghan staff. By the time we got there in the late fall most of the plants had withered, but there were still a few smallish green tomatoes clinging to the vines. I got permission to take a few and fried them up for one of my housemates who had never tried a fried green tomato.

In the spring men appeared in the fields, "harvesting" the weeds (alfalfa?) for feed. They were using scythes.

And then in May we got this:

Dear All: We have just received a security alert that the new campus property may be a target of terrorist activity. For this reason; until further notice the new campus property is off limits to all AUAF Staff, Faculty and Students. All activities planned for this site are hereby cancelled until further notice. We regret this inconvenience and will let you know as soon as access can be restored.

I had just finished taking some spring pictures of the blooming flowers on the property. There was a new dog in the area that seemed to have adopted me. At least he followed me around one day. By the time I posted the pictures we had received the security alert and I ended my post with "I hope I get to go back before I leave."

I didn't. On May 18 there was a car bomb attack: eighteen killed and one woman lost her head. It was just outside the new campus property and blew a hole in its wall.

I didn't have a chance to go back to see my new friend the dog or the rest of the spring blooms.

12

Security Revisited

*...it is a fantastic day ... and I'm about to go take a walk with a new
acquaintance* (Email from a friend, December 1, 2009)
*Going for a walk, huh? No scarf. No leers? Nobody thinking kidnapping
thoughts? No security concerns? I will never never never take for granted
the so-called simple pleasures, like being able to take a walk alone.* (My
reply)

At one point in my pre–Kabul conversations, I asked about the difficulty
in getting around if I didn't speak Dari—would I have trouble "mingling"?
I actually used that word. I had visions of myself wandering through open-
air markets, enjoying the hustle and bustle, the sights and sounds of the Kabul
streets, perhaps stopping at a sidewalk café for a glass of wine. I was delu-
sional.

My mentor laughed. "Oh, no, you won't be mingling," she said. And
how right she was. No mingling. Apart from the car bombings and suicide
bombers, there was also the issue of women walking on the streets alone.
Unaccompanied women are often verbally harassed and even grabbed. The
sentiment (in some minds) is that a woman on her own is a prostitute or at
least has adulterous actions in mind.

So we didn't mingle—even the men did not wander the streets. We were
transported back and forth and out and about by a university van (or SUV).
The university hired a security firm which provided guards at the gates and
escorts for us in the van; the drivers were hired by the school.

This "protection" seemed theoretical, however, for I noted that neither
the escort nor the drivers carried weapons: no guns, no batons and no pepper
spray. The guards at the school gates and at the guesthouse were armed, but
not the men in the vehicles. I was told that they had special martial arts training. When I tried to verify this information, however, I got laughs. So ... the
question was: how were they protecting us? And in case you feel like asking:

I never saw any money change hands. Somehow the men's presence made a statement to would-be attackers: These people are protected. Additionally, although our vehicles had no AUAF markings on them, I'm fairly sure that our license plate identified us to checkpoints and troublemakers alike.

Security measures were imposed primarily to thwart kidnappers. We joked about wearing signs that said, "My family doesn't want me back" to deter abductors. But just before I arrived, a Western woman was shot on a street close to our neighborhood. Bad things did happen. I did not dwell on this thought. None of us did.

Several of us would ask regularly, "When was the last kidnapping?" And the answer was, "Can't remember." Were kidnappings infrequent because of the security measures or because there was actually little threat of kidnapping? Then we heard that often kidnappings were kept quiet so as not to disrupt ransom negotiations. There were moments when many of us thought the risk, if there was one, was greatly exaggerated. What the security measures did, in fact, was isolate us from life on the Afghan streets.

When I first learned the security rules, I abided by them ... most of the

Friday was family day in Kabul and the balloon sellers were on the streets, particularly in front of the zoo.

time. Perhaps it was all a self-fulfilling prophecy: impose restrictions in response to a perceived threat and the threat becomes real.

The Taliban were blamed for many things — rightly so, in many cases, I'm sure. But some of the procedures intended to deter Taliban attack didn't make sense. For instance, changing the times of transport — couldn't the Taliban wait for another 15 minutes? — was bizarre. I thought sometimes we were part of a video game. We were the good/bad guys and the other good/bad guys were trying to get us and we were trying to hide from them. But not really, because everyone would clock out at the end of the day and go home to their families. Remember the old Ralph the Coyote and Sam the Sheepdog cartoons — enemies during the day, neighbors at night.

How can you protect a walled facility, even with guards in towers, from a short-range missile? You can't. And you don't try. But you set up a system so it looks to be safe, and feels safe because all the trappings are there: guns, big men, more guns. But it was a charade. And we all went along with it, because we had no choice. In any case, we were all injected with a healthy dose of caution. And I was warned before I came: Afghan life is like an onion: peel one layer and there's still another beneath. I was never quite sure what that meant, but it sounded profound and appeared to describe the layers upon layers of life in Kabul. And one of those layers involved security issues.

In practical terms it meant we were not encouraged to "mingle" with the local populace. (In fact, it was in my contract that I agreed to comply with AUAF's policies, which included security procedures.) We were driven everywhere and generally accompanied on the street by an Afghan escort. Whether or not there really was a constant underlying risk to living in Kabul, we lived as if there were.

13

Out and About in Kabul

We're on lockdown or whatever tomorrow. Why? No one knows. "Security" is all we're ever told. Anyway, I plan to ... what am I talking about? I will be in all day and will try and call you. (Email to a friend, November 7, 2009)

Introduction

The work week started on Sunday in Kabul, as it does in most places in the Muslim world. Friday is their holiday; we would call it the Sabbath. Families spend time together on Fridays. I saw them entering the zoo that we passed on every trip into town. I saw them at Babur Gardens having a picnic or sitting in the tea house. Fridays are the big day of the weekend for many families since some Afghans work on Saturday.

But for Westerns, just as the weekend got to Sunday and "kick back and relax," it was time to go back to work. (I don't think anybody from the West ever gets used to Sundays being Mondays.) The work week starts on Sunday and goes through Thursday.

I taught Sundays through Wednesdays, from early afternoon to early evening, but most days I went to school in the morning. I was up early thanks to the animals and the children and the muezzin's call to prayer and I was ready to conquer the world. I didn't like hanging around the guesthouse on workdays as I felt isolated (and I was).

At school, however, I was part of a bustling community and it invigorated me. The students were challenging and my other faculty activities were energizing. I loved the "being at school" part of my life in Kabul.

But the days were long and exhausting, and when 7:00 P.M. came I was glad to climb into the van for the ride home. That short ride with my colleagues was fun. That's when we wound down and told silly stories about our students or about the mouse hiding in the bookshelf, or about the broken (again) refrigerator. We'd bitch about the administration, and bemoan the inability to get anything done in a reasonable amount of time. And we would try to support each other in the insular world in which we found ourselves.

After arriving home, my first order of business was a glass of wine — a large one. I planned dinner, read my emails, ate and maybe watched some TV. Then I went to bed, read, and slept. I was not bored with my life in the guesthouse; I enjoyed my solitude. (Although in a guesthouse with up to eight other people solitude was a matter of interpretation.)

We had a television, but sitting down for a night of television was problematic. No TV guide, for one thing, and the English-language paper did not publish TV listings. Three or four stations showed movies in English; the rest were in Dari, Pashto, Urdu, or Hindi. The movies from India — the Bollywood movies — were lively enough to warrant a short look, but generally I stuck with the movie channels. Again — no schedule.

On one station a particularly obnoxious emcee-type would announce the next movie time and then go back to a celebrity meet and greet. Unless I was lucky or willing to stay up really late, the chances of seeing a movie from start to finish on a given evening were minuscule. Some nights I would sit down for a few minutes and watch while eating my dinner. Often one of the other houseguests might join me.

DVD's were the main source of viewing entertainment. All the guesthouses maintained a stock of recent and classic movies, some trashy biker films and at least one copy of *Animal House*. A large living area was on the first floor, and some evenings we would all gather there to watch a DVD.

Mostly I learned to watch movies on my laptop, on the short couch in my room, curled up with a glass of wine and one of the (possibly illegally acquired) movies supplied by my student Aziz.

I also played bridge online and read a great deal. The library had a decent collection of popular novels and I had brought books with me, so I traded books with at least one student and several of my colleagues.

The weekends started on Wednesday night for me. I didn't have classes on Thursday, but usually a faculty meeting or committee meeting was scheduled and I went in to school anyway. Some Wednesday nights I would go out to eat.

On the weekend we went grocery shopping — an Event. And sometimes I would go "tourist" shopping: for clothes and trinkets and such. Sometimes I would go to a restaurant/bar. Often I went by myself — there were always people at the bar to talk with — or a group of us might plan an outing.

Shopping, eating, and some sightseeing: that was life away from school We passed a cinema on the way into Kabul, but no one was ever seen going in or out and there was no billboard list of coming attractions. The rumor was that the cinema was a meeting place for homosexuals looking to make a connection. Or maybe it was just closed. I never found out.

As far as special events in Kabul: Since *The Afghanistan Times*, which was written in English, (more or less) had no information about coming attractions of anything (perhaps because it seemed wise not to broadcast where a large number of people would be, particularly a large number of foreigners who spoke English, and just might be Americans), the only way we heard about them was through the "grapevines" which operated through the international and university communities.

I subscribed to "What's Happening," an online newsletter which included a "personals" column. Once there was a message from an Englishman looking to find a Buzkashi game (the "polo" type sport with the dead animal). I contacted him; I wanted to go as well. Nothing ever came of it, though. Special events were rare, but the ones I found out about, I attended.

Weekends in Kabul, unlike those I was used to at home, were not a continuum of sleeping in, hanging out, riding my bike, shopping, taking a walk, coming and going, uptown and downtown and around the town. In Kabul the weekends were made up of isolated events, all of which had to be choreographed through the school's transport office. Want to go to a restaurant? Call Transport and arrange a ride. And then hope they remember to come. Want to visit some other friends? Call Transport, and make sure to get directions, arrange times and hope they remember to come.

But that was life for most us outside of the school environment. As it turned out, having to be driven everywhere provided me with a wonderful opportunity to see and photograph life on the streets of Kabul.

Kabul

Kabul is the capital of Afghanistan and is approximately on the same latitude as my home in Charleston, South Carolina. Unlike Charleston, it is a mile high and landlocked — as is all of Afghanistan. It is nestled in the hills of the Hindu Kush range, part of the Himalayas; the Kabul River runs through the city.

I was warned that the altitude might cause breathing problems, at least initially. It didn't. I was more concerned about the air pollution, which, I had read, was severe. Jane (my mentor) told me it only affected those with preexisting conditions. Hmmm. In any case, it took me two months to come down with a lung infection.

Kabul is crowded, being a city built for three million people that now

Top: Houses high on the hill had a great view, but no piped water. *Bottom:* Afghans fought Afghans for control of Kabul in the early 1990s leaving behind bombed and scarred buildings which are still in evidence.

We were always admonished to close the windows of our security van as we traveled through the streets of Kabul — forcing me to take my pictures through a pane of glass.

houses close to five. Afghans move in from the provinces, particularly from the south, to escape the fighting. Many end up in refugee camps living in tents — for years. These people are considered "internally displaced," not refugees from another country. Since they're not "true" refugees, the United Nations is not responsible for them. They're Afghanistan's problem, and the problem persists.

Some newcomers take up residence on the hills around town. Sandy-hued structures perch on the hillsides and steep and rugged paths wind to the top. Unlike in western countries where "high on the hill" implies wealth and view, in Kabul it means poor and no piped water. Children and their donkeys walked down the hill every morning and filled up water bottles at the public pumps and toted them back up the hill to sell. They did it every day of the week and it took them all day. These children did not attend school regularly.

The houses of Afghans living on the outskirts of town were versions of our guesthouse, two- or three-story buildings with a garden, each surrounded

Flocks of schoolgirls in black tunics and trousers with white head scarves were out and about throughout the day.

by a wall with a gate and a gateman. The garden almost certainly would have rosebushes. In one area on the outskirts of Kabul, new housing projects were being built. But in the city proper many people lived behind gated and rusting metal walls and down dirty and littered alleys.

Kabul is not a pretty city. Bombed repeatedly during the civil war of the 1990s, it has not recovered. It still bears the scars: buildings with gaping holes and pitted roads. Many buildings were left to crumble, and crumble they did.

The remains of the Soviet Cultural Center, a sand-colored building with pockmarked walls and no roof, were still visible along the main road into Kabul. I was told that the building and the land belonged to the Soviet government, which is problematic considering the breakup of the Soviet Union. It was unlikely that any cleanup or tear-down would occur any time soon. And so it sat.

There were a few multistory buildings in Kabul, but not many, and several of them had the bombed-out look of recent terrorist activity: charred walls, broken glass and barricaded doors.

In the center of town, concrete blast walls lined many streets and circled many public buildings, particularly the embassy complexes.

Although I had several maps of the city, I never got a sense of direction — where certain restaurants and stores were in relation to each other and to our neighborhood. The maps were never terribly clear to me and that was not entirely because of the language problem.

I guess since everybody — at least all the Afghans — knew where they were and how to get around, they did not see the need for detailed maps. (At first, I thought perhaps the absence of a good city map was a ploy to keep the Taliban uninformed in terms of streets.) I never knew the address of the guesthouse where we stayed. In fact I didn't know the name of the street where it was located either. I'm not sure it had a name, as a matter of fact. When we called for pizza, we would call one of the guards at the guesthouse to take the phone and give directions.

Kabul has districts, and I knew I lived in *Karte See*, Fourth District, but that's it.

Street names, if they were present at all, were vague, such as #2 Street. Some of the houses in our area had a number on the gate.

Work seems to have stopped in this picture. Perhaps the men are working on a plan to move those rocks — either by hand or by cart.

Ninety-nine percent of the time, the driver, the escort or Transport would know how to get anywhere in Kabul. But not always. Here's an example of directions to an evening of bridge: "If you are using Cab Company A, the house is Adrian's House. If you are using Z or GT cab company, the house is John's house (behind Adrian's house). If you are driving and you know the Kathay Inn, if the inn is on your left, take the first right immediately after the Kathay Inn. Then take the first left. The street will turn to the right. When it straightens out, we are the first group of guard boxes on the right. In all cases: we are at the end of the alley on the left. Feel free to call for directions and I can put one of our staff on the phone with your driver."

Once I had gotten to a place following directions like these, I could only pray that the driver would be able to find it again when I called to be picked up.

My mentor, Jane, had told me about a tailor that she liked. She didn't know his name but she knew where his shop was located, or so she thought. In fact she did not really know where he was, except somewhere around a specific restaurant in our local area. We went back and forth through one particular intersection, round and round a traffic kiosk searching for the tailor whose name we didn't know. I finally gave up and asked to be taken home where I had a hissy fit. Sometimes life was frustrating.

14

Streets and Traffic

Hi mom. It's Saturday and Steve and I are going skating at some secret spot. Well I'll talk at you later. Love. (Email from my son, November 28, 2009)

When we weren't at school or in the guesthouse we were mostly in a security van being driven through the streets from one enclosed space to another enclosed space.

The number of cars and the condition of the streets generally kept speed to a minimum and so a trip of ten miles into town could take an hour. One could bring a book, catch up on gossip, stare out the window or take pictures. I took pictures. After I had been clicking away for some months, one of my compatriots asked me if I hadn't taken all the pictures I could ever want of the streets of Kabul. My reply: "Absolutely not."

One day an attempt was made to restrict my picture-taking. Habib, one of the younger escorts, told me the faceless "they" at school had announced I was not to take any more pictures. I smiled, Habib nodded. He had passed on the message; I heard the message. I ignored the message. It wasn't Habib's problem and nothing more was said.

So I continued to take pictures as we traveled to and from and around the city, and I tried to capture on film the life on the streets of Kabul.

In our street the children (mostly boys) played in the road and flew kites from the rooftops. Flocks of schoolgirls in their black tunics and trousers and white head scarves paraded down the main road throughout the day. There was a playing field nearby and children were always there kicking a soccer ball.

Sometimes I got a glimpse of a toddler peeking out from behind a gate. I took a picture of a grimy little girl (four or five) with a dirty red dress and a lime green head ribbon, leaning against the wall and looking to her left up the street. A few books were hugged to her chest. Often I would see a group of young people hanging out on a fence. Once or twice a young (and presumably prepubescent) girl would be part of the group.

One of my favorite shots was of a little girl in a bright pink bonnet and short pants and sandals. A smaller boy stood apart from her, looking at her in her garish and revealing clothes with an expression that might have been saying, "You're not going out dressed like that, are you?" She was standing as tall as she could and staring back, perhaps saying defiantly, "Oh, yes, I am!"

The main roads outside our neighborhood were filled with shops. Street

These ditches, for snow runoff, I was told, line many of the streets in Kabul. I suspect that more accurately they were for whatever fell into them, including sewage.

vendors operated from carts, kiosks or open doorways. Some vendors walked with their wares. I could barely make out one man who was hidden amidst blue water jugs slung from his arms and shoulders. I thought at first that the containers were watering pots for plants, but they were water jugs for people. Another fellow was strolling and selling balloons. I hoped he got some business, but I wondered who bought balloons in Afghanistan; perhaps someone bought them for their children.

Some young people worked in the shops along the street, at least part of the day. I have a picture of my kite seller, a youngster about nine, in blue jean overalls. He had a crew cut and looked like a grownup with his serious, worried face.

In the warm weather, children sold ice cream from tiny carts. And every morning I'd see a young chef along the highway, sitting next to a smoking grill, waiting for customers.

The street vendors and shop owners were out and about early and stayed open all day, every day. I wondered sometimes how much of a living they could make selling on the street. I thought of the man with the decorated

I wondered as we passed this establishment regularly: could it in fact be the "perfect" restaurant?

horse who waited by school selling buggy rides. Who were his customers? Not tourists. Everyone else was in cars or taking buses or even walking. I never saw anyone take a buggy ride. But, the man with the horse and buggy was always out there — he was employed — he had somewhere to be. I suspect "work" was more of a thing to do and a place to go for many of the vendors rather than a life-sustaining activity. I don't know how some of them survived.

Along Darulaman Road, which ran beside our neighborhood, construction crews were always at work — men with shovels and dump trucks. Move the rocks, dig the dirt, and spread the dust.

Groups of men worked on the mysterious concrete ditch which ran along the roads throughout Kabul. We were told it was for snow removal. No one actually confirmed it in writing, but I suspect the ditches were not only for snow runoff, but for whatever fell into them — like trash. One day I went shopping with a housemate for a microwave and a vacuum cleaner. The salesman ripped off the packaging for us, went to the open door of his store and tossed the paper and cardboard into the ditch.

I also suspected these ditches were the sewage removal system as there was no formal sewer system in Kabul. But this subject was not discussed with the internationals. Perhaps this was another instance of Afghans being hospitable and "not wanting to upset their guests." "Snow runoff" was good, environmentally sound and all that. Besides, none of us really wanted to consider what happened to our waste once it was flushed down the toilet. In fact, it went into a cistern and then to parts unknown.

No matter where in the city we rode, building construction (or destruction) was ongoing. Often it was hard to tell if a building was going up or coming down — I saw men on buildings with ladders and hammers and wheelbarrows. Nothing seemed new, nothing was finished, nothing changed. And sometimes, there was just no knowing what was going on. For instance: the three-story strip mall which was under construction the whole time I was in Kabul. The first floor appeared finished; the second story had wooden sticks (not beams or joists or studs, but sticks) supporting the floor above, which was riddled with rebar pointing skyward. The sign on the building was already completed and maybe predictive. It read, in English: "All Day Shopping Center."

Building signage was a constant source of both amusement and befuddlement. A restaurant touted itself as the perfect restaurant by calling itself "The Perfect Restaurant." A neighborhood grocer's sign read, "Be Happy All the Time." And then there was the shop advertising disposable dishes which had "door" in both English and Dari printed on its entranceway. I now think the signs were not meant to be cheery or self-congratulatory or even explanatory. Rather they were the results of Afghan translators missing some of the nuances of English.

The signs advertising Western food, although written in Arabic script, were transliterated from English. I remembered some of my elementary Arabic and could often sound out some of the words; for example, I might see "ch," "eee," "ssss," "br," "g," "r," and realize I had just read a sign advertising "cheeseburgers."

Billboards spotted the roads. Those that featured people as part of the message used Western-looking men in Western garb and, of course, women who were not wearing burkas or even head scarves. A huge disconnect existed between who was pictured on the signs selling products and the reality of who was on the streets reading the signs. For instance, one sign which was seen all over town advertising a gym depicted a well-oiled, muscular and near naked man — not a usual sight in the streets of Kabul. And, I wondered, how could the image of a bare-chested man flexing his muscles be acceptable in a place where women wore burkas covering virtually all of their faces?

As the road moved into the city, the shops thinned out and we got our

All manner of conveyances populated the city streets.

Top: Brightly-decorated pedicabs were another mode of transportation, but for Afghans, not internationals. *Bottom:* Kabul has sidewalks, but many people insist on walking in the street, making for a complicated interaction between pedestrians, conveyances and animals.

Top: Many of the shops along the way to town looked like recycled storage units —
and probably were. *Bottom:* This head-laden women enshrouded in blue is not trying
to get into the car; she has her hand out for alms from the driver.

Top: This graffiti-pitted wall lined the main road into Kabul. *Bottom:* One of many trash collection/deposition points in the city, this dump was on the main road into town.

first look at the hills which were the backdrop for all life in Kabul. They faced us to the north as we left our neighborhood — green with trees in the good weather and snow-topped in the winter. Once we had circled a crumbling traffic kiosk and headed into the city, the hills turned rocky. Houses of mud, brick and concrete perched on the cliffs, and shops lined one stretch of road at their base. Some of the shops, which may have been recycled storage units, had garage-like doors that could be closed at night. During the day the doors were open and tarps, supported by wooden posts, were strung as awnings. Everything blended together: hills, houses, stalls: all dusty and brown. Now and then colors burst from those monochromatic hillsides: a pale pink house partially hidden by its drab neighbors, for instance. Or a vendor selling plants displayed in brightly-hued clay pots. Another vendor had painted large blue and red flowers on his wall.

Even closer to the city the road became more and more congested, not just with cars and all matter of moving contraptions, but also with people. Everyone walked in the street. I have a picture of a turban-wearing older gentleman strolling in the midst of the traffic. A Western-dressed father with a tight hold on his toddler son stands in the middle of the street. In the background are cars and buses and more people in the street. Women in burkas scurry about, some with heavy loads balanced on their head, and in the far background sits a buff-colored mosque with two minarets poking into the dusty blue sky.

The road suddenly narrowed and became one way as it veered to avoid another empty traffic kiosk — this one painted with red and white stripes. A heavily pitted wall splattered with what was possibly graffiti in Arabic script edged the road, and the cars and people competed for traveling space.

The traffic jam slowly moved along, turned at a corner covered with trash, passed a mosque and traveled along the Kabul River for about a mile before it turned again and headed into the city. The trash was always there and in a somewhat defined heap. More piles were seen on other street corners and in other open areas. Garbage collection was nearly non-existent in Kabul, although large collection bins were seen here and there and were emptied more or less, now and then. Sometimes a lone garbage man could be seen moving stuff from one container to another. Or he may have been a scavenger. Our houseman removed our guesthouse refuse by walking it around the corner and dumping it in the street in what was presumably the dedicated neighborhood dump. Goat and sheep soon appeared, herded in by their young caretakers, and, *voila!*, recycling. Rudimentary, but effective.

Around the corner and across from the mosque was an open courtyard

The drinking water in Kabul is bacteria-ridden, but the Afghans drink it anyway. And for many it must be obtained from a public pump.

where pigeons strutted and smartly dressed men stood about having serious discussions.

A public water pump sat near the mosque. (Not only was Kabul water bacteria-ridden; in many cases it had to be pumped out of the ground.) The pump was always busy. Once I saw an Afghan family: Dad, in traditional dress, looking casual, was watching the street. Mom, in her burka, was watching the two sons, who were wearing Western gear and busily pumping water.

A beggar was always sitting on the corner near the mosque. He was a big man, bearded, wearing sandals, lolling on the ground half asleep, with his possessions in plastic bags strewn around him. Usually another man would be seen crouched down with his head resting in his arms, still another sitting and holding his stuff.

The Kabul River bed runs through the city. It held no water in the fall and winter months of my stay. Instead it held garbage — and goats and sheep grazing on the garbage. When snowmelt swept down from the mountains, the river filled and the garbage floated downstream, but more garbage always appeared to take its place. Now and then a group of internationals

Top: Goods for sale are spread out on the footbridge across the Kabul River. *Bottom:* All manner of items are for sale along the road. Note the sign for the gym with the well-oiled muscleman.

Top: Sometimes goods were displayed along the sidewalk. ***Bottom:*** This gentleman with his dray helps move goods into the city.

would try to clean up the river bed by picking up the litter. Their efforts didn't last. Afghanistan has more things to worry about than (fill in the blank).

The river side of the road was lined with vendors selling mostly clothes. The clothes, well-used by the look of them, were laid out on the bridge railings and on the footbridge crossing the river.

On the other side of the road were shops — tiny, grungy and dilapidated — and vendors who had spread their wares on blankets in the street: from nuts to housewares. Several tailors had shops and animals' skins hung outside. An optician had his sign out and a stall displayed shoes. Some men sat in wheelbarrows watching; others strolled about.

Across the river a line of shops could be seen, but we never got close to them. From a distance they suggested what Kabul may have been before the bombs and before the Taliban. Perhaps cafés thrived there once and people promenaded along the river on a Friday afternoon. At least I hoped so.

But now, for us, there was no way we would be allowed to get out of the car, even with escorts, in that environment — too many people, too much hustle and bustle, too dangerous. So, we peered through the van windows and watched as life went on — outside.

All manner of moving vehicles and all manner of creatures clogged the streets. Goats and sheep were herded through the crush of vehicles, children raced between cars, and carts drawn by skinny horses took their time getting from here to there. Boys on the streets would wave tins of burning *espand*— the seeds of a wild plant — offering to ward off evil spirits for a few Afghanis (Afs). Some would try to clean the windshield. A few young girls would be out and about selling gum or showing a quick smile.

There were bicycles and motorcycles and mopeds and the ubiquitous Toyota cars and trucks. Now and then a solitary donkey could be seen making its lonely way along. Or a few of the hundreds of local feral dogs would be lying in the sun waiting for the dark and their time to prowl. (There was no SPCA in Afghanistan and no animal control officer in Kabul.)

Sometimes a horseman could be seen maneuvering through traffic. And before the festival of Eid, the sacrificial lamb — actually a ram — was on display, decorated in henna for his part in the festivities.

Buses and vans dodged here and there, crammed with passengers. This wasn't public transportation for most of us — no Westerner that I knew traveled in them.

Dusty-clothed men with large flat-bedded carts or drays shouldered their heavy loads into Kabul. (Apparently big trucks were not allowed inside the city limits. These men with their drays were hired to "tranship" goods from

Top: Animal flocks mingled with the traffic on the streets of Kabul. *Bottom:* A solitary donkey searches for friends along this dusty road.

This sacrificial ram has been painted with henna for its part in the Eid festival.

the city limits into the city proper.) Street sweepers could be seen now and then — bent old men sweeping the streets with brooms.

A scholar or two was always sitting on the sidewalk on a prayer rug, reading, probably the Qur'an. Sometimes two men sat in the road, discussing. And now and then, a man with his back to the street, peeing.

Men predominated in the streets. They were the majority of the vendors, the shoppers, the strollers and those hanging out. There were some burka-clad women shoppers and women in modern dress on their way somewhere, but they were not on the streets in numbers like the men and, in Afghanistan, they certainly did not hang out. The men did. No matter what was happening: changing a tire, moving a load, selling shoes or digging a ditch, extra men were always standing around and watching. Sometimes a group of men would be clustered on the corner, crouched and waiting.

Of course there were men who did not spend their time in the streets — who worked in the banks and the schools and the hotels and restaurants. They were the ones I saw on the street walking quickly and with purpose — like one young man, smartly dressed in black pants and a brown leather jacket

Top: Scholars were often seen on the road discussing the finer points of the Qur'an.
Bottom: Men predominate on the streets.

When the men are not shopping or walking about, they're hanging out.

walking down the street, holding a blue notebook in his left hand. He had
somewhere to go. He passed two men sitting on a blanket next to a wall. One
was wrapped up against the cold; the other was begging. No place to go.

The men mostly wore the traditional *shalwar kameez*—in gray, brown
or black. Some wore Western-style suits. Once I caught a picture of a young
man in bright yellow pants. He was striding out accompanied by a woman
in a blue burka—the traditional color of burkas in Afghanistan. I took a picture of an Afghan man in traditional dress and his two burka-clad companions.
(Wives, presumably.) They were standing next to several blue plastic fuel containers which matched exactly the blue of the women's burkas. The scene
startled the eye.

Not all the women wore burkas. Some wore skirts and long coats, usually
in dull colors, along with a scarf for their hair. I saw one older, traditionally
dressed woman clutching the hand of her daughter, who was dressed in jeans
and a bright shirt and no scarf. Now and then a departure from tradition
emerged on the streets.

And, not to be forgotten—an important segment of the population on
the streets: the military and paramilitary. Men with guns were everywhere.
Checkpoints were maintained throughout the city and always near the U.S.

The signs behind this mom and her determined child advertise a pharmacy and an X-ray clinic.

Embassy. Army vehicles were parked (amidst razor wire) at several street corners. Green police jeeps were perched on the hill leading into the city and red-bereted Afghan National Army troops watched over everything. And in the sky, the NATO blimp — the all-seeing eye above Kabul. It never made me feel safe ... just watched.

The streets were filled with movement and life and rare bits of color. Unlike in the West where streets are mostly for getting from here to there, in Kabul the streets are daily life for many. Not just buying and selling and working on the streets, but socializing and reading and studying and hanging out. While so many of the images were dusty and drab, life on the streets was endlessly fascinating and no, I never felt that I had taken all the possible pictures of the streets of Kabul.

Working women don't wear burkas, but they are usually covered up in dark and drab colors.

Traffic in Kabul

Kabul was a jumble of shops and roads and people and animals and people on animals. Add to the mix every imaginable means of transport: cars, trucks, wagons, mopeds and Pedi-cabs. Set the whole thing in motion and you get the traffic jam of the city's streets.

Traffic crawled in Kabul, too many cars and too few roads, some of them barely roadworthy. Some days a member of Parliament would decide to take

Some young women choose to jazz up the customary cover-ups with jeans and bright stripes.

a drive. Then traffic would be rerouted and roads closed to protect him from attack and traffic would crawl even slower. There was nothing to do at such times but sit and wait. Backing up and going another way was out of the question; there were few options for getting in and out of Kabul. Go straight through town or circle town and approach from the other end; neither option was ideal and both took time.

Contributing to the problem were the ubiquitous checkpoints. From the guesthouse or from school there were two ways into the city center of Kabul. One, the shortest way, went through the area where the palace and the U.S. Embassy were located. Here traffic was restricted and the area was heavily guarded. All vehicles going through were stopped, including ours.

I felt sure that the checkpoint people recognized the university vehicles, I'm not sure how — perhaps by license plate. Certainly once they saw a group of us in the van, they realized that we were internationals with foreign passports. But we were stopped anyway. We could still be potential bombers, I guess. We were often asked for our university identification card. I didn't have mine, having conveniently lost it once I saw how awful I could look. One officer was particularly insistent that I show an ID even though I showed him my passport. Finally our escort and the driver convinced him that I was who I said I was and he let us pass. Habib and Ahmed, our two guys, were pissed. "They can't even read," one said. "Trying to be a big shot," said the other. I asked if they would go back after dropping us off and beat them up. I thought I was being funny, but nobody laughed. American-style sarcasm does not play well in Afghanistan.

Many times when we came to a checkpoint, it was "old home week" between our guys and the checkpoint officers. It was my impression that all Afghan men of a certain age, in Kabul at least, knew each other or were related. Our guys would drive up, high-five (or the Afghan equivalent) the officers, who would laugh, and maybe they'd ask us for an ID, maybe not. It amused our guys that we had to produce IDs considering the general illiteracy of the officers.

But the officers had the guns. And we didn't.

Checkpoints were not the only bottleneck in town. The area near the mosque where the road turned to follow along the Kabul River was particularly problematic, especially on Fridays. The mosque was not large enough to accommodate all the Friday worshippers, so the crowd overflowed into the street, more or less totally blocking this main artery into Kabul for long periods of time. I never saw road rage however. Everybody just waited. Some got out of their cars and waited. I took pictures.

I asked my mentor, Jane, about driving in Kabul. "Oh, you won't be driving," she said. She didn't really tell me why. It turned out that very few women drive in Kabul, but I think what she meant and why most internationals don't drive in Kabul is that it takes a video gamer's skill to navigate in traffic with no pattern and few (if any) rules.

Convenience was the watchword, particularly with the concept of one-way streets, which are only one way if drivers choose to honor that definition. On one memorable morning on the way to the National Gallery of Art, our driver wasn't buying into the concept. Two routes would take us to the gallery: the long route around a few blocks and the short route, down a one-way street — the wrong way. I seemed to be the only one in the vehicle reacting to all the cars whizzing by and pretty much dodging us. Everyone else remained calm-ish, but I had yet to develop that Zen place in my inner being — or whatever.

Many things in the U.S. that seem really important take on a different hue in Afghanistan. The prevailing sentiment for most of us was that Afghanistan offers a lot more to be concerned about than one-way streets and which way people travel on them.

After that first time traveling a street in what I considered the "wrong way," I just closed my eyes and thought happy thoughts.

Traffic flow was erratic and was not guided by any principle of traffic management known in the West. Traffic lights, for instance. I remember spotting my first traffic light and commenting on it to one of our guys. His reply: "Oh, there are several traffic lights in Kabul." Several? In a city of 5 million? This particular traffic light was flashing red and then green, but it did not seem to be controlling traffic flow, which moved whenever it was possible to move.

The route into town was marked by several roundabouts or traffic circles, and a bright red and white striped traffic hut or kiosk would often be in the center. Sometimes a traffic guy would be standing or sitting around. Sometimes he would be directing traffic. Not all traffic circles had traffic kiosks. One had a dilapidated structure of some kind and was a gathering place for feral dogs. Another had a huge sculpture of oblong shapes sprouting from the dusty ground.

Not all traffic kiosks were even separated from the traffic. They could be plopped right in the middle of an intersection — taking up space in the lanes and forcing the traffic into swerving maneuvers to avoid the hut or the traffic "director."

Generally the traffic moved counterclockwise around these traffic circles. Except when it went the other way — or both ways. As I said, its flow often depended on convenience: the fastest and easiest way to get where you were going.

Some roundabouts had no clearly defined center — just a large open area in the middle of an intersection with no traffic lights. Vehicles and people and the frequent flocks of animals just headed across the space and hoped for the best.

Parking and where it was allowed depended in large part on how many cars could fit along the often non-existent curb while still allowing for a measure of traffic flow. In some areas in town, cars would be triple-parked. Or a virtual parking lot would spring up on the side of the road. The big problem was getting a car "de-parked" once it was time to leave. An ad hoc form of parking management sprung up in these areas; some money exchanged hands as well.

In my mind, traffic was a mess. Violations abounded in my Western head: parking violations, one-way street violations, general disregard-for-any-kind-of-order violations, but no one got tickets. I asked once about this and I was told that sometimes a parking ticket would be issued and that was about it. In fact I never saw any police that were doing anything but standing around looking military.

Traffic is not really a mess in the Afghan mind. Afghans are a group of people who do not see time as linear, as Westerners do: One thing happens and then another and then another. You take a turn and then it's my turn. In the U.S. we take turns while driving — the person on the right has the right of way, for instance. In Afghanistan it's whoever gets to point "A" first. And that is not by queuing up, but by "funneling in." There is no forming a line to turn a corner, but the forming of a funnel of cars that culminates at the corner and allows the first car there to turn. The rest of the cars keep edging in and new cars are added to the outside of the funnel and eventually everybody gets to make the turn. It was new to me, but everyone else knew the routine and it worked.

Drivers had to be on a constant lookout for cyclists, carts, trucks, and animal-drawn vehicles, the odd herd of goats or sheep, the occasional donkey and the pedestrians. Kabul had some sidewalks and a few pedestrian bridges, but generally people walked in the street. Their attitude towards cars was cavalier, to say the least. In most countries, including the United States, pedestrians, while rude sometimes and reckless, generally recognize that cars are bigger than they are and can be potentially lethal, so therefore try to avoid collisions with them. Not so in Kabul. No fear. Pedestrians acted as if they were the only presence on the road. They moved across the street and along the street as though they owned it and rarely checked to see if a car was headed their way or even in their way.

I had an opportunity to cross the street several times in Kabul. I tended to stand back and wait for the traffic to stop for me. That was not the way it was done. My escort would urge me to start crossing and the cars would stop. One hoped. Another harrowing experience.

When I first got to Afghanistan I was jumpy and terrified to varying degrees while riding in the city. Once or twice I shrieked when it appeared that a collision was imminent. But we always managed to dodge the other car or the moped or the child riding the bike or the goats. I soon quit paying attention to the driving. Resignation can be a good and healthy emotion: what will be, will be. I took pictures instead.

Rarely did a mixture of cars and people and bikes and wagons and buses and animals have such an amiable experience on the roads. Yes, it was a mess, but not a desperate mess.

15

Shopping

The weather is still cool here. I am still having issues with the barking dog next door. (Email from my son, September 10, 2009)

Grocery Shopping

Friday was grocery shopping day—a noteworthy occasion considering that most of us went from guesthouse to school to guesthouse to school—and that was all—for at least four days of the week. Entertainment during that time consisted mainly of doing laundry and watching DVDs on our laptops. By Friday we were ready to party.

Grocery shopping may not sound like a party, but believe me, a break in routine and a chance to travel out of our "prisons," even for a short time, was like the first day of summer vacation—freedom!

We could also go grocery shopping on Wednesday afternoons, but only in the local shops and at the local street vendors; we couldn't go into Kabul city. I'm not sure I ever got an adequate explanation for this: just another thing that was done and could always be explained as a response to security issues. Maybe the Taliban or kidnappers would be more active on Wednesday afternoons than Fridays since Friday is the day of worship and even bad guys take a day off. But that doesn't explain why Saturdays were also deemed to be safer than Wednesday. Just another mystery of life in Afghanistan.

The problem with Wednesday shopping in the local stores was that the stores were small and had a limited selection. Also, I often felt the owners did not want us there. I don't know if it was a security problem or whether they didn't like foreigners or they didn't like me.

Weekend shopping, on the other hand, was different. For one thing, it was the only time that we didn't have to arrange for transport. The school scheduled it for us; we simply had to sign up by Wednesday.

Vans came at 9 A.M. and noon on Fridays and 10 and 1 on Saturdays. I

121

suspect the runs were short because there were no public bathrooms. (Actually, that's not quite true. One concrete structure labeled "public toilet" was on the edge of a dusty park near our guesthouse. Considering that most internationals would not consider hanging out in this open, unguarded area, I wondered who would use those facilities.) In any case, we all "went" before taking any trip into town — just in case.

Usually the morning runs were for groceries (and beer, once I located the secret source). Afternoons we could do "real" shopping — clothes and stuff— or go sightseeing or visiting. I usually chose the 9 A.M. Friday run for groceries. I wanted to get stocked up early since there would be no opportunities to run down the street to the corner grocer for forgotten milk or chips. We had to buy everything we needed on these arranged shopping ventures.

Several stores in Kabul catered to the international crowd, and we were always running into other Westerners as well as our colleagues from school — there usually were at least two AUAF vans out grocery shopping at any one time.

The clerks and other personnel at these stores were always friendly, and even if the owners only wanted our dollars, I always felt liked by their staff.

At least one of these stores had an ATM machine which worked most of the time. When it worked, it never made a mistake; for that, I was thankful. Cash was in U.S. dollars or in Afghanis (Afs). ATMs were the only source of cash for most of us. Some AUAF employees had all or part of their salaries deposited in a local Afghan bank, but then the problem was how to extract it. Checks were not accepted as legal tender; neither were credit cards, and coming up with cash was a continuing annoyance.

Additionally, the stores provided security in the form of an armed guard at the door and often one inside the building. Our driver stayed outside with the van; our escort came in with us.

These stores carried a wide range of snack foods, hair products and canned soup. I dined on soup several times a week — a particular favorite was mushroom bisque.

They also stocked a large selection of cheeses, including the "Happy Cow" variety, and a goodly supply of canned meats, including Spam. I never stooped that low, although I was tempted. I did buy lots of anchovies, sardines and fish that looked like sardines. I also stocked up on Kit Kat candy bars. I thought they were past their "due date," being crumbly and with a whitish cast, but I didn't care. Chocolate is chocolate!

The other thing they carried, until I bought them all, was steak and kidney pie. It came in a tin which was opened and placed in the oven, where it commenced to rise and cook and it was yummy. The answer to my query about when they would be getting some more was, "It usually takes four months for shipments to reach us." Transport of goods was a real problem in Afghanistan, particularly if trucks had to come from Pakistan through the Khyber Pass, which was under the "supervision" of varying factions, including the Taliban.

I also bought some prepackaged Pakistani meals, many with lentils (*dal*). One in particular was really tasty and I bought it every week — until the supply ran out. No new shipments of my two favorites arrived while I was there.

And then there was another Afghan challenge to be met and won: how to transport eggs. It had never been a problem in my previous U.S. life. Here, eggs were not packaged in cartons, but sold separately. The clerk carefully placed them in a tiny plastic bag. Or you could try to put them in the bag yourself. The first time I bought eggs I broke all of them on the way home when they clanged and banged about in my bag during transport.

I always chatted with the egg man, and I told him I was a teacher at the American University. I was quite proud that I could say this in Dari. It turned out he was a student, but at Kabul University. After that we always exchanged greetings, me in my stumbling Dari, he in stumbling English, and he always smiled.

Although often inconsequential, there were deprivations to living in Afghanistan. I consider myself a good camper and generally can cope with adverse living conditions. After all, I lived in England when a shilling bought hot water and baths were twice a week. In those days I had to put Jello outside the kitchen window to set because we had no fridge. I was prepared, I thought, for "deprivations" in Afghanistan. I knew, for instance, that getting alcohol might not be as easy as walking to the corner pub. I might also have to go without pepperoni. But I knew hot water was available, and soap, so I didn't think laundry was going to be a problem. But it was. Not a serious problem, but a problem nevertheless.

Our guesthouse didn't have a dryer so we had to hang up our washed clothes to dry. As they dried, they stiffened. (I'm still not sure why that happened.) So one weekend at the end of a particularly tiring week I had reached my tolerance limit for stiff sheets and stiff underpants. I wanted "soft" clothes again and I thought maybe I would try using a fabric softener. I had never used one in the States; it didn't seem necessary. Now it sounded like a good idea.

When we went to the store, I searched around in the cleaning/washing supply section but didn't see fabric softeners. I felt sure that they would carry them, since they carried room fresheners and Oreo cookies and other Western staples. I finally asked a clerk. "Do you carry fabric softeners?" He looked at me and smiled. (Afghans smile a lot when they're trying to be polite while thinking you're nuts.) "Fabric softeners?" I repeated. He smiled some more and then called over another clerk. They exchanged a few words in Dari, and I tried to explain to them what a fabric softener was. "Y'know, softens your clothes." I got more smiles.

The light finally dawned! A fabric softener, for God's sake? In a country with no potable drinking water and an open sewer system. What was I thinking? (I had several of those "What was I thinking?" moments in Afghanistan.) I suffered through stiff clothes from then on — in silence.

Other than the lack of fabric softeners and steak and kidney pies, these stores tried hard to accommodate us. One had an entire wall of breakfast cereals — not something on the menu for most Afghans, I suspect. Another carried every type and color of fruit drink. They also stocked fish and meat, both frozen rock-hard and wrapped in cellophane. I tried what was called a T-bone steak once. Actually, it was a solid chunk of meat cut from the T-bone area of the cow; it was not a "steak" and it did not taste like any T-bone I had ever had. (Again, this was due to slaughtering practices wherein the animals are bled out and, thus, have no "juice" for gravy or flavor.) I didn't buy the fish since I doubted its freshness. Afghanistan is landlocked and the river passing through Kabul could not support any edible lifeform.

When we were ready to check out, the clerk would tell us the total in dollars or Afs. It was computerized and we got a receipt and you could pay in either currency. All stores that dealt with foreigners had an adding machine, in order to exchange money as needed. When we were done, we gathered our packages and waited in the van until everyone else had finished shopping. I was usually first done, never last. For at least one of my colleagues, grocery shopping was an attempt to recreate "home" with all the attendant familiar foodstuffs and cleaning supplies and personal products and anything else that caught her eye. She bought a lot and it took time.

One of these international grocery stores is also where I got my first look at the "Queen Bee." She looked American, but could have been from any Western country. She had learned not only that she was blond and beautiful but also that she was due homage from all lesser souls. She would exit her big black (or white) SUV, often with UN emblazoned on the side, with her artfully arranged scarf barely touching her tousled hair. She marched regally into the store, trailing her entourage of burly men with mean faces. Apparently she saw her arrival with driver and escort as a sign of social status, removed from the ragtag rest of us and certainly removed from the Afghans in the store. Some of us saw the constant presence of a driver and an escort as the signs of our imprisonment, not of our special status. Anyway, I didn't want to meet her. I had the feeling she might be an "Ugly American."

The worst part of the shopping trip was waiting in the van for the rest of our group to finish. Standing around outside the store and around our vehicle were beggars — mostly children and mostly boys. Some went to school part of the day and then the rest of the day they worked the street to support their family. They sold gum or maps or just held their hand out. There was one beguiling young girl, in a bright pink jacket with a fur collar. She had straight cut hair that stuck out every which way and a plain face until she started her pitch. Then she put her hands on her hips, flashed her eyes, pursed her lips and charmed the pants off all of us. I usually gave her something for her performance.

One enterprising young man sold a local "What's Happening" guide. The guide, however, was actually a free publication and could be picked up at several locations. This was an example of begging in disguise.

Begging was not just the purview of children. Sometimes burka-clad women would approach the van. That's when I learned the true meaning of begging. It is not just asking for something once, but over and over and over again. "Please, miss, please, miss, please, miss." The women would reach out their brown and lined hands; sometimes they would lift their burkas so we could see their faces. Finally, after we turned from the window with "help me" in our eyes, our driver or escort would take pity on us and say something to the women in Dari and they would leave us alone. Or we would roll up the windows.

And then there were the women with their babies, huddled on the street hoping for anything.

We all gave to the beggars, not all of us all the time, but everyone forked over some money to either the women or the children.

After we left the grocery store on these weekend shopping trips, we would stop on the way back to the guesthouse at the stalls along the street to buy fresh fruits and vegetables. Again, no mingling, but we could at least get out of the van and move down the road a bit and eye the carts of produce. The escort was on the street with us, warning us to stick together, not to wander too far away, herding us. We stayed near the van, which was usually parked between us and the traffic.

For me, here was an opportunity to stand outside and look around and be part of the street scene, for an instant at least — but not for long. We were hustled through our shopping. The feeling was that it was not a good idea to be outside for very long in one place — it gave a "wannabe" a chance to call his Taliban buddy and tell him about the *khareji* (foreigners) that were hanging about. The security issue created an urgency about shopping on the street, so it was not as much fun as it might have been.

I always bought something from one of the stalls, even knowing that I might not get around to eating it. Again, I just wanted to be out on the street. (I did eat the pomegranates, however. Wonderful fruit!) I pointed and nodded when asked, "One kilo?"—I didn't really need over two pounds of anything, but it was simpler to agree. When I was done everything was placed on a scale and weighed together. The counterweight was once a spark plug, another time a big rock. It didn't matter; the total was never very much.

I wondered sometimes what the vendors on the streets thought of us. A van pulls up; a beefy guy gets out (no weapon) followed by several foreigners, including some women with headscarves. I wondered if they thought we were afraid of them. I wondered if they were afraid of us. I could drive myself crazy sometimes.

Other than having our movements restricted, the worst thing about shopping on the street was again the beggars. The children dodged in between us and the women in their burkas followed us with their outstretched hands. I tried to give the children something. Some of us would buy the women and children fruit rather then give them money. I didn't often give money to the women. I don't know why.

Dealing with the beggars and particularly the women was difficult, and I'm not proud of my reactions. We all had to make our own peace with them. I still feel guilty about seeing it as a problem — for me. One American woman told me that the women in burkas who were beggars were all prostitutes. I thought this was a remarkable comment since the women were obviously not flaunting their "wares"— they were wearing burkas, for heavens' sake. And, too, if they were prostitutes — why? Probably because they were widows and their husband's family did not want them. They were forced onto the street to survive. The government certainly was not going to help them. Someone else said that the children were employed by a "pimp" who sold them the gum or maps or whatever and at the end of each day he got a cut of the take. I don't know if that was true, but I suspect it was.

Further down the road were several butcher shops. They had their wares skinned and beheaded and hanging from hooks outside their doors. One weekend we were in a lockdown situation — not going anywhere because a VVIP was in town (a Very Very Important Person) and no one was allowed to go into Kabul. As security put it, there was "a credible ongoing threat" and there were roadblocks and ID checks everywhere.

To celebrate that I wouldn't be going out to dinner that night, I decided to visit one of those butchers and try for some fresh lamb. (At school, the mystery meat was billed as "lamb." If it was, it was very old lamb). So that afternoon, I looked for lamb — a young and tender leg of lamb or a lamb chop. I pointed at one slab of meat hanging overhead and asked what it was. The butcher pointed to the sidewalk and to the decapitated head lying there. It looked like a lamb to me. I bought it; I did not care for the taste. I went back to my beans, rice and canned sardines regime after that.

On weekend grocery trips we made two other stops on our way back to the guesthouse. One was at a French bakery, which was called The French Bakery. They sold meat pies and donuts. The other stop was at a French restaurant that also sold bread and, on some memorable days, meringues. There is nothing quite like a crisp clot of whisked egg whites and sugar to make the day seem bright and beautiful. I loved those Fridays, particularly if it was a meringue day!

Other Shopping

Sometimes on Friday or Saturday the grocery shopping morphed into Real Shopping — the stuff that we really didn't need, but as "tourists" were compelled to buy.

Chicken Street was the place. Some of the streets in downtown Kabul were named for what they originally sold. Flower Street sold flowers and Chicken Street, well — chickens, I guess. When I was there I saw no chickens, but that was the area where the internationals went for leather goods and furs and knick-knacks and whatnots and DVDs.

The DVD store was a regular and important stop. Considering the scarcity of English-language TV shows coupled with the inability to know when they were scheduled, watching movies on DVDs was a major form of entertainment for most of us. DVDs sold for $1 (or 50 Afs), and there was a break in the price if 10 or more were bought. The store was minuscule. A few young fellows were always hanging around the counter and then there were three or four or five us from school. Cramped quarters, indeed.

We were always stared at. The stares didn't feel hostile, just curious. The only experience many Afghans had with Americans and other internationals was what they had read or heard of us — many had never seen a "real" American or talked with one. I often felt that people on the street and in the shops were really curious. Ah, so that's an American! That's how they talk and how they interact with one another and how they treat women. And, again, all of us women were anomalies. Objects of wonder, I'm sure, to an Afghan who was not used to seeing women on the street or hanging out with men who were clearly not their husbands, brothers or fathers.

After the DVD shop, the other major stop in the area was a grocery store that sold alcohol. Some Afghans do drink even though alcohol is proscribed by the Qur'an, but they do so in secret. A male colleague who was an Afghan could not come into a restaurant that served alcohol unless one of us internationals "signed" for him. Alcohol cannot be bought in most grocery stores and is only available in those restaurants that cater to the internationals.

Periodically, the Afghan president, Mohammed Karzai, bowing perhaps to pressure from some of his constituents, would close the "international" restaurants or make it otherwise hard to get a drink. During one of these "sieges," Dee and I were in a restaurant and ordered beers. The waiter tried to tell us something which we didn't understand. When he came back to the table, he put two coffee cups down. Questioning, I looked up to the big smile on the waiter's face and looked down and saw that it was beer in the cup. That was how the restaurant circumvented the "don't sell alcohol" rule — they hid it in coffee cups. Afghanistan is a wonderful place.

Shortly after I arrived, I realized that finding a steady supply of alcohol was going to be a priority. Word was that there was a place in town where one could buy it all: beer, whiskey, wine. The drivers and escorts, I'm sure, knew all about where to buy whatever, but they didn't offer the information. I don't think discussing alcohol was *haram* (forbidden), but we didn't talk about it. One of my colleagues who had been in Kabul for a while found the store, and he soon directed me and others to it. I always had a hard time remembering exactly where it was, but if I could get the van in the area, the owner would flag us down.

The wine came in quart-size boxes that were hidden behind the quart-size boxes of juice. The beer was hidden under the refrigerator. The owner also sold vodka, but its alcoholic content was questionable. I stuck with the wine.

I'm sure that everyone on the street knew what was being sold in the store. In many ways, Americans and other Westerners were catered to — if we wanted alcohol, for instance, Afghans would provide it for us. But we were discreet and most of us tried to protect the anonymity of our supplier. One day a new university employee was introduced to the store. She was a recent arrival in Kabul and hadn't quite got it that alcohol was illegal — really illegal. She marched into the store and loudly asked where the beer was located. The store owner took it with good grace and smiled. The rest of us just looked apologetic.

Our escorts, of course, came with us into the store, and, of course, knew what we were doing. We made sure to buy them a soft drink or whatever. We did not discuss our purchases with them.

The purchase of alcohol, although a weekly event, was not the only item I purchased on my forays into town. On one shopping trip with the indefatigable shopper Dee (I think she shopped in her sleep) we went to a leather shop for bags. I found one I liked, but it was $55 and more than I wanted to pay. I told the shopkeeper that we were going to look around some more and I might return. In fact, I did return and the owner dropped the price to $45 because "you came back," he said. I tried to get him to lower the price further, but stopped at Dee's warning look and her silent accusation that I was being cheap. I was never much good at bargaining.

Our escort accompanied us along the street and into the stores. Window shopping, as it were, was a hurried event: move along, don't loiter and don't call attention to yourself.

One Saturday afternoon some of us talked our driver and escort into dropping us off in Chicken Street and coming back for us later. This was not an "approved" arrangement, but since one of our companions was a large man, well over six feet tall, I suppose we were considered to be relatively safe. I did not feel safe, however. We were stared at, and one of our group kept going off by herself. We were forever trying to round her up so she didn't get lost or abducted or whatever. And the beggars clustered around.

Whenever we were on the street the child beggars would soon find us. Suddenly a gaggle of little boys, sometimes with a little girl or two, would appear. Usually a boy would attach himself to one of us, looking cute as a button. "I'll be your bodyguard," he'd say. The first time, I must admit, I was charmed, and I let a young fellow sell me a map. But I told him that I didn't want the creased and grimy copy that he was clutching. I wanted a new map. Off he went. And a slightly less crinkled map appeared. I didn't have the proper change. Actually I had a rather large bill. He'd get change, he said. Off he went, again, with my money and my map. "Uh oh," crossed my mind. But soon he was back with my "newer" map and my change. All was well. Then everyone wanted to sell me a map.

The beggars soon lost their cuteness and became irritating. There, I've said it. I knew that most of the children were helping to support their family by begging. Some, like the youngster who sold me the map, went to school in the morning and begged in the afternoon and did his homework at night. Some children sold gum and candy, some just begged. But that didn't alter how annoying they became. They buzzed around us on the streets, like flying insects. Sometimes they tried to touch us, grab our arms or our hands. We dodged into stores to avoid them as the store owners did not allow the children in the store. We gave them money; we bought them fruit or a bag of chips. But it was an impossible situation and I didn't know how to make it better.

My friend Dee collected a flock of street boys the first time we ended up on Chicken Street. Over the next few months she revisited the area and rounded up about seven of them. She petitioned her friends in the States and they sent warm clothes — hats and mittens and coats — for the children. One day she took them to a little grocery story in the area and bought them all milk and cereal. They looked like they needed it.

Dee was an artist and she bought the children colored pencils and paper and encouraged them to draw. She hoped to be able to arrange a showing of their art in the States, which was a wonderful idea, but difficult to implement. In an effort to provide them with a warm and safe place to draw, she talked with one of the restaurant owners in town who seemed to be sympathetic. But when it actually came time to allow these children into the restaurant — children who were mostly dirty and smelly and in tattered clothes — well, the owner, said, she was sorry, but it just wasn't such a good idea after all.

Dee finally became discouraged with her project and the children went on to find other soft-hearted foreigners to buy their candy and their maps and do what they could to help.

Not all of our other shopping was in the Chicken Street area. There were at least two mall-type conglomerates in Kabul. Not really malls as Westerners might understand the word. Not a sprawling suburban store-opolis where window-shopping was a contact sport and the young could see and be seen. For one thing these were urban malls, located in high rise buildings, and for another, young people did not hang out in them.

One of these shopping complexes was the City Center — a modern glassed structure on the backside of a fancy hotel. It catered to internationals and rich Afghans and had the only escalator in Afghanistan — which did not work all the time. One nice thing about the City Center was that once we were inside the building, we could walk around by ourselves, without an escort. It was a small pleasure, but still there was a thrill in moving about without a tagalong. Mind you, to get into the building, we went through a metal detector and had our bags checked.

We sometimes saw young women shopping, but very few. Mostly men were there and they looked at us — not with hostility, but curiosity, again. I don't know why we didn't see couples shopping or women shopping on their own in the City Center.

The stores sold DVDs, electronics, jewelry and cameras. In fact, this was the only recommended place to buy cameras. I was warned that if I wanted certain items, cameras, for instance, it was unwise to buy them on the street for fear of rip-off products that carried the name of well-known manufacturers but not their reliability or performance.

There were a few stores for women and one in particular that we always visited; the owner was quite gracious. Even though they sold women's outfits, they didn't seem to have a dressing room. The owner showed us how he would hang some material up as a curtain to provide privacy if we wanted to try items on. We declined. But I did buy one particularly beautiful head scarf.

The salespeople were all men, even in the shops selling women's clothes. They tagged along with the shoppers and did not seem to understand the concept of "just looking."

There was also an indoor café—not really a café but a collection of tables where you could sit and eat an ice cream or drink a coffee bought from the nearby kiosk. Dee and I tried to sit there one day and relax and watch people. We were the watched ones. It was not relaxing.

We went to another mall one day, one that catered to Afghans who could afford to buy clothes from a store rather than from a market. This "mall" consisted of four or five floors of tiny shops, mostly selling women's clothing. And here's where we saw women on their own. Lots of women. I'm not sure why the women were at this "mall" and not at the City Center; perhaps because it did not generally attract Westerners, and in particular Western men.

That day there were four of us women from the university and one escort. We all ended up buying something—again, "just looking" is not translatable. Our escort's job was to keep us all together and, presumably, under his protection. In other words, we were his "flock." It didn't work out well. Four women have four different reasons to go shopping and insist on going in four different directions. Noori, our escort, fretted about the problem and alluded to the "danger." While feeling his misery, we ignored him.

We also visited a women's co-op regularly. It was through a guarded gate and behind walls. Our van would drop us off and come back later to pick us up—another small measure of "freedom." The co-op sold clothing handcrafted by Afghan women, as well as handbags, scarves and some jewelry. On our first visit I struck up a conversation with one of the men behind the counter. Turned out he was from the Panjshir Valley, the home of Massoud, the famed Mujahideen leader. I had brought to Afghanistan a copy of an article on Massoud which also included some wonderful photography of the valley and its environs.[1] On a subsequent visit I brought the article and showed it to him. I hope he was pleased.

There were vendors on the street and in several large outdoor markets but we were not encouraged/allowed to shop in these areas—too many people, too much risk. ISAF (International Security Assistance Force), the NATO coalition that was "keeping Kabul safe," had its own market on Fridays where the local women would bring their hand goods to sell. Unfortunately, right after I arrived in Kabul a bomb went off across the street from the area and it was closed down — too dangerous.

One Saturday, Cindy, a colleague and an "old-timer" in Kabul, offered to take me to an area she knew where we could buy clothes similar to those in the co-op, but considerably cheaper. The escort was not pleased when he found out the shop was down a crowded alley where the car couldn't go. He kept urging us to hurry. His nervousness made me nervous. I was not sure about what. Cindy, on the other hand, simply ignored him. "Just down here," she'd say. Or "Let's try here." And in each shop Cindy made the owner pull out dress after dress and scarf after scarf. I bought something early on in an attempt to speed up the shopping spree, but Cindy was in no hurry. On and on we went, further and further away from the safety of the main road and our security van. Finally, the escort had reached his limit of worry and told us, "We have to leave," and I was happy to do so.

The bright red embroidered tunic that I bought that day shrank three sizes with the first wash.

Finding tunic tops and pants was not a problem. Finding shoes was. There seemed to be only one shoe shop in town — in the expensive mall at the City Center. I was told I could have shoes made, but I never got around to that. I ended up buying shoes in Dubai on one of my trips.

I also had some tops and slacks made by a tailor. There were tailors that specialized in women's clothes, but I didn't care for the colors of the cloth that they displayed. I visited instead a men's tailor (two of them, in fact), which was problematic. If they measured you, the garment would be large as the tailors would not touch a woman to take measurements. It was best to take a pair of pants or a top that fit and let the tailor use that item for measurements. That's what I did.

I went several times to one tailor. The escort negotiated for me. They did good work and I was pleased with the price. But I don't think they wanted me there; I always felt rushed. At another tailor, after the third visit or so, it became apparent that I was not welcome. Suddenly no one could speak any English and for some reason our escort couldn't or wouldn't communicate with them in Dari or Pashto. I don't know what the problem was, but my presence was not wanted. I got the message and didn't go back.

One afternoon I accompanied Mary, who taught at the university, and her husband, Carl, on their search for a winter comforter. They planned to go to an open-air market where we could walk around a bit and shop. Walking around without an entourage would have been a treat and I jumped at the chance to go. Unfortunately, that day the road to the market was closed. Plan

B was to try another market that they had heard about but weren't real sure where it was. We rode around a bit and finally it became apparent that we had wandered into an unfamiliar area. The street was filled with men selling goods, hawking them, displaying them, and everything seemed to be animal in origin: live animals, dead animals and animal parts. And, once again, we were stared at — three white people (and two of them women) in the "wrong" section of town. Here the stares weren't just curious, they were hostile. It was unnerving. While trying not to scare his wife and me, Carl found his way out of the area with all due speed.

Late in the spring, just before I left for home, I had one of my few opportunities to walk down the street unaccompanied by a security guard. Three of us (all women) decided to go to lunch and then run a few errands. And we were determined to walk through several streets to do those errands. We didn't have far to walk from the restaurant to the travel agency, which was the first errand, but it was through some back streets and we were stared at, of course. This time I felt real disdain sweeping off some of the men we passed. How dare we be on the streets unaccompanied? Who did we think we were? Not everybody, of course, reacted that way, but enough did so that it was an uncomfortable experience.

Probably the best shopping trip I had was on a morning in the cool fall. I was out with Elaine — and our driver and an escort, naturally. The escort, Habib, was a university graduate but probably making more money with a security firm than in his chosen profession. I didn't know anything about the driver except that his name was Amin. Elaine had a video camera and wanted to do some taping around Kabul. So we asked the guys to just drive around for a while before we went where we were scheduled to go. In other words, we wanted to play hooky. The next thing we knew, Habib had "borrowed" the camera, and was pointing it at anything and everything, the radio was on and loud, playing lively Afghan music while we were careening around the streets of Kabul, having a grand time. We never got to see the video. There was difficulty with downloading it — too large a file, I think. It didn't matter. We never did any shopping that day. That didn't matter, either. That bright morning was one of my best experiences in Kabul.

Rug Shopping

Everybody buys rugs before they leave Afghanistan. I was no different. Sean and I wanted to shop for some, and we asked Kama to come with us to help. She spoke Dari and was from one of the "stan" countries and knew well the bargaining techniques that were essential in many of the market settings.

Bargaining was not really the practice in most of the stores in the City Center, particularly for high-end items like cameras. I had occasion to buy a new camera (having spilled what was probably beer on the one I brought from the States). I bought it at a camera store in the center; the extent of my "bargaining" was asking if the quoted price was the lowest price. (I'm really not much good at bargaining.) I don't think price negotiating was expected there, but I could be wrong since so much is negotiable in Afghanistan.

Bargaining, however, was expected in the markets and in shops in the Chicken Street area. Bargaining was also part of the "game" when buying rugs.

We planned to try more than one rug shop. However, after our experience at the first one and the positive (so we thought) outcome, we went no further.

The rug shop we decided on looked like most rug shops. The floors were covered in rugs; those for sale were folded and stacked along the walls and up to the ceilings. The young salespeople scurried about, and at any indication that a certain rug was something we liked, they'd pull it from the stack and unfurl it with a flourish to the floor. "Too busy," I'd say. Apparently they knew that expression. "Too much red" or "Maybe" or "How about that one." We were offered chairs and tea. We, of course, accepted both. Rug shopping is an event! More rugs and more "Perhaps," and "Keep that one out." A man who must have been the owner and patriarch of the family finally appeared, sat and took over the proceedings and the negotiations.

We finally had a group of rugs, several for Kama and for Sean, one for me. We were told individual prices for the rugs. "What is the price for all of them?" we wanted to know. What kind of total price could be negotiated? We then took the offered price, which seemed to be less than the sum of the individual prices, and apportioned it to each rug. It was then up to each of us to negotiate the price for our own rug or rugs. I don't know if I got a deal or not. It doesn't really make any difference. I liked the rug I chose and it was the price I was willing to pay.

Gifts are often given to customers after a purchase. My gift from that outing was a necklace — and another happy memory.

16

Sightseeing

They were expecting some trouble and we were not allowed to go into Kabul yesterday. (Email to a friend, September 9, 2009)

After a few weeks in Kabul, I was more comfortable with my classes and with the students and guesthouse living. Now it was time to get out and about and see some of the city's sights — other than the grocery stores.

Kabul, Afghanistan, however, is not a tourist stopover. It wasn't that there weren't places to see, but it was a war zone, and going anywhere other than grocery shopping and dining out took a steel will and a pioneering spirit. Security concerns were the name of the game.

Sightseeing excursions into the city had to be cleared through the school's security office, which liaised between an outside security firm and the school administration. And it was never easy.

My idea of a joke was to ask if I could go to Mogadishu and walk down the street naked. Ha ha. I thought it was funny because maybe it would have been easier to get permission to go to Somalia than it was to visit the zoo or an art gallery in Kabul. I guess it wasn't that funny, but it amused me.

Darulaman Palace

One of my first Saturdays in Kabul I arranged a trip to visit the Darulaman Palace. Kabul does not have a lot of places of interest to sightseers; the most impressive and the first one on my list was the palace. Several of my coworkers were also interested in going, so we arranged with Security for a driver and an escort.

This was the first time I had met the escort, Jafar, and he became a favorite of mine. I didn't know his story, other than he was from a wealthy family. He had a wonderful smile and was gorgeous. He also had a look about him that was far too resigned for his young years. I wish I could say I knew

The original magnificence of Darulaman Palace is still present despite the holes for windows and the missing pieces of its roof.

more about him, but there was a distance between us, as there was between most of us internationals and the staff, that was rarely breached.

We were lucky that day, I think, to have been given permission to visit the area. We must have been the first group of internationals who had asked to visit the palace and perhaps Security had not really considered the dangers involved. For one thing, as the site was also used for some of the NATO offices, it could have been a target for attack. The grounds did not have a gate, so we would be relatively unprotected. As it turned out, the NATO guard left his post to walk around with us — more out of curiosity on his part than any commitment to our protection, I suspect.

The palace, now bombed out, perches on the hill at the end of Darulaman Road and sat in the far background as we traveled to school each day. It had been built in the early 1900s by the reformist king Amanullah Khan. (He also built a Queen's Palace, which is smaller and stands behind the main palace and higher in the hills.) Since its construction, the palace has been burned, repaired, burned again and then bombed — the latest damage done by Afghans fighting Afghans after the departure of the Soviets in the early

1990s. It was still standing, though. The rooms had all their walls and many of the floors and ceilings remained, but it felt like pieces of history were missing.

To reach the entrance we had to climb a short, steep and pitted road. The palace walls towered above us on our right. A sandy, dry and barren area enclosed by three walls was the remains of the palace courtyard. If I squinted a bit, I could almost see the palace in its original magnificence — marble walls intact, towers complete and windows glassed in. Perhaps at one time the courtyard had a fountain and benches and flowering plants. But now, Dari graffiti was scrawled on some of the walls and gray, low-lying succulents had taken over. Jafar knew the common names of many of the plants and he wrote them for me — in Dari. I couldn't read or pronounce them. No matter. Many were blooming and I took hope.

Inside the palace, devastation reigned. Some rooms had "no entry" signs. We assumed that meant unexploded bombs were present or perhaps the flooring was unstable. One room, maybe a ballroom, was circular and the scarred columns were still supporting the remains of the ceiling. The statuary had

This now-scarred ballroom still retains some of its past grandeur.

lost their heads and stairways ended in midair. Ragged holes where windows had once been looked out on what was left of the gardens where local sheep now grazed.

I don't know what the Afghans thought of that trip. I think it was the first time that Jafar and Hanzala, the driver, had ever visited the palace. I guess sightseeing is not a priority for anyone in a war zone — including the Afghans. Talk among us all that day was minimal. We ooh-ed and ah-ed over the bombed-out grandeur of the palace, of course, but other talk, for me, was difficult. I didn't really know what to say. It was my first experience (and one of the few) being with Afghans in a part of their history and I was afraid to say anything that would hurt or offend.

In many parts of the world, this old palace would have been preserved and renovated and tickets sold and concession stands opened. Benches would line the replanted gardens and children would race along the paths. Not here. There was no one there that day but us.

Efforts have been made recently to save the crumbling buildings and restore them, but there is just so much broken in Afghanistan that I suppose there isn't enough will or money available to rebuild this piece of the past.

We all took a sample of the marble rubble scattered about. I still have mine.

National Museum

My second foray into the world of Kabul sightseeing was the following weekend. A group of us decided to visit the National Museum.

The museum was just down the hill from the Darulaman Palace. Unlike the palace, where pretty much anyone could wander onto the property, here there was a fence and body searches.

The men in our party were searched by the guards at the gate. The other women and I were herded into a tiny shed off to the side. No door, but a filthy, threadbare curtain "assured" our privacy. An ancient woman smiled and smiled and smiled as she went through our bags and then patted our breasts. This was my first of many pat-downs in Afghanistan. It was not pleasant and it never got any better.

On the other hand, the gardens were beautiful.

In October the roses were still blooming, as were purple asters. A stone reportedly from Mecca and carved during the time of the Prophet Muhammad, 14 centuries earlier, was displayed outside, as were the remnants of a train that ran from Kabul to the palace in the early 1920s.

Inside the building were the remains of the museum's collection. Here's an excerpt from their webpage.[1]

For thousands of years, Afghanistan was a crossroad for trade from India, Iran, and Central Asia. As a result, many treasures and artifacts have been discovered and collected. The Kabul Museum housed the most comprehensive record of Central Asian history. Many of its pieces have been dated as far back as pre-historic times. One of the museum's largest displays was the magnificent Bagram Collection. Discovered in 1939, by archaeologists excavating a Kushan fort, it contained an amazing 1,800 pieces from India, Rome, Greece, Egypt, and Central Asia. The Kabul Museum also had one of the largest displays of Greek and Roman coins found near Kabul. This collection was a historical treasure, as it contained coins from numerous civilizations dating from the 8th century B.C. to the late 19th century.

These treasures and many others were tragically lost when the Kabul Museum was bombed in 1993. At first, only the upper galleries suffered losses and looting. The remaining artifacts were transferred to lower leveled, steel-doored vaults. In 1994, the United Nations attempted to stop the looting by repairing the doors, and bricking up the windows. Disappointingly, these attempts failed, and looters continued to plunder 90 percent of the museum's collections. Both private collectors and antique dealers from as far away as Tokyo have purchased stolen museum pieces. Looted artifacts have shown up all over the world, and they bring in large sums of money to the criminals.

In early March 2001, the Taliban decided to destroy all pre–Islamic statues and objects in Afghanistan, after an edict was announced by their leader Mullah Omar in late February. The Taliban destroyed numerous statues in the museum which survived the previous looting and destruction as a result of war.

And a final plea on the site:

It is our deepest hope that the beautiful treasures of our country can one day be found and returned to their rightful home.

There were very few exhibits and many of them (or their remains) displayed signs which read "destroyed in 2001."

The plaque outside the doors read, "A nation stays alive when its culture stays alive."

This museum was trying very hard to do just that.

This was another sad day on the sightseeing tour of Kabul.

The Zoo

One of the stories about Afghanistan that charmed me was the story of Marjan the lion and the Kabul Zoo. Marjan was born in 1976 and was given to the zoo by the Germans in 1978.

One day during the Taliban regime a young yob seeking to prove his manhood, perhaps, climbed into Marjan's cage and began to pet Chuchu, the lion's mate. Marjan apparently did not appreciate this familiarity and attacked and killed the young man. In retaliation the fellow's brother later threw a grenade into the cage, blinding Marjan and leaving him permanently disabled. But he survived. He died in 2002 at the age of 25.

The lion had survived and so had the zoo, thanks to the dedicated zookeepers who saved what animals they could during the civil war and in later days often went without food in order to feed them.

The zoo was on my "must see" list.

Sarah, a housemate, also wanted to go and we started the tedious process of getting permission. Apart from the ever-present threat of kidnapping, apparently the zoo is not just for families enjoying the day out, but also a haven for young thugs who are looking for trouble and maybe don't like Westerners. We could have taken a taxi, but then we would have been without protection and that was really a last ditch alternative. Finally, after signing a release form that we knew the dangers, etc., etc., we were given permission and assigned not just a driver and one escort, but two escorts. Rather than on Friday, we would go on a Saturday, when presumably the crowds would be less and the danger minimized. We were told if there was trouble, I, being the older, would be pushed to the ground, and Sarah was to fall on top of me as protection. Not something to look forward to.

Nothing untoward happened, however, except that we were stared at — which happened all the time and, while disconcerting, was not terrifying.

The zoo was a sad, sad place. A young man sat atop the statue of Marjan at the entranceway. Personally, I thought he was being disrespectful of Marjan and the lion's prominence in the zoo's history.

The open courtyard at the entrance had a central fountain that was not working. The geese and some seldom-flying birds were milling about a large open area with trees and water, on dry and dusty earth. We paid extra to go into a separate building to see the fish, but there were only two tanks. An alligator cage was also in the building, but no alligator. Instead a large model of one sat in its place.

The ferris wheel was not working. The wolves paced and eyed me with hungry eyes and the ostrich pecked and tore at the wire on his cage. He wanted out.

The elephant house had no elephant. It hadn't made it through the "troubles" of the civil war in the 1990s. Mujahideen fighters shot the elephant and ate the deer and rabbits, and incoming shells shattered the aquarium.[2]

Two lions are now in residence, but they were hiding the day we were there.

A sign, in Dari, displayed Mickey Mouse warning visitors not to feed the animals.

And then there was the pig—*khanzir.*

Afghanistan's only known pig trotted out of quarantine Saturday, two months after he was locked away because of swine flu fears, to bask again in the mud at the Kabul Zoo.

The pig, a curiosity in Muslim Afghanistan where pork and pig products are illegal because they are considered irreligious, was quarantined because visitors to the zoo were worried it could spread the new H1N1 flu strain, commonly known as swine flu.

"Our people did not understand that the disease only passes from person to person and felt that the swine influenza might even be spread from the zoo because we have a pig here," zoo manager Aziz Gul Saqib told Reuters.

"Other zoos abroad told us not to worry ... when people began to realize the disease doesn't come from the pig itself we decided to release the pig," he said.

"It is very *haram* (forbidden) and should not even been looked at. I don't think it should even be in the zoo," said a ... visitor named Nassim.

But others were intrigued.

"I think it's an interesting animal in terms of the way it looks. You can't really use it for anything ... it is haram and you shouldn't eat it," said 22-year-old biology student Fatemeh.[3]

That day the pig was seen in a little house in a big fenced area that he shared with several goats.

A young man, full of warring hormones, finally worked up nerve to talk with us—mostly to pretty, young Sarah, I suspect. He wanted us to take a picture of him, which I did.

Except for the staring noted earlier, there was no trouble. I think the guards enjoyed the outing.

I'm glad I went. But it was sad. It was just not a zoo as I knew them from the U.S. It felt like the pieces of a zoo that had been left over from some tragedy—and, in fact, that's exactly what it was.

National Gallery of Art

One bright Saturday morning in early fall, I arranged a trip to the National Gallery of Art.

It is a smart-looking white building with blue-green trim that we passed (and admired) every time we went into Kabul. Many of the buildings on the road were single-story with flat roofs, either falling down or seriously leaning. Many had pieces of all sorts of junk, even tires, on their roofs. And all were brown. This bright building sitting back from the street always caught my eye.

The gallery was enclosed by an iron fence, and we drove through a gate to its parking lot. Gardens surrounded the property and everything was in bloom. Afghanistan in so many ways is dusty and brown, making gardens here and there bursting with color seem even more vivid in contrast. Among the blossoms I noticed flowers I had seen in South Carolina in bloom — Four O'Clocks, or *Mirabilis jalapa*, I think. One in particular was two-colored: yellow and pink.

We were the only patrons that morning. Entrance was 250 Afs ($5) and a ticket was written out for each one of us. Not only is Afghanistan a cash-and-carry society, it is also a handwritten one. No preprinted tickets ripped off a roll, but one-half of a printed form that was hand-signed with the amount and a date inked in — and officially stamped.

We left our shoes at the door and put on a pair of the gallery's sandals. We were told if we wanted to take pictures of the paintings it would cost 50 Afs per. A docent was assigned to us; she was an older (but probably not that old) woman who spoke little English. We didn't speak much Dari, but we had our escort with us to translate.

The gallery was dark; most of the light came through the windows. The

The Taliban's misogyny resulted in torn pictures of women which were displayed by the National Art Gallery with a sign "210 Destroyed Relics of Taliban Regime."

collection included some pictures of Afghanistan painted by Afghan artists, but we also saw works by French and German artists — a lot of them. Some paintings had no labels; some of the picture frames were damaged. A few paintings were hung and well-lit, but one was propped on a chair next to a window. At one point, the docent wiped her hand over a painting to remove the dust.

These paintings were what remained of a much larger collection. I suspect the Taliban were to blame and we soon saw proof of at least some of their destruction. An aquarium sat in the main hallway. Inside (instead of fish) were torn paintings, mostly of women. The sign on the glass, in English and Dari said "210 Destroyed Relics of Taliban Regime."

There was one painting, however, that the Taliban had not destroyed. It was a cartoonish illustration of four women in burkas, which didn't quite cover their legs or their stylish high heels. The date was 1956, when times were good for Afghanistan — and for women.

I'm glad I visited the gallery, but it was terribly sad. Again, like the zoo, it was what was left after a national tragedy.

Shah M Bookstore

While a bookstore might not be considered a stop for sightseers, the Shah M bookstore was on my list.

Immortalized in Asne Seierstad's *The Bookseller of Kabul*, it is the only shop specializing in English-language publications in the city. It and the zoo were two places on my Kabul "bucket list."

So one Thursday afternoon not long after I arrived in Afghanistan, I decided to go. I planned to go alone. No school transport — no school escorts — just me being a big girl. I figured I had come to Afghanistan by myself, so I certainly could be brave and travel into Kabul by myself.

I arranged for a taxi to pick me up from school; some taxi firms were approved by the university and we were urged to use those firms. Once again I never got a clear picture of what that approval entailed. Didn't the Taliban know how to drive a taxi? Or was this another instance of everybody in on the joke, except us silly foreigners? Maybe there was some kind of quid pro quo arrangement between the university and these companies. After all, everything was negotiable in Afghanistan, and I suspect our safety was as well.

In my pre-trip preparation I found out that the fare would be $5 (or 250 Afs). As it turned out, the fare to anywhere in Kabul was $5. I planned to give the driver a tip, so I felt prepared at least for that exchange. I did not tell the dispatcher where I wanted to go, which was a mistake. The driver, as it turned out, didn't speak English. I didn't speak Dari — except for "how are you" and "I'm fine" and "thank you." We were able, however, to agree that I wanted to go to the Shah M Bookstore.

I was off for an adventure that afternoon and I was relishing my freedom from school and from the school's security measures.

I was expecting to be dropped off at a normal bookstore — like a Books-a-Million or a Barnes and Noble. However, the driver pulled over to the curb on a street packed with dusty storefronts and pointed to a doorway indistinguishable from the rest of the doorways. It had a barely discernible sign over the door — Shah M. "Uh-oh," crossed my mind.

I paid, thanked the driver — *Tashakoor*— got out of the cab and the cab drove off. I was now on the sidewalk in the middle of Kabul — alone.

Here goes, I thought, and opened the door to a long, narrow hall lined with bookshelves. At the end the hallway bent to the right and in the bend was a desk. And the only people in the store were men — Afghan men.

It hit me that I was not exactly expected. (Something like a black person in a whites-only bar in the 1960s or a woman at an all-male club any year.) Here I was not just a woman, but an unaccompanied one. Thank God again for the three-sex concept in Afghanistan: men, women and foreign women. Foreign women were generally treated with respect, and what would be considered inappropriate behavior by an Afghan woman, was tolerated in us and often met with bemusement.

I've been in other places in the world where I probably should not have been. When I went to London in the 60's, I went anywhere I wanted, including into the pubs, which was not totally accepted behavior at the time. I never had a problem. I went to Mexico and ended up in the wilds of the Yucatán in a taxi with a driver who spoke minimal English while I was only mildly conversant in Spanish — *una cerveza mas, por favor*. Would he rape me, kill me and bury me in the sands of Cozumel? No. He found me a great cabana at a great price.

So, just as I did when faced with a bar full of men in London, I barged forward — and began to browse. Eventually I made my way back to the presumed owner. It turned out he was the son of the bookseller, had been to Canada and spoke excellent English. We had an entertaining conversation about Afghanistan and its problems.

I bought a couple of books, one a biography of Amanullah Khan, the reformist king in the 1920s, by a reporter who was alive and in Afghanistan at the time. The book was published in Pakistan in 1932. It's an unusual book: brown sticky labels are glued on the front and the spine with the title, *Amanullah Ex-King of Afghanistan,* and Roland Wild (the author). Was there a makeshift factory at that time where workers sat and attached sticky labels to books? Maybe so.

I was able to charge my purchases; the store had an old slide credit card machine. As it turned out, this was the only time I was able to use a credit card in Afghanistan. The country is a cash society. It could be dollars or Afghanis, but cash. Cash on the street was fluid. If the storekeeper didn't have change, he would send his son next door or down the street.

After wrapping up my purchases and throwing in a free postcard or two, the young owner called me a taxi and at my request walked me out to the street. It was a great experience and I ended up going back a couple of times. The credit card machine, however, which worked the first time for me, never worked again. I'm still not sure how they can break, but apparently, in Afghanistan, they do.

On the way back from the bookseller that day the taxi ran out of gas. I heard it coming. Car dies, crank crank — nothing. The driver's English was limited to knowing that I wanted to go to the American University; my Dari was limited to saying "thank you." He tried to tell me that he had to leave the car (and me) to go get gas. I got the message when he got out, grabbing an empty can.

And there I was: In Kabul, in a war zone, in a cab. By myself. I had a phone, but I had no numbers stored on it as yet — no security numbers from the school. So ... I had no one to call. Based on the rest of the services that seemed to be missing in Afghanistan, I doubted that calling "information" or "911" would help, so I just sat there and wondered what I should be doing. People walked by and cars drove by. Some people looked at me; some didn't.

Finally the driver came back, filled up the tank, grabbed a few guys on the street for a push and off we went. And nothing bad happened. When I think back on it, what did I think would happen? We were told we should be worried about kidnapping. I was more worried about being a stranger in a strange place.

When I told the story about running out of gas, my colleagues thought I was brave. Foolish, more likely, but I didn't have any choice really. Perhaps there was a risk that the Taliban or the criminal element would whisk me away, but people are essentially good so there was also the chance that no harm would befall me and everything would be just fine. And for me, that day, it was.

Lake Qarghur

Qarghur is a manmade lake just outside of Kabul and a favored destination for families on Fridays when the weather is warm. We had heard from the locals that it was a sight to see.

The first time we tried to visit the lake — get permission, arrange a car, driver and escort — we were told it was too dangerous. That was early in my stay, and there were still areas in Kabul that I wanted to visit, so I put the lake trip on hold.

It soon became apparent, though, that there were only so many places in Kabul that we were allowed to go. Having reached nearly the end of that list, one rainy and coldish Saturday, Dee and I decided to try to visit the lake again. Permission was granted. Apparently the Taliban don't like rainy and coldish days.

It wasn't really raining. More like a heavy mist that was being dragged to earth: cold moisture all around us but not actually falling. In the nine months that I lived in Afghanistan, it rained maybe twice. That is, rained as we think of it here in parts of the United States — persistent. In Kabul, however, the rain was short-lived.[4]

I remember once in April a storm seemed to be coming. The houses I could see from our balcony were dark, but there was a bright light on the hills all around, filtering from the gathering clouds. Then the clouds moved in and overtook the sun and the hills turned dark. No thunder and only a drizzle of rain. A surprise of a rainbow appeared on one slightly misty afternoon. Once in downtown, when it was raining lightly I noticed an umbrella that seemed to be floating on the sidewalk. It turned out that a worker in a ditch was holding the umbrella while not digging.

And so on that moist Saturday we made our way to the lake with a driver and escort. The scenery turned green and hilly soon after we left the outskirts of town. The first thing we saw as we rounded the curve towards the gate was a billboard featuring a group of smiling Western-dressed people sitting around enjoying "a quality product of the Coca-Cola Company." The women in the advertisement were not wearing scarves and showed much more skin and curves than is considered appropriate in Afghanistan.

The road went along the lake shore and cut through several picnic grounds, including a semi-covered concession area. The park was surrounded by rolling hills, green and damp, sprinkled with scrawny pines and covered in litter: paper, bottles and garbage. No anti-littering signs and no trash barrels to be seen. My mantra again: Afghanistan has many things to fret about. Littering is not on the list. But it was sad, nevertheless.

The lake had swan boats all lined up and ready for a swim. Afghanistan is dry and dusty and brown a great deal of the time. But here on this gray day were bright colors: lime green swans and bright red and blue and pink ones.

No customers, however.

Brightly-colored swan boats awaited their spring visitors at Lake Qarghur.

The lake itself looked full of smoke: a trick of the eye from low clouds reflected in the water.

Dee and I pressured our guys to stop and let us walk about. Many times it was clear that our Afghan employees thought we were nuts. Here was an instance: Why would we want to get out of a nice warm car and traipse around in the cold and mist? They didn't ask and we didn't have an answer anyway.

Dee and I split up — which always made the men nervous. I walked out on a wooden pier that led to a concrete hut in the middle of the lake. Below me on the rocky shore was a young boy picking up bottles and cans and other valuables. Dee stopped for a drink at one of the kiosks. I watched some feral cats argue with a wild dog over the remains of some animal. A park guard stood about looking like a policeman, and a worker was shoveling what looked like cement mix into a wheelbarrow. He had several piles yet to shovel; no other workers were to be seen.

We were the only visitors to the lake that day except for the cats and the dog. But maybe they lived there.

I also watched one armed guard signal (or so it seemed) another man who was carrying a rifle, both of them glancing at us — the two old foreign women wandering around with little protection. I was probably being paranoid, but I got nervous and wanted to go. Apparently so did our escort and driver. We left soon afterwards.

Perhaps in the summer the lake is a joyous place, with families and children and happy noises. On that day it was dank, dark and miserable.

On the way back into town we passed a refugee camp where several tiny children were playing along the road. Dirty faces, dirty clothes. Behind them was a fence and behind that were tents and more tents. We stopped to take pictures, I'm ashamed to say. I'm not sure why I am ashamed to admit to taking pictures of these children. Perhaps it is because it sounds exploitive or demeaning. I was not proud of myself.

Dee and I gave money to the escort to distribute to the kids as he thought best. Quite soon a few older men appeared. I thought that the money should be given to them rather than to the children. Ahmed, our escort, said the best thing to do is to give money to a child who has no father. The money will then go to the mother who, as the escort said, can't work. (Translation: is not

A camp for internally displaced peoples — that is, a refugee camp on the outskirts of Kabul.

allowed to work.) The men on the other hand are, of course, allowed to work and are therefore not assumed to be quite as needy as the women. Here was another sore spot for many of us: thoughts of the billions and billions of dollars sent to Afghanistan and still there were camps filled with homeless and starving people and dirty and helpless children. I was ready to get back to our warm, safe and dry guesthouse. Overall it was a distressing afternoon. I felt depressed about my helplessness. It seemed that saving the world was going to take longer than I had thought.

17

Special Events

Visited Babur Gardens last weekend—That's Babur for God's sake—he came here and fell in love with Kabul and wanted to be buried here.... the place reeks with history—and old history. (Email to friend and history buff, September 25, 2009)

Babur Gardens

Babur Gardens is approximately 30 acres of garden, including an art museum and a conservatory and the final resting place of the first Mughal emperor, Babur, who constructed the "avenue garden" in Kabul around 1528 C.E.

The first time I went was on Peace Day, September 21. It was also the first time I was out in a crowd in Kabul and the first time I saw how nervous crowds made our escort.

Too many people were milling around and, of course, we did not apprehend the danger, which added to his nervousness. He would not let us mingle with the crowds and made us stay on the periphery, which made hearing the speeches and being part of the "celebration" difficult. That day I was introduced to what it was going to be like as an international in Kabul—segregated!

Instead of hanging about with the crowd, we visited the rest of the gardens. It was a bit of a climb up the stairs of the "avenue" to the gravesite. Along the way on the various terraces, flowers bloomed and people were gathered, sitting on blankets, having picnics and listening to the speeches.

At the grave there was an elderly Afghan who was happy to guide us around and point out items of interest—in Dari, which no one but our escort understood. I don't think he was an employee of the gardens, just a visitor proud of the history of his country.

Afterwards, we made our way to the tea house which also doubled as a conservatory. My interest in plants necessitated my oohing and aahing at the collection.

At one point our escort drew over a young boy, about nine, who wanted to speak to me to practice his English. His father stood by, full of pride, as the youngster and I exchanged names and he told me what he wanted to do when he grew up — study business. And I told him I was a teacher at the university. Boy, did I feel special.

We sat and were served tea — my first experience with the omnipresent tea served at all social settings. Our escort finally started to relax and enjoy himself once we were away from the throng, and it turned out to be a pleasant afternoon.

I visited the gardens one other time just before I left Kabul. The occasion was an exhibition of drawings, prints and photographs by European visitors to Afghanistan from 1830 to 1920. I enjoyed the showing, but the experience was flavored by the other visitors' reaction to us.

We drew more than our normal quota of looks that day. We had, of course, a male escort and we were four women: all foreigners. One of us was a large woman, another was missing a leg and walked on crutches, there was Dee who wore her head scarf in a most unusual and unflattering manner, and then there was me.

The staring was not actually hostile, just curious. Who were we? Why were we there? And didn't we look different? (In retrospect, I guess we did.) I find it hard to imagine, what with the Internet and YouTube and all the technological avenues that open up the world, that internationals would be such an oddity. But we were.

I never turned down an opportunity to go someplace or do something new in Kabul. But sometimes it was not as much fun as it could have been. Rock stars and movie stars and politicians might like being stared at, but it is not a pleasant experience for the rest of us. Trust me on this.

Music Festival

The Second International Music Festival of Kabul, a presentation of musicians from Pakistan, India and Afghanistan, was scheduled for September, shortly after I arrived. I heard about it from the sister of a U.S. Embassy employee who knew everything that was going on in town — which wasn't a whole lot. But here was a three-day festival and I made plans to go to several of the events.

The first one was a Friday night concert held at the French Cultural Center, and I went with a couple of other women. The musicians came from

Badakhshan, the northernmost province of Afghanistan — next to its border with China. The musicians sat on the floor, with stringed instruments and small drums, and sang in the local language. To my virgin ears the opening few notes of each song sounded suspiciously like the opening few notes of "Dueling Banjos." For some reason there was a young boy on the stage with the musicians. Babysitting issues, perhaps?

One singer encouraged the mainly male audience to clap along with the music. We women, not knowing any better, clapped along as well. We found out later that the song was about the charms of women: their voluptuous hips and honey lips and other stuff. (I was due to start Dari lessons the following week.)

The next event was the following afternoon at a preservation site called Turquoise Mountain. The concert was held in the courtyard of one of the old buildings. Everyone sat on rugs and pillows that were strewn about on the ground — reminding me of my rock concert days. The music was Hindustani; the singer from India. I didn't hear words in what she was singing, only sounds, which fused with the sounds of the instruments to produce the sounds carried by the wind through trees in a mystic garden at twilight. Haunting!

And the last performance I attended was on Saturday night at the Goethe Institute Garden, attached to the German Embassy. Security was particularly tight that evening; German elections were Sunday and warnings had been received from Al Qaeda and the Taliban that retribution might be forthcoming for Germany's presence in Afghanistan. At each of the other events, bags were checked and there was a security gate. On this night there were three separate security checkpoints and I was searched (by a wand) twice.

The singer was a Pashtun, the largest ethnic group in Afghanistan. They live in the south of the country and in parts of Pakistan. The high point of this event for me was the Attan dancers. (This was my first exposure to Afghan men dancing; I saw more of it at school later in the year.) I thought at first it was simply some young men who were overtaken, as it were, by the music and decided to get up and dance. I found out later that it was a planned part of the evening and even though the dancing appeared rather loose-limbed, the steps are actually ritualized. Not quite as "in step with one another" as perhaps Greek men dancing, but every bit as rhythmic. And fun to watch.

This concert was my first foray out in the evening by myself. I had arranged for Transport to take me there and to pick me up when I called them. The problem was that Transport did not come inside any compounds (restaurants, hotels, embassies) to let us know when they had arrived. Instead they sat outside in an unmarked van and called us on their cell phone to announce their arrival. And that night I had to go outside and stand around (in the dark) and hope they would spot me (before a Taliban or a kidnapper or any other bad guy did). They then had to signal me somehow because I surely couldn't spot our van amongst all the other vans waiting for their passengers.

It was scary.

Except for that little bit of terror, overall it was a great festival and it was free.

Invitation to Lunch

Everything you read about the people in Afghanistan always mentions their hospitality and I was exposed to it in many small ways while I was there. But never was the hospitality quite so up front and personal as it was the day I was invited to lunch.

Connie (a colleague of mine) and I were invited to visit the family of one of her students for a meal. The student's name was Masouma and I had met her and some of her friends at a gathering earlier in the year. The meal was either lunch or dinner at her auntie's house — whichever would be best for us. Connie said we should plan on lunch — dinner was likely to go on quite late.

The lunch was scheduled for a cold and miserable Saturday and I really didn't want to go out. It is quite easy to hunker down in Kabul — stay in the warm safe guesthouse and shut the door and watch videos and drink wine. But the number of Afghans that I had met and talked with was countable and I knew I couldn't refuse this invitation. So I went and I'm so glad I did.

My friend Dee had also been invited but was sick and couldn't go, so it was just Connie and her husband, Phil, and me. We bought pomegranates as our contribution to the meal. Once we were in town, Connie had to call Masouma to notify her we were on the way and ask her to stand on the street and wave us down. Finding where anyone lives in Kabul is a problem: halfway down the street on the left between the green and the brown doors and like that. While some Afghans lived behind walls and in nice houses, others lived behind storefronts or behind metal doors set in a street of metal doors and storage units. And there were no gardens.

The apartment was three largish rooms and a place to cook. I think there was a bathroom, but I can't remember where. Masouma introduced us to her auntie, who was an older woman, heavyset and bent over, who just kept smiling and nodding at us. She was cooking on what looked like a gas heater and had laid out the finished food — meat and vegetable pasties — on a bedsheet in another room.

In that same room was a low table (a *sandali*), which was covered with a blanket and surrounded by cushions. Underneath the table was a brazier of charcoal that on cold evenings was lit. Family members would lie down on the floor with their backs to the table and pull the blanket over them, warming their backsides by the fire.

While the aunt was finishing up the meal preparations, we were shown into what was probably the parlor — the only room that had furniture, as I knew furniture to be: a few large comfy sofas and some chairs. The room was icy cold. None of us had removed our coats, but it was still uncomfortable. A heater was subsequently moved from another room and cranked up and we started to thaw. (I think now that the aunt gave up the heater that was warming her as she prepared the meal.)

Masouma introduced us to her two sisters who were still in high school and a third who was attending Kabul University. Conversation was in English and Masouma acted as translator since no one else in the family spoke English. Unfortunately the three of us spoke Dari with only limited ease.

For some reason one of the girls centered her attention on me and my marital status, perhaps because I was unaccompanied by a man. I told her I was divorced and she asked why. I said we just had some problems or some other vague answer. The young girl persisted however and asked how come I got married in the first place. Not one to mince words, I said I was pregnant at the time and that's why I got married. Masouma looked at me and asked, "Do you want me to translate that?" No, I guess not.

One of the sisters was kind of engaged. Her betrothed had promised her a car if she would marry him. The other girls thought it was a "bribe." They knew that once their sister was married there was a good chance her new husband would not let her continue her education. It was telling that these young women realized the perils of getting married and, more importantly, the perils of quitting school.

We finally moved into the eating room. The food, lots and lots of it, was spread out on the floor on a cloth and cushions were arranged around it. There was nothing else in the room except for some posters on the wall. The striking thing about the living quarters was their sparseness. The sleeping room had the *sandali* and cushions; the eating room had cushions and the sitting room had a few chairs and sofas. There was little clutter: no books, no knickknacks and no plants. None of the "extras" found in Western houses.

Handwashing bowls were passed around and the meal began. The food was really tasty — the best Afghan food I'd had so far. Everyone ate with their fingers and sometimes, using their fingers, the girls would scoop up food for their aunt or for each other. The meal had an intimacy about it unlike dinnertime in the States.

These girls and their auntie were from a northern province. Their family had sent them to Kabul to live and go to school. Their auntie came with them as chaperone. Connie intimated that the "auntie" was probably one of the father's wives, but thankfully I didn't ask. As an all-woman household they were an oddity in Kabul and their neighbors frowned on their living situation. Households without males were suspect. The family put up with the street's disapproval and perhaps the dangers associated with it in order that the girls could receive an education.

Conversation was general, mostly about the girls' school and what was going on at the university.

Connie had a backache — sitting on the floor for meals is hard for some of us. Her husband offered to change positions with her so she could lean against a wall. The girls were curious about the interaction between the two of them, asking if all married couples in the West were like that — actively and publicly helping one another. Here was another example of the deep divide between Western culture and Afghan culture with respect to men/women relationships.

While we were there, word came that the father was in town and was on his way. Suddenly there was anticipation in the room: "Father's coming, Father's coming." And soon he arrived.

He was a tall lanky man with graying hair and a lined face. We were told that he had retired from teaching but Connie was not sure whether he truly retired or whether he couldn't teach any more for some other reason.

He had traveled all the way from the North specifically because we Americans were there. He acted as if it were an honor to have us in his house and eating with his family. He brought gifts for us as well — nuts and fruit.

Masouma, who appeared to be the favorite daughter, sat by his side with her hand on his leg and smiled at him. She had to translate since he did not speak English. Throughout the ensuing conversation the father watched his daughter when she spoke, obviously incredibly proud of her achievements. And she looked at him with all the tenderness of a beloved daughter. It was so obvious that there was a closeness between the two — one that I had rarely seen in my lifetime and certainly not in my relationship with my own father.

For some reason we started discussing cheating. Both Connie and I had experience with the cheating problem at the university and we were curious what the Qur'an had to say about it. The father, through his daughter-translator, explained that there were three times in the Qur'an where it was permissible to lie (a form of cheating, perhaps). The one response that I remember: lying was acceptable if to tell the truth would hurt another person. I got interested in the topic and was asking, again through his daughter, for more information. Connie's husband sotto voce suggested I stop; he was getting the feeling that the conversation was becoming uncomfortable for our host. (I think now the discomfiture might have arisen because there is some question as to whether lying is OK, if to infidels.)

And then we got onto the belief in God. And did we believe in Allah? Phil went first — appropriately since he was a lay minister. He emphasized a oneness between the Christian God and Allah and was incredibly diplomatic and kind in his response. Some of the girls shared their thoughts, and soon after, the afternoon broke up and we packed up to leave. Connie told me later that she and Phil were afraid that last conversation would come around to me and I would respond "I don't believe in God," which would not have been appropriate.

I can still see in my head the way the auntie bowed and nodded and smiled a sweet smile. I can't adequately describe all that the smile conveyed to me. She made me feel like a queen and that she was incredibly honored to have me in her house and at her table. I'm embarrassed to say that I never sent her a thank-you note. I am bad about sending notes in the States, but I should have sent one that time. I hope the auntie is still glad that I came.

This invitation revealed to me a common misconception about women's rights in Afghanistan. Not all men in Afghanistan are tyrants. Not all men in Afghanistan think women should be in the house or be dead. And not all men in Afghanistan think their daughters should not go to school. All the young women at the university were there because of the support of their families, particularly their fathers. These were men who saw the importance of educating their daughters as well as their sons. I had now met one of these fathers.

And I had now truly experienced the hospitality and generosity of an Afghan family.

Women's Study Group

I went to Afghanistan to save the world — in particular to save the women.

I knew about the usurpation of women's rights in parts of the world, in particular the Middle East. I had read books by Saudi women telling of being prisoners in their own homes and being horribly punished for adulterous sex. I read Hosseini's *A Thousand Splendid Suns*, about the plight of women in Taliban-run Afghanistan, and I had read of the stonings. I knew in some countries women couldn't drive or wear shorts, but then in some of those countries women were prime ministers. It was all confused in my head. And, of course, as an American woman I had no idea what it really meant to be discriminated against.

Oh sure, as a secretary years ago I brought my boss coffee in the morning. I didn't *have to*— it was just done. And it wasn't until the 1970s that women could wear pants to the office. I was called "honey" too many times, and "young lady." But that was discrimination LITE. We could drive, we could vote, we could refuse to marry somebody and we could marry anybody. In most areas, adulterous sex was not punishable by stoning. And we could walk down the street with a fair assumption that we would not be sneered at or touched or jostled.

Not so in Afghanistan. Although women have equal rights under their constitution, in reality in some parts of the country, even after the Taliban were removed from power, women continued to be chattel.

And they wear shrouds of blue. I knew I was in Afghanistan when I saw my first burka-clad woman. Not just a picture of a blue apparition with no face ... a real one.

One day on a shopping trip I was asked by one of our drivers if I wanted to buy a burka. While in Herat, Dee and I and our escorts passed a shop that sold burkas, and the fellows wanted to know if I wanted to try one on. As though there would be nothing unusual about my wanting to cover myself up and become invisible. I didn't think so.

As I found out later, wearing a burka can ironically give a woman a great deal of freedom in Afghanistan: freedom from being harassed on the street. With your face showing you are visible and recognizable and exposed. Wearing a burka allows a woman to move through the streets and the market without being seen.

So knowing about the burkas and the second-class standing of women in Afghanistan, I was on a mission to straighten out the whole problem. The first thing to do, I thought, was find a women's group to align myself with. And the Yellow Pages were the place to go. "Let your fingers do the walking," as they say.

Well, phone service in Afghanistan is mostly by cell phone and there are no phone books, and, of course, no Yellow Pages.

On to Plan B. I started putting the word out: I wanted to get involved, I wanted to help, I wanted to meet women. During the course of putting out those feelers, I found the trivia game on Monday nights and through that connection, found other card players. And, through a long, long unplanned layover in Dubai, I found the mother lode (as it were) of networks: Dr. Red-ding. She was a woman in Kabul who put out a newsletter and was the go-to person if you wanted to publicize women's accomplishments, issues, troubles, anything. I still receive her newsletter.

My first round of "talking up" my wishes went out to the women at school. However, some were still getting settled in and many of the "old-timers" were submerged in their own lives in Kabul. Finally one teacher (Jennifer) told me she was trying to get a women's study group started and would I be interested in joining. Yes. Yes.

The first Saturday there were only four of us, Dee and I and Jennifer and one of her students. But the next time, even though one young woman commandeered the meeting with an interminable monologue on women's rights being human rights, there were more women. And then one Saturday it was a full house. Some Afghan women, students and a few older women, plus quite a few internationals: a woman from Sweden, one from Germany, another from Malaysia, and me.

The talk was about men and women and the unequal rights of women in Afghanistan. There was an older Afghan woman there. She had removed her scarf, and her long black hair was done in a single braid. She did not speak much English, so her young friend translated as the discussion raged. But it was obvious she knew what we were talking about and was following our gestures and facial expressions and angered voices. And then at a pause in our ranting she said, in English, "Allah is a man, Muhammad was a man and my husband is a man." And we all agreed — that pretty much summed up the situation.

They told me that they could not read the Qur'an since it was in Arabic, and they had to trust the mullahs to tell them what it said. I mentioned that the Qur'an has no reference to women wearing a veil except in the one section[1] referring to the Prophet's wives: when you ask something from one of them, do so from behind a veil (or curtain). Nowhere else is the topic of veiling women mentioned except in this one reference. They did not know this.

At another meeting I gave a slide presentation on women in the Qur'an in which I quoted words which not only say that men and women are equal, created from a single being,[2] but words which also conferred on them divorce, dowry and inheritance rights.[3] It was a learning experience for all of us.

The young students told us that they were from the provinces and sent to Kabul to go to school with the blessings, of course, of their fathers. But the girls were under tremendous pressure to marry when they went home. Not from their immediate family perhaps, but from the rest of the village and the elders. And they knew if they were to marry, that would be the end of their life, in a sense.

We talked about marital and societal abuse of women. I asked if there was a spiritual advisor — I started to say "priest" — whom they could go to for help. What a dumb question. They reminded me that the spiritual advisors, the mullahs, were all men and would probably not take the side of a woman in any dispute.

I was pleased that I had been invited to join this group; it was one of the few times I had a chance to talk with Afghan women. I was frustrated that I could do nothing except listen.

18

Kabul at Night

Poker's at my house this Thurs if y'all can make it. Let me hear from you.
(Email from a friend, September 7, 2009)
I'm not going to be able to make it— I'm trying to stir up a game in the guesthouse.... Mind you, gambling is ILLEGAL *in Afghanistan, unlike alcohol which is tolerated for foreigners. So I might have to wire you guys for bail money. Have fun.* (My reply)

Kabul at night was dark.

In the winter, the sun had gone down by the time we left school. There were no street lights along Darulaman Road. (Power was scarce in Kabul, and it was not used for lighting the streets.) The shops were set back from the road, and what dim light shone from them did not break the darkness.

Some of the street vendors were still out in the early evening, but their carts were lit only by a single bulb hung from an awning pole, powered by a battery. The light did little more than highlight a face and a cart along the way. It felt claustrophobic to me.

The roads were packed on the way home, as they were in the morning, with weaving bikes and racing children, burka-clad women shopping, men walking and Toyotas. But now they were hard to see. Shapes were backlit by traffic.

When we went out later in the evening, Darulaman would be nearly empty. Maybe a lone seller of *naan* (the traditional Afghan bread) would still be open, with his battery-operated, light-bulb-lit cart. They were usually the last to abandon the dark street.

Along the road into Kabul, the nearby mountain twinkled with lights from the homes perched there ... mostly dim and yellowish. The homes on the hills had power — power, but no running water. First things first, I guess.

In the center of town some of the restaurants or shops would still be open and light spilled outside their windows. In the back streets there was no light. Dwellings were within tall walls and behind tall gates and little light escaped. The potholes and boulders in the streets were easy to hit in the darkness. Rides at night were always rough.

Alcohol Procurement Adventure

During my first week in Kabul several of us (women) in the guesthouse decided we needed alcohol. We were told about a place that the UN ran that had a buffet, a hair salon, a bar, a swimming pool and sold alcohol to go. Off we went.

Like every other place in Kabul at night — it was dark. Upon entering I saw what looked like, and in fact were, bunkers. That was probably my first "ding dong" moment — war zone!

Inside the complex it was also dark — solitary lights here and there but not enough to light the walkway. Moving around inside was mostly stumbling towards lit areas, in this case, what looked like a bomb-proof building with a solid door. Inside were wood-slatted shelves with perhaps 25 bottles — total — displayed.

The shelves held bottles of white wine and red wine and there may have been whiskey and beer by the case. We all bought wine; it was fairly reasonable, as I remember. But it didn't really matter. We wanted it and were willing to pay whatever. There was also a bottle of crème de cacao, of all things, on the shelf. I bought it. It was Plan B. I still have that bottle; I brought it back to the States with me and it sits in my kitchen cupboard. That night we all had a shot of crème de cacao to celebrate. It's pretty bad stuff!

After that trip, which made it clear that obtaining alcoholic beverages was not going to be easy, we looked into making our own wine, but never did.

We went back to the UN facilities several times, but the prices escalated to $45 for a bottle of cheap red or white wine. By that time we had found the blessed grocery story that became our "supplier."

More Night Ventures

Getting out of the guesthouse on my off time was super important, as it was to most internationals. Once the museum and the art gallery were closed and the clothing shop shuttered, the only places to go were bars and/or restaurants. (Movies were not an option.)

There were several bars/restaurants in Kabul that were "approved" for the international community. Turns out there actually was an official approval given based on the level of security provided by the establishment: height of the walls, number of guards, and so on. And most of those establishments served alcohol. Oh frabjous day!

It was not easy getting to many of the restaurants at night, however. One was particularly difficult: it was down a muddy, bumpy road with no lights at all along the way. We would get out of the security van and stumble towards a dim light denoting a guard shack. A uniformed guard would materialize — he was not there and then he was. He would open the door and usher us inside. It had quite the feeling of a John le Carré novel. Inside we did more stumbling around in near dark until finally — a door with light peeking through. As it turned out it was a good restaurant, and I ate there often.

Dee (my shopper friend who also liked to eat and drink) and I went to a place one night that we're sure now was not on the "approved" list. We had heard that the food was good, but perhaps that was in the daytime with sunlight and people around. At night it was somewhat different.

Our van left us at the entrance to a driveway with the instructions that the restaurant was in the rear of the building. They did not want to drive in with us or walk us in for some reason; we should have known something was not right at that point. But Dee was determined to try out the restaurant and I wasn't that scared — yet. It turned out that the restaurant's foyer was an empty room where we stood for a few minutes, wondering what we had gotten ourselves into. An Afghan man appeared and apparently realized we — two foreign women — were there to eat and he began bustling around to accommodate us. We didn't see any other diners or, in fact, anybody else. We left quickly with apologies.

When we arrived back at the main road we found that our van had left us. Now we were stuck — in the middle of Kabul, at night, on a dark street, alone. We tried to be as invisible as possible while we waited for transport to come back for us. "Why didn't you tell us what that place was?" we asked. Once again in the hospitable way of Afghans, they just shrugged and indicated they thought that's what we wanted to do.

With no street lights and dim to even dimmer, possibly battery-driven lights the only illumination of doorways, entering most of these restaurants at night was a challenge. We were grateful when an armed guard would emerge from a shadow and direct us inward. Sometimes we had to turn over an ID or a passport. Other times a search of our purses was the routine. And sometimes the guards would just smile and say good evening, we'd say good evening and that was it. In several places, managing to make our way inside the gated walls was only part of the journey; locating the actual door to the restaurant remained. Again dim lights, coupled with uneven paving stones and my dirty bifocals, made navigation risky. I really did not want to fall.

The fear of falling was not inconsequential in Kabul. The sidewalks were rough and at night dimly lit at best; even at school the walkways were rugged. My dignity seemed important to me and falling down was not something I wanted to do. One night I had that misfortune while returning from buying wine at the UN store.

Trenches lined many of the streets, and that night I tripped into a trench (actually a ditch), crashing to the ground, skinning the hell out of my leg and breaking a bottle of wine. (I saved two out of three.) I remember my escort trying to assist me as I attempted to stand up and gather my dignity. "Let me help you," he said. I'm still struck by the kindness of his words.

On the way back to the guesthouse, my bag with the broken bottle of wine leaked onto the carpet, producing an unwelcome stench, I'm sure, for our Muslim staff. Another mortifying moment.

Even if visiting these restaurants/bars offered some logistical difficulties, we were all eager to get out and about on the weekends or whenever there was an opportunity. Sometimes the food was good; sometimes not. One night a large group went to a Chinese restaurant (that's right — Chinese restaurant in Kabul, Afghanistan). The company was great, the booze was welcome, the food was mediocre.

I liked one particular restaurant the most. I was introduced to it in the fall when the weather was lovely and we could sit outside and enjoy the garden. As the weather changed, people moved inside and then there was the warmth of a real fireplace — very cozy and very Western. I always ordered beef carpaccio, which was terrific. Some thought it was strange that a raw meat dish would be a menu item in Afghanistan. (As it turned out I did get sick, but not from beef carpaccio.)

One of everyone's favorite restaurants served Lebanese food. And a French restaurant in town sold pepperoni pizza which was pretty tasty; however, I'm still not sure if the "pepperoni" was pig-derived.

Menus in these restaurants were in English, of course, but English as written by a non-native speaker, which made for some interesting offerings. My favorite was the menu listing for a "sated aborigine." I was tempted, I must admit, but actually it was the Afghan version of a lightly fried eggplant.

I usually drank wine, since ordering vodka and tonic did not necessarily mean there would be vodka in the drink. The wine choices were usually white or purple. I always went for the purple. It was the best buy. Beer was also an option — Heineken or Heineken.

As mentioned before, Afghans were generally not allowed in places where alcohol was served. The other customers at these establishments were the international set in Kabul: expatriates primarily from the States, Australia,

Britain and Canada. Some were in their 20s, but most were in their 30s and 40s. Many worked at the embassies and some at the various NGOs (non-governmental organizations). And then there was us — the faculty and staff from the American University. We saw very few military personnel.

Included in the international set were the "Testosterone Men." Men swagger everywhere, but they flock to, flourish and swagger big time in war zones. Every time I went to one particular restaurant there would be a pack of them standing at the bar, posturing and telling their stories of adventure and daring. And the unspoken game was always, "I've been in a more dangerous place than you." High points were given for Somalia and Iraq. And, of course, they were earning points by working in Afghanistan.

Safi Landmark Restaurant

One night "adventure" was an abortive visit to the Safi Landmark Restaurant.

The City Center mall is connected to the Safi Hotel, the only four-star hotel in Kabul. Dee and I had heard that they had a great restaurant so we made plans to go.

The City Center has the only escalator in Afghanistan, and it happened to be working that one evening. It also had an elevator with glass walls that went to the restaurant on the top floor.

We didn't know if they served alcohol; in fact, we didn't know anything about the place. Our transport guys said, "Safi, you want to go to Safi?" And that's the only indication we had that perhaps our plan was not a good one. Our second indication that this was really not a good plan came when we walked into the restaurant and realized the place was filled with men — Afghan men and no one else. No families, no dating couples, and no women. It was clear we were not expected.

We found a table, however and sat down. Our waiter did not know what to do and neither did we. We started to ask if we could get a drink, looked at each other, shook our heads, thanked the waiter and left. It was quite embarrassing.

Again, we asked our transport guys," Why didn't you tell us?" And again, they said they thought that we really wanted to go there. Turns out where we wanted to go and did finally go that night and several other nights was the Sufi Restaurant — not Safi! This was a fine place — comfortable and dark, with Sufi music on Wednesday nights and beer by the glass or wine by the bottle. They also served a thin form of their traditional bread (naan) stuffed with spinach, which was delicious.

Cards

I like to play cards, and in one of my early communiqués with my mentor I asked not only if I could get a beer but if anybody played bridge or poker at the school. She knew about the beer availability, but not whether or not anyone played cards.

Once I arrived in Kabul and had settled in a bit, I started getting itchy — card-playing withdrawal symptoms had set in. I sent out a general memo to my colleagues at school to see if anyone was interested in getting together to play — bridge, poker, name-the-game. I got no response.

I persevered, however, found a few channels to put out the word, and finally located a Monday trivia game and got two nibbles about possible card games.

One event was a "secret" poker game. Gambling is *haram* according to the Qur'an[1] and Muslims generally don't gamble. Some do, but they don't advertise it. So the game was secret and the location was revealed only right before the event and only to those who were preapproved. Quite cloak and dagger, but I didn't mind. I was ready.

The secret location turned out to be a local restaurant. The game was Texas Hold'em, which I had played only a few times, but it didn't matter. There was a $50 buy-in and the money was to go to one of the women's groups in town. Food would be provided and alcohol could be bought. Perfect.

For the $50 I got not only food, but an allotment of chips. I could buy more chips if I needed them up to a certain hour. After that time, no more chips could be bought and everyone played until they ran out. Real money went to the top three players; the rest of us just had fun and drank and ate.

There were seven long tables with nine people at each table. I was one of three women in attendance. Most of the men were internationals, but quite a few were Afghans. We played an hour or so and I did OK. By that I mean I didn't have to buy any more chips. After we ate, the game turned serious. And, suddenly everyone but me got to be a much better player. It took a few hands and I was out. The Afghan with the better hand apologized for beating me. I didn't care.

As another ploy to raise money, they auctioned off each of the player's ability to stay in to the end and be the big winner. I'm not sure how the payout worked, but if you thought a certain player was likely to "take all," then you put up your money to bet on him. I think. Anyway, some of the players were obviously well known, and apparently had won in previous years. They "went" for nice sums. For me and others like me who were new and whom no one knew, our "résumés" would be beefed up. "Now we have Penny

Travis, she's a doctor, folks, what do I hear bid on her?" Dreadful silence, until some blessed soul finally offered $20.

The evening was great fun and I felt I was part of a community.

My second nibble for card playing was through a fellow at the trivia game who knew of a weekly bridge game and put me in touch with the leader. I went — one time. That night only the host and I knew how to play. Two people sat in the same easy chair and necked and tried to play cards and the fifth tried his best to catch on. In the midst of the game, the lights went off — not an uncommon occurrence in Kabul. Candles were lit and we continued to play. No problem. It was a pleasant evening, but the card playing wasn't.

Not long before I left Kabul a poker game was arranged with some of my colleagues — all men. We played for pennies and nickels and I won — a whopping $8. We never played again.

Towards the end of my stay, one of my housemates and I arranged a weekly bridge game at our house. Two of us knew how to play and we were teaching the other two. It had the makings of a good game, but I didn't stay long enough to find out.

Trivia

My most regular fun time in Kabul was the weekly trivia game.

Finding entertainment in Kabul (other than grocery shopping) was difficult. When I first got there I put the word out — as we all did — to let me know what's going on, I'm up for anything, and so forth. After being "locked in" at the guesthouse and "locked in" at school, I needed to get out! One Wednesday early on, I grabbed one of my colleagues and said, "Please tell me someone's going out tonight — I want to go."

There was one fellow at school who seemed to know everything that was going on in Kabul. He told me about the trivia game that was held each week and promised to put me in touch with the organizers. That never happened. (He talked a good game, but his follow-through was poor.)

Then one night I was invited to play cards at the home of a colleague's friend. I am a big card player — not particularly good at any game, but I love the surprise as each hand unfolds, be it bridge or poker or even canasta, in a pinch. (Before I left the States I played weekly — both poker and bridge.) At the time of the invitation I had not played any cards in Kabul and I was excited about holding cards again. As it turned out, it was not really a card game (I had heard what I wanted to hear), but a game of tokens or something. A silly game, but sometimes you take your entertainment where you can get it, which was certainly true in Kabul.

During the course of the evening, the host and hostess mentioned a weekly trivia game and said they played. I told them I'd love to join in, but didn't know anyone. Linda's comment, bless her heart, was "Well, you know us."

So, what the heck — I decided to go by myself and see what it was all about. I arranged for Transport to take me and told them I'd call when I was ready to be picked up. I was dropped off at a guard shack, my bag was searched and then I was free to stumble through the entranceway, across a dark and stony path and into the International Club, wondering, not for the first time in Kabul, what had I gotten myself into.

As it turned out, my host of the previous evening was sitting at the bar when I arrived. The game hadn't started yet, so we had a good introductory talk. I asked him, for instance, why he was in Kabul. His rather glib response was, "You've got to be somewhere." So much for that conversation. But it does highlight an attitude difference among those who have a partner in Kabul, a husband or wife or lover. This fellow was married and he and his wife had great jobs that provided them with good feelings and sustenance. They had a house and friends and a routine and if they had to restrict their movements for security reasons it was OK — they had each other. And their adult children came to Kabul to visit. Just like down home. For the rest of us single people, life in Kabul could be confining and sometimes lonely. And definitely celibate.

I ended up playing with his team that first night.

Also that first night I ordered a ham and cheese sandwich, as advertised on the menu. As eating pig is *haram*, pigs and pig products are not generally available in Afghanistan. A certain French restaurant had pepperoni pizza on the menu and another restaurant served bacon for breakfast, but even in the stores catering to internationals, no pork was available. So I was pleased to see the offering of a ham and cheese sandwich.

The young sweet-faced waiter informed me, with a shy smile, that they didn't have ham. Well, I thought, I could have guessed that. "But," he said, "We have bacon." So that's what I had from then on — a bacon and cheese sandwich. Each week I would order "ham and cheese"; the waiter would say "No ham, but bacon." And I'd say, "Fine, make it a bacon and cheese sandwich." And we'd both smile. Sometimes you take your entertainment where you can get it.

I would also order a glass of wine. It was served in a water tumbler and was a very big drink. I usually had two. I did not have to drive home.

The manager always smiled when I came in and he remembered what I liked to drink. I'm sure he appreciated our business, but that's OK. I felt like a valued customer.

The players were all internationals — many Brits, a few Australians, Canadians and Americans. A Frenchman and his Swedish wife also played regularly. Each week a team from the previous week would come up with some questions for the game — usually five or six rounds of ten questions or so. Some questions were simply read by a leader, others were passed out as pictures to be identified and some questions were snippets of music. Each group had its own unique style, which produced unique groans from the other participants. One night there was a round of ten questions on Napoleon. Most of us knew Josephine and Waterloo, but these particular questions were obscure — maybe not for a true Napoleonophile, but they stumped all of us. Then there was the retired biology professor who centered a round of questions on little-known parts of little-known animals. But it was a break from routine and almost like home.

Except no ham.

There was a friendly rivalry around the trivia game. The winning team got bragging rights. It cost $5 to play and the money that winter bought fuel for one of the orphanages in town. The team that won also decided which team would come up with the questions for the next week. It wasn't always the winning or the losing team that got the next question-writing duty — sometimes the team that came in second or next to last won the "honors."

One night the festivities were interrupted by an announcement that trouble was expected in the vicinity of the hotel and the suggestion that we might want to leave for our respective guesthouses. No one left. We all knew we could just as easily be blown up riding to our guesthouses as sitting where we were, so we decided to take our chances and stay and play.

I continued to go every Monday night, and eventually a team from school was formed. The game started at 8:00 and by 9:45 it was over. Most everyone had to be back to their residences relatively early; our security van had to pick us up before 10.

We were in a war zone and everyone knew that life was more dangerous than not, but on Monday evenings between 8:00 and 9:45 we got a break — we were with compatriots and friends and it was a lot of fun.

I still get a reminder every Monday from my Yahoo calendar — "8:00 P.M. Trivia International Club." I haven't gotten around to removing it. It reminds me of a special time.

Travel at Night

Most forays into Kabul at night were arranged with the Transport Office. We could also arrange for a pickup or simply call when we were ready to return. Generally the latest that transport would pick us up was 10; on the weekends, it was midnight.

The ride home was always an adventure, particularly after trivia. A few of us would be a bit tipsy and sometimes we sang. Other times we were silly and laughed a lot. Our antics seemed to amuse our driver and escort. And they always seemed "looser" at night as well.

Speeding wasn't really an issue on the streets of Kabul during the day — too many cars. (And as far as I could tell, there were no speed limits, anyway.) Not so at night, particularly later at night when cars and people were home and off the streets. Then our drivers turned into amateur Dale Earnhardts and we zoomed around Kabul. It was scary, but fun.

On one memorable occasion at night, we rode down a one-way street going the wrong way. Seems this was the quickest way to where we were going. The driver and our escort thought it was great that we were all loudly concerned, as it were. "What are you doing?" and "Wrong way," and "Watch out!"

We didn't have to use school transport; we could call a taxi to pick us up and to bring us home. Some of the clubs were open until the wee hours for the international crowd and then it was necessary to use a taxi service. Again, several taxi companies were "approved," which, I gathered, meant they were not run by the Taliban or other kidnappers.

I always took a taxi to the trivia game on Mondays. This involved my calling 30 minutes before my last class ended to arrange for a taxi to pick me up. It usually took at least 30 minutes for one to arrive and the "gate" at school would call me when the taxi was outside. When I stepped outside into the darkness it was never clear which car was the taxi, and although they were supposed to identify themselves to me, they never did. I simply got in whatever car moved up to the door and flashed its lights. The ride cost me $5, plus tip. (Again, it cost $5, plus tip, to get anywhere in Kabul.) Some of us probably overtipped. We were told this was not a good thing because it wreaked havoc with the Afghan economy; this argument was too convoluted for me to follow. I continued to overtip.

I usually had interesting conversations on the way to trivia. The drivers all spoke reasonable English and at least one had spent a lot of time in England.

One taxi driver told me they had a special "permit" that allowed them to go through some sections of the city and not be stopped. One night on the way to the trivia game I noticed that the taxi did not seem to be stopping at checkpoints. He said, "They don't check cars with older women in them." To which I replied, "Don't they think an older woman could carry a bomb?" which was probably not a wise remark for me to make. The driver didn't respond, but I bet it made him think!

It was always fun to get out and about in Kabul, particularly at night. But I was always glad to get back to the safety and lights of our guesthouse.

19

Trip to Herat

Judy called about playing bridge, but didn't leave her number. In the weird chance that you get this instantly, do you have it? How was Herat? (Email from a friend, September 25, 2009)

Afghanistan is really different from England or Mexico or Australia: all countries I have lived in or visited extensively. That seems obvious: a different language, different customs and a different look about the people. And, as I was to find out, taking a trip to another city in the country was also different and not easily accomplished.

Afghanistan is not a tourist hotspot — except perhaps for ecologists looking for the snow leopards or hikers looking for a mountaineering adventure. Historians and archaeologists also are perennial visitors. But for the standard tourist, it's not on their list.

There are security issues, and, in Afghanistan, there are "How are we going to get there and get back" issues. All out-of-town trips had to be cleared with the security office. No trips were allowed to the south: to Kandahar, for instance. No one wanted to go there anyway.

Bamiyan was my first choice of a place to visit outside Kabul. The giant Buddhas used to be there — before the Taliban decided to blow them up. Taliban Mullah Mohammad Omar stated at the time: "All the statues around Afghanistan must be destroyed."

> Because God is one God and these statues are there to be worshipped and that is wrong. They should be destroyed so that they are not worshipped now or in the future.[1]

I knew there was a restoration project going on and I somehow wanted to show my respect. And I knew that the governor of Bamiyan province was a woman[2] and that the area was populated primarily by the Hazara, an ethnic minority which comprised most of the Shiite Muslims in Afghanistan. The countryside was said to be breathtaking and the newest park in Afghanistan at Band-e-emir was in the same province.

I asked about official transport to Bamiyan. "Absolutely not," they said. Too dangerous. But ... we could always hire our own transport and armed guards. There was some interest at school in doing that, but we never made the plans. The feeling was it just wasn't worth the risk to form a convoy to go to Bamiyan to see what remained of the Buddhas.

So travel by road was problematic. Another option, however, was to fly to Bamiyan. But as I was to find out, flying was not terribly reliable. Not to say that once in the air you don't arrive at the planned destination. It's getting in the air that's the problem — knowing when the plane is scheduled to leave, and if it will leave on time.

There are four airlines in Afghanistan (Safi, Pamir, Kam Air and Ariana) none of which at this writing is allowed into Europe, due to the unsafe conditions of the planes. When I was in Afghanistan, Safi flew into Frankfurt. You could get to Dubai from Kabul and to New Delhi. And that was about it. And you could fly within the country if you were lucky enough to be at the airport when a plane was about to leave.

I found out that a plane did fly to Bamyan. One of our colleagues went there over what she thought might be a long weekend. Turned out it she was there for a long week. One plane flew in and one plane flew out, all on the same day and only once a week. This meant spending seven days in Bamyan province: a long, long time with essentially little to do but visit the archeological site. To get anywhere in the area you would need a driver. You might want to pay an escort as well, in case you wanted to get out of the car. Remember an international, particularly an international woman, is not expected to walk around by herself. And one of the favorite pastimes of all tourists — shopping — is severely limited. There are no bright shiny malls or drop-in pizza places or cozy bars for a quick beer. And window shopping is just not the same when you are hurried along by an escort who wants you off the street. So going to Bamyan lost much of its appeal.

Just three weeks after arriving in Afghanistan, Dee and I decided we would go to Herat, a large city about 400 miles to the west of Kabul. We had a few days off and thought it would be nice to see a bit more of Afghanistan. La di dah. A few other coworkers were going as well, but for some cliquey reason we all were not going together. (This may have been the start of the deteriorations of relations amongst housemates which was looming on the horizon.)

We made arrangements for a hotel room. Again, arrangements for most anything in Afghanistan are not easy. To start with, calling on a cell phone and trying to communicate with someone when you don't speak their language and they don't speak yours is a challenge. We thought we were calling a certain hotel and we thought we had reserved rooms. Not exactly, as it turned out.

The first part of the adventure was at the airport in Kabul. After our driver and escort dropped us off we then stood in line — a long, long line — to check our baggage. It was a line which, as I found out later, is not so common in Afghanistan. Storming the counter is more the routine and there was always someone right at the counter hoping to edge in. I encountered one of these "line crashers" when I was almost to the front of the line, and I could see how his "edge into the line" maneuver was going to work. But I stood in front of him and his family and claimed my rightful next place for service. I knew at the time I was being childish, but it was a long, long line and I was thirsty and had to visit the bathroom.

Baggage check-in was our next obstacle. We had tickets, but once they were handed over, they seemed to disappear. Then the clerk could not remember having seen them. He, of course, had laid them down while he was talking to one of the several men who were standing about with phones in their ears. Dee was getting irate and slightly shrill and finally nagged our way past the baggage clerk with a receipt that we hoped would allow us to reclaim our stuff at the end of the journey. I was getting nervous. The next stop was the waiting room. It was packed and no one knew exactly when the plane would be there. We were all there at the so-called arranged time, but the plane was not and so we sat and I tried not to think about this trip being a big mistake.

In the waiting room I was exposed for the first time to a Western woman who apparently did not realize she wasn't in her backyard. Or maybe she did and simply didn't care. In any case, there she was: heavy, tight-fitting top and jeans and no head scarf and leaning up against the wall with the kind of sullen expression that would have made my mother say, "Fix your face." She appeared to flaunt her unconventional appearance — in a country where many women wore burkas and most others wore scarves and all women dressed modestly. It was the custom. The mantra for us was to never draw attention to ourselves. Although we didn't wear burkas, we still tried to be invisible. This woman was not invisible and I was somehow embarrassed.

That young woman was not really my big concern. I was more worried about when I should take my secret pill — the one that would get me through being confined on an airplane without screaming. I don't remember much about the plane trip, but assume it was fairly uneventful. I mainly sat there and was calm.

The car that met us in Herat was not from the hotel that we thought we had called, but another one. The first one had closed, we were told. When?

No one was sure. It was a bit stressful but the driver convinced us that he was not the Taliban. We didn't have a big choice being in a strange town in a strange country, and being unfamiliar with the language increased our emotional stress. We decided to believe him and hoped our remains would eventually be recovered.

Baggage collection was in the parking lot of the airport and centered on a cart piled high with luggage from the plane. There was no revolving carousel surrounded by patiently waiting passengers — rather a crowd made up of men only (and us) pushing and shoving and grabbing. We realized afterwards that we should have paid a couple of the young boys hanging around to push, shove and grab for us.

So far I was not having a good time.

The hotel was nice and the staff polite and helpful. By the time we got there I really needed to use the facilities and was directed to a bathroom off the lobby. Seeing that there was no toilet in the bathroom, only a porcelain-lined hole with places for two feet on either side, I returned to the desk to

Herat is more conservative than Kabul; more women were covered in burkas, for instance. But Herat has fewer bombed-out buildings.

This is the beautiful Friday Mosque in Herat. We were allowed to wander about the halls and visit the workshop.

ask for the women's bathroom. Well ... that was the women's bathroom. I just didn't see how I was going to manage to relieve myself over a hole in the floor and still remain dry when I was wearing slacks. Thankfully the bathroom in my room was of the more conventional and easier-to-use variety. It's one thing to read about different customs in other lands — bathroom facilities, for example. It's quite another thing to meet them on a personal level.

One custom I was introduced to in the hotel was the provision of a prayer rug for the guests. What a nice idea!

We decided against eating at the hotel that night — the restaurant doubled as a barber shop, so looking for another place to eat seemed to be a good idea. We ended up with a taxi and an escort from the hotel; I'm still not sure how that was arranged, but it was and they took us to the "Thousand and One Nights" restaurant for dinner. It was high on a hill overlooking Herat and seating was available either outside under a huge canopy or inside the restaurant proper.

We decided to sit at one of the outside tables. Actually we sat on the table, which was a raised and rug-covered platform maybe eight by eight in area. And there we sat, Dee and I and our driver and escort, atop one of the platforms, trying not to think about looking foolish. Before we sat down we looked to see if there were any other women outside. There were and we decided it must be appropriate for us to eat outside. The men did not say one way or another. We were told later that we should have gone inside; that women are not allowed at the outside seating. I guess those other women outside didn't know the rules either.

We ordered a pizza. Looking for the comfort of home, I guess. It was not exactly a pizza as I had remembered a pizza, but it was close enough to provide the comfort I was seeking. It was like the innards of a ham and cheese sandwich with added mushrooms spread on pizza dough. And we drank Cokes. No alcohol in Herat. But I had brought a bottle of wine, just in case. I should have brought two.

The next morning I saw my first mynah bird, on the sill outside my window. It was black and pacing and pecking on the glass. I thought it was a mean-looking bird.

That day our first stop was the Friday Mosque or the Mosque of the Day of Assembly. It was awesome. I did get a chance to visit Agra and the Taj Mahal before I left Asia. The Friday Mosque had the same beauty — bright and shiny and perfect. We were allowed in and left to roam about by ourselves, through the main courtyard and surrounding hallways. In the central area for prayer there were stacks of bricks placed here and there to hold down the prayer rugs on a windy day. Smart!

We also had a chance to visit the workroom where replacement tiles are constantly being made. It was primitive. The only light in the workroom came from the windows and formed patterns of sunshine and dark, sunshine and dark. Dee talked to the curator about buying some artifacts; I talked to the gardener who was tending his plants. I was only able to greet him, but I tried asking him for a cutting of one of his plants. That didn't work, so I made a scissor motion with my fingers, smiled and pointed at the plant I wanted — the universal language of plant lovers. He understood and gave me a cutting.

We went shopping after we left the mosque. Again with our driver and escort. We were stared at everywhere. In Kabul, the capital, many women, while covered, did not wear burkas. Not so here — most of the women on the street wore burkas or were heavily veiled. Our headscarves could not hide our Western origin and someone tapped me on the rear. At the time I thought it was a mistake; later I thought it was probably intentional. One of our colleagues said her wrist was grabbed on the street by a man who then pointed at her bare forearm. Afghan women are often harassed on the street, often to discourage them from being on the street. I could see how that would work.

I bought two necklaces, each with a large agate. I also bought a traditional dress, or so I was told. Dee assured me it was old and that the bodice had been salvaged from another dress. I wondered later why I had bought a used dress that, as it turned out, had several holes in it.

That night we had a good meal at the hotel and that was the end of the fun times.

It turns out that as we were on holiday so were a lot of other people. It was the end of Ramadan and the festival of Eid had just started. All the shops would be closed the next day so that everyone could spend time with family. And the holiday went on for a week. Who knew if the shops would also be closed for a week.

We drove around Herat that afternoon and started thinking about whether or not we really wanted to stay more than another day or so. Even though our original plan was for a four- or five-day visit, we could see that we had pretty much run the gamut of tourist attractions. And, again, we couldn't simply wander the streets or stop at a sidewalk café and order a latte or a beer. Certainly not a beer and there were no sidewalk cafés. And I, for one, did not feel comfortable on the streets without a male escort. There were too many stares and the random jostling. I had visions of spending the next four days confined to the hotel with nothing to do, nothing to read and nothing to drink. Here's when I started to panic.

We checked with the desk about changing our return tickets to Monday from Thursday. We were told that, yes, there was a flight on Monday, but no one knew when it was to arrive or leave. Swell. But we were told someone (?) would call someone (?) on Monday and find out what time the flight was.

Dee and I decided to visit the local airline office the next morning (Sunday), to get a better idea of what was going on. A pleasant and smiling young man told us that, in fact, there were no flights on Monday and not for the next three days. Trapped.

When the clerk said "no flights for three days," I said "You've got to be kidding." He didn't understand my words, but he understood my expression. "Wait," says he. Let me make a phone call. Chatters into the phone—in Dari. I realized he could have been talking to anyone: his mother, his sister, his bookie and not necessarily anyone who knew anything about plane arrivals and departures. At last he hung up and smiled.

"I have good news. One flight today."

"When?"

The nearly empty airport in Herat — just my friend Dee and I and an Afghan couple. Here the husband and Dee are looking for any sign of activity: people, airplanes, anything.

"Oh, you go to airport in half hour, maybe hour and half."

"When does the flight leave?" I try again. He smiles and shrugs.

Here's where the situation morphed into one of those wartime spy "escape" movies — à la *Casablanca*. Get the right documents, hurry, hurry. Run for the plane, the bad guys are close behind. Whew ... just made it! The End and Closing Credits.

Off we race to the hotel — quick, check us out — pack up — hurry hurry. The taxi driver races to the airport — hurry hurry. When we get there the only people around are four or five armed guards at the gate.

This is one of those times I thought, "Uh-oh."

The driver talked to the guards (Dari again). When I started to say something, the driver made a "shut up" motion. I could take a hint; I let him do the talking.

Anyway, apparently there was a flight, but when? was the question. The driver couldn't come into the airport grounds with us, so Dee and I entered the gate alone. There was an empty parking lot with bright wildflowers poking through the cracks, an empty guard shack, a fence in the distance, a closed snack shop and a yellow bench. And no people. No One.

And no planes.

And once again, "Uh-oh." Well, I sat and waited and Dee went looking for food. After a while a well-dressed man and his chador-clad wife appeared. They seemed as confused as we were, but since we didn't speak each other's languages, it was hard to tell. Dee went off with the guy, looking for airplanes or signs of any activity. The wife and I sat together on the bench and she offered me some of the nuts from her lunch: almonds and pistachios. I demurred, but she kept offering until finally I had a lapful.

I was feeling more optimistic about our chances of escape.

Finally an officer showed up and opened the canteen and more passengers arrived and we were assured that a plane was coming and that it would leave for Kabul at 2:00.

Eventually, we were hustled into the derelict building to have our luggage weighed. We stood in line some more, our bags were searched, we were searched, we stood in line again, walked for a goodly distance — all with our bags and finally got to the main airport building and there was a big plane. Yippee. That was my other concern: if a plane showed up, would it be a tiny thing? But here was a big plane with big wings. I was so glad.

I went off looking for a restroom. The one I was directed to — language problems again — was filled with men. A very nice young man motioned me inside and smiled, seeming to indicate that I was in the right place. When I got a gander at the hole in the floor and the buzzing flies, I decided I wasn't in the right place, if you know what I mean. I decided that I didn't have to go after all. (I think all women in Afghanistan develop larger than normal kidneys in response to the dearth of usable public toilets.)

By the time I got back to the waiting room, all the women were missing. Imagine my concern. Turned out they had all been ushered into the women's waiting room. It was dark and unpleasant, but apparently kept the women (and me) safe from men's prying eyes.

Finally we were hustled onto the plane and it took off for Kabul — at 1:30, a half hour earlier than "scheduled."

Our other colleagues returned to Kabul a full 24 hours after we did. They were surprised to see us and wondered how we had gotten back so fast. They apparently were in a different movie.

20

Trip to Jalalabad

*Lucy and I are going to see "The Last Station" Monday afternoon at 4:20
at the Terrace Theater. Would any one like to join us?* (Email from a
friend, March 28, 2010)
I'd like to, but I'll be on the road to the Khyber Pass. Omigod! (My reply)

Traveling to areas outside of Kabul was a problem. We were able to fly
to Herat, but road trips were mostly out of the question — "too dangerous"
or "security concerns" were the reasons. There was always the threat of kidnapping — either the Taliban or some other group for money or notoriety.

In April, however, one of our Afghan colleagues offered to take some of
us to Jalalabad by road. His family had connections in the area, which meant
he knew or was related to everyone living in the province, and he was going
to provide security for us. As it turned out we rode in a bus with an armed
guard, in a convoy led by a police car. The armed guard was provided by our
colleague, and the police car was probably driven by one of his relatives.

In all, there were ten of us, including our escorts.

Considering how few opportunities there were to see any of Afghanistan
other than Kabul, I jumped at the opportunity. Jalalabad is along the road to
the Khyber Pass and Pakistan. All goods traveling between the two countries
travel along this road, which runs through the Kabul River Gorge and may
be one of the most dangerous roads in the world. Some of my students lived
in Jalalabad and made the trip there and back every week. One fellow told
me he did not drive. Too dangerous.

Our colleague neglected to mention the dangers of the road, but instead
dwelt on its beauty. I was glad because here's an article I had a chance to read
before I took the trip.[1]

> Even in a nation beset by war and suicide bombings, you would be hard-pressed
> to find anything as reliably terrifying as the national highway through the Kabul
> Gorge.

A billboard advertising Land Rovers, a man sitting on the street and a horse and cart, all on the way to Jalalabad.

The 40-mile stretch, a breathtaking chasm of mountains and cliffs between Kabul and Jalalabad, claims so many lives so regularly that most people stopped counting long ago. Cars flip and flatten. Trucks soar to the valley floor. Buses play chicken; buses collide.

The mayhem unfolds on one of the most bewitching stretches of scenery on all the earth. The gorge, in some places no more than a few hundred yards wide, is framed by vertical rock cliffs that soar more than 2,000 feet above the Kabul River below. Most people die, and most cars crash, while zooming around one of the impossible turns that offer impossible views of the crevasses and buttes.

The lethality of the roadway stems from the unique mix of geography, the road itself, and the drivers' disregard for the laws of physics.

The two-lane highway is barely wide enough for two cars to pass. On the inside lane, less than a yard outside your window, stands a wall of treeless rock that climbs upward in a nearly perpendicular line. A foot-high ledge guards the outside lane, behind which lies a valley floor as far as 1,000 feet down.

...The cars zoom at astonishing speeds, far faster than would ever be allowed on a similar road in the West, if there was one. Like Formula One drivers, the Afghans dart out along the sharpest of turns, slamming their cars back into their lanes at the first flash of oncoming disaster. Most of the time they make it.

The danger is heightened by other things. On paper, the government of

Some of the magnificent scenery in the Kabul River gorge on the way to Jalalabad.

Afghanistan requires that drivers pass a test to get a license, but few people here seem to have one.

Then there are the cars themselves, battered Toyota taxis and even Ladas from bygone Soviet days. A typical Afghan car has bald tires and squeaky brakes — not exactly ideal for zigging and zagging through the mountains.

But perhaps the gravest threat, apart from speed of the cars, is the slowness of the trucks. The massive tractor-trailers that move cargo in and out of Pakistan are often overloaded by thousands of pounds. They cannot move fast; if they are climbing one of the gorge's thousand-foot hills, they cannot move at all. They get stuck. They fall back. They fall over.

So the cars and their drivers stack up behind them, angry and impatient, and rush and maneuver and pass them at the first chance.

And so the cars crash, one after the other.

I was no fool. Storied mountains, gorges, hairpin curves? I made sure I had plenty of "be calm" pills just in case I panicked. At least one other traveling companion had the same idea.

I knew it was about a three-hour journey given no traffic problems. I now know that meant no traffic accidents. And, of course, no shootouts.

The plan was for us to go up early one day, spend the night and come back the next day.

The scenery was every bit as magnificent as promised, and scary. Here's where I saw small children in the middle of narrow, hairpin turns, directing traffic. And Afghan trucks brightly decorated, many with wooden doors. One was piled so high with bags full of stuff it was amazing that they remained aloft. We saw a bright blue truck that had missed a turn and was nosed into a wall separating the road from infinity. And we saw a bus resting in a ravine after having missed its turn. I saw a camel and a Brahman bull and families of Kuchis, the nomads of Afghanistan. There were green hills and rolling sand hills and great expanses with tiny villages nestled within. And in the distance were the snow-capped mountains of the Hindu Kush range.

The Kabul River, which forms the gorge between the mountains, also meanders through the city of Kabul, where it is a garbage repository and a feeding ground for herds of goat and sheep. No one would call it anything but ugly. In its gorge towards Pakistan the river tumbles and sparkles along its way and it is beautiful.

The scenery going to Jalalabad was breathtaking and terrifying.

We ate at a restaurant on the river. Arrangements had apparently been made for our arrival and we were given a private room, actually a porch that served as a room and overlooked the water and the children playing in the water. We sat on the floor and a bright blue plastic tarp was laid down in the center for the food: rice, naan, meat, and cans of Coca-Cola. Everyone's bare feet were alarmingly close to the food, but no one seemed to care.

Some of the children swam over and plates of food began to disappear.

We revisited this site the next morning for a boat ride. When we returned there was a crowd waiting for us on the levee. Once again we were drawing stares.

On the top of the levee several snooker tables were set up and young boys were playing. Snooker? On the banks of the Kabul River?

I had forgotten to bring my battery charger and had to buy some emergency batteries for my camera. "Don't buy batteries," everyone said. "They won't last. They're cheap Russian throwaways." I didn't listen and bought several packs in the tiny store on the river. I should have listened.

It's amazing that Afghanistan has managed to survive at all over the past

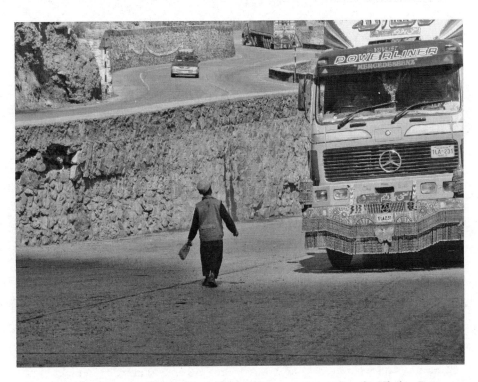

A young boy directs traffic on the winding and dangerous road to the Khyber Pass.

A woman and her baby beg on a street in Jalalabad.

few years; so many of the products that find their way into the country are defective or broken or worthless. Including batteries. Luckily one of my colleagues had extra chargeable batteries so I didn't lose the opportunity to take more pictures on the trip.

Unlike Kabul, Jalalabad had not been bombed. Buildings were whole, and streets were relatively pitless. We visited a park and saw Afghans strolling about and visiting. One young man was sitting in the midst of pink rosebushes with shards of pomegranates strewn around him. We visited a gushing river and had tea and visited a shrine and admired the roses. And we climbed around on a sand hill and never figured out what it was or why we were there.

That night I had one of my best restaurant meals in Afghanistan. At least I'm guessing it was a restaurant, because it didn't look like one. It was an upstairs room over an ice cream shop, but somehow a wonderful meal appeared for all ten of us. One of the best parts was their version of *montoo* — a ravioli-type dish, this time stuffed with spinach. We drank Coca-Cola — again.

We stayed that night in a hotel that had been grand in years past but now was just shabby. My room was adequate, barely. I asked for a night light so I could read in bed; I got a bemused stare. The small-screen TV was perched

This camel train was stuck in the same traffic jam as our van.

on top of the minuscule refrigerator and the bathroom needed care. I did not use the shower and I did not sleep well.

I wandered the grounds of the hotel early the next morning. There was a sweeping lawn with large old trees and a still lovely garden with a pond and a fountain. The gardener was at work sweeping his walkway. I could imagine the hotel and grounds in a better time.

A pile of garbage was hidden behind the hotel. I doubted that there was a pickup service — unless one counts the goats and sheep.

Breakfast was served in the hotel's dining room and was most strange. Tea and bread and one fried egg — for all of us.

We had planned on going further east towards Pakistan that day, but apparently "they" knew that "we" were in town and that appeared to be a matter of concern. It was unclear exactly who "they" were, but "we" turned around and headed back to Kabul. And I was told to stop waving at the small children. We were to be invisible.

Lunch that day was in a village of tiny streets and open shops and more stares. Once again the ubiquitous blue tarp was rolled out and food appeared. We wanted fish and we got fish. Chunks of fish and Coca-Cola. This establishment seemed rough to me, but I imagine it was not any different from many other eating places scattered around the countryside. The kitchen facilities were rudimentary. No electric stoves, no refrigerators, an open grill of some kind and the head of whatever was being served lying about somewhere nearby. And at this restaurant the skin and attached fur of an animal had also been discarded on the steps. I did not look closely.

We, the women, needed a bathroom. There was one across the street, down the hill, next to an open kitchen and behind a shop. One of the guards stood watch as we singly tried to use the open pit facility. It was not designed well and we hosed it down first. It is safe to say that there are few arrangements for women in public in Afghanistan. In particular, no bathrooms. Presumably women are not supposed to be out and about long enough to need a bathroom and if they do, as I was told, one "holds" it. Men, on the other hand, can relieve themselves anywhere, anytime and often did.

We stopped on the street to buy fruit. A young man wandered around with a scale on a pedestal slung over his shoulder. If you needed something weighed, he was the go-to guy, apparently.

A goatherd wraps his face to keep from breathing the dusty and dirty Kabul air.

On the way back to Kabul we got stuck in a traffic jam approaching a tunnel. We never found out what caused the delay; no one seemed to care. But it was an hour at least without moving, and it was hot and the bus was not air-conditioned. A dead body was being transported in the vehicle next to us. Muslims bury their dead as soon as possible after death and they do not embalm the body. There was a smell and although we were told it was disrespectful to look, we all did.

Also stuck in the traffic jam was a truckload of bulls which were not happy with the delay and the heat. A happier crew was some camels and their driver. The young man smiled and posed for us. His camels were snotty and could not be bothered. Camels are like that. As a big city kid, I was fascinated. A camel, for God's sake.

All in all it was a great trip: beautiful scenery and a brief look at another city and one that was not bombed. And one wonderful meal.

And thanks, we think, to the fish meal, I had my first experience ever with food poisoning. Only two of us got sick; we had eaten off the same plate of fish chunks. My fellow sufferer was found by one of his housemates clutching the floor of their bathroom and was taken to the hospital to be rehydrated. I made the trip from bed to toilet, bed to toilet until I had rid myself of most of my GI tract and the world finally came back into focus.

Afghanistan is not for the weak in mind or body!

21

Health Issues

Don't panic when you see how thin I am — I am not sick; just recovering from a few bacteria that took up residence in my gut. (Email to my son, May 30, 2010)

Kabul is not a healthy place. And not just because of the random car bombs and suicide bombers. The air is polluted with dust, fecal matter, car exhaust and other noxious fumes.

According to the Afghanistan National Environmental Protection Agency, a main cause of the air pollution is the surfeit of old and smoking vehicles. It is estimated that there are 900,000 cars in Kabul. Additionally, in the winter anything and everything is burned for heat, including tires and plastic. Diesel fuel is used to generate electricity. Many of the poor people live high on the hills surrounding Kabul. There is no piped water to these houses and sanitation is lacking. When it rains or snows, the runoff carries dirt and soil as well as fecal matter to the streets below where it is ground down and then whipped into the air with the rest of the dust from the many unpaved roads throughout the city.[1] And then there are the brick kilns which burn rubber and old car tires and discharge their toxic gases.

I often saw men (and some women) clutching scarves or masks to their mouth to keep out the dust. The women wearing burkas held the cloth tight to their faces.

And then there was the nonpotable water supply. We all drank bottled water, but it is nearly impossible to keep from swallowing water in your daily life, particularly if you take showers and forget and let water splash your face and dribble into your mouth. Which I did. And at school they served tomatoes and other fresh vegetables, which I suspect were washed in the local water. Many of us unthinkingly (or stupidly) ate the vegetables.

We all got sick — and over and over for some. Coughs, colds and intestinal problems. Lots of intestinal problems. Some of my colleagues were not just physically fatigued, but psychologically fatigued by the constant onslaught of bugs. Others tried to get through the experiences without embarrassing themselves. One of those was me.

Most everyone picked up *Salmonella typhi*, the causative agent of typhoid fever. I was vaccinated against typhoid before I left the States, but you can still contract the disease — though an attenuated version. In my case, I had no symptoms. Other colleagues were hit hard by the disease. In fact, one had to be "medevaced" out of Afghanistan for treatment.

The other common infection came from *Helicobacter pylori*,[2] a bacteria that lives in the stomach and is strongly associated with peptic ulcer disease and gastric cancer.[3] It is endemic in countries with a poor water supply and generally is asymptomatic.

There were two places in Kabul where internationals went for medical care. One was a hospital, down the road from school, called (oddly) Cure Hospital. The other facility was a clinic run by a German group. I visited the clinic on several occasions; the first time was in November when I picked up a lung infection.

Generally speaking, my colleagues and I spent most of our time inside and were not exposed to the rotten air. I was really not conscious of its bad quality and had no particular problem breathing due to the pollution or the elevation. I did walk outside on the new campus property several times a week, but that was the extent of my outside activities. However, in November we were granted a "vacation" when all the schools were closed in response to the swine flu scare. During that free period, my exercise buddies and I went to the new campus every day to walk and run. My contention is that the increased time outside upped my risk of picking up an airborne infection. Which I very quickly did.

I coughed and coughed. And my right lung hurt. And I coughed some more. I did not eat much. After four or five days of lying in bed without any magical healing taking place, I called my mentor, Jane. "Please, could you come get me and take me to the clinic?"

And she and her driver did. By that time I was extremely weak, with barely enough strength to walk downstairs to the car. The driver did not really know where he was going and so the first place we stopped was not the clinic, but I still had to make my way through the entranceway in order to discover his error. Finally, we found the place and I got checked in. Everybody in the waiting area let me go in front of them. I probably didn't look well. The doctor confirmed that I had a lung infection, gave me a prescription and I left and got better.

The next time I went to the clinic was to get drugs. I had an American prescription for some Valium-esque drug that made it easy to fly if you were terrified of heights and/or enclosed spaces. I was going away for Christmas and would be taking several flights, and I knew I would need drug help. The young man at the clinic's reception desk told me that I didn't have to see a doctor if all I needed was a prescription filled. The pharmacist was not terribly interested in checking my prescription; she just asked me how many pills I wanted. (Prescription laws seem to be lax in Afghanistan.) At first I thought maybe a dozen, but then I thought what the heck: "Could I have two dozen?" I held by breath. "No problem," was the response. And off I went with my happy pills.

And the last time I visited the clinic I found out I was carrying around a dose of both *Helicobacter pylori* and *Salmonella typhi* and got the worst scare of my Kabul stay.

It was just before I was to return to the States, and I decided to go to the doctor about my inability to put back on the weight I had lost during my lung-infection, non-eating days. To my surprise, she hit my chest a few times (and she had a boxer's punch) and declared my lungs clean. She also took some blood and when those results came back, she casually announced that I had not one but two bacterial infections. And here was the kicker: one of the tests was a screening test for cancer in the GI tract and it had come up positive. Well, there I was — in a German doctor's office in Kabul, Afghanistan, hearing that maybe I needed to go get an ultrasound to see if I had a cancer growing in my abdomen. It was a great moment.

When she found out I was going back to the States, she suggested I wait and have it done there — this is Afghanistan, after all, she reminded me. I announced that I would like to know now rather than in a month if I had cancer, thank you very much.

She gave me a note and the "address" of a place where a sonogram could be performed: "In front of Jamhoriat Hospital." I showed the paper to Kareem, the escort, and after some discussion, he and the driver decided they could find this doctor. Oh, this did not sound good. Once they found the general area of the address, the van pulled over and Kareem and I got out and began walking down the street — a street of only men — I in my headscarf and my escort, who looked like a bodybuilder, thank God.

He peered at storefronts and now and then stopped and asked someone a question in Dari. Finally we were directed up a dark and dirty stairway and down a bleak hallway. (The approach reminded me of a secret abortion clinic.) A door at the end opened to a room that the word *barren* doesn't begin to describe. A man sat behind a desk — the receptionist. Actually "greeter" might be more appropriate. His desk was empty. No pencil, no paper, no files, no computer — nothing but a cell phone. Three benches and a chair lined the room. A few men were sitting along one wall and a few women (one in a burka) were sitting along the opposite wall.

Kareem explained to the "receptionist" that I wanted to see the doctor and showed him my paper from the clinic. I was directed to a chair — not with the men on the one wall, or the women on the opposite wall, but to a chair on the third wall.

And there we all were, the men, the women and me and my escort. Kareem did not know where to sit, or rather with whom to sit, and so he stood. And we all assiduously looked at our feet. As I've already mentioned, I'd been told that there were three genders in Afghanistan: men, women and foreign women. Here it was in full play.

During the course of what turned out to be a short wait, several men showed up, which necessitated a total shift in the seating arrangements — since men are not — that's ARE NOT — going to sit next to a woman in a public place. The women all moved to the bench next to me and we got back to staring at our feet.

Then the doctor came out and asked if I was the American woman who needed a sonogram. I thought it was pretty obvious that I was the American. Foreigners, particularly white-skinned and brown-haired foreigners, tend to stand out in Kabul. I think he'd gotten the word that there was a *khareji* (foreign) woman waiting to see him and he wanted to check me out. He said if I was in a hurry (an understatement, for sure) he could take me first. I looked around the room to see how everyone felt about me jumping the line — one man said it was OK with him. May that man's soul rise to heaven.

So I was ushered into the doctor's office/examination room. Knowing that men and women generally didn't touch in Afghanistan, I was wondering how this particular procedure was going to work. Usually with a sonogram it is necessary for the device to be placed on the skin, and I didn't think a layer of clothes in between was going to help the diagnosis. Besides, the area of concern was my intestinal tract, which could be deemed more personal than checking for an ear infection. For some reason he placed a blanket over my covered legs; it was unclear why.

The doctor told me that he worked at Kabul University — which I took as his attempt to reassure me that he knew what he was doing. When the sonogram was completed, without any undue embarrassment on either of our parts, he filled out a letter to the clinic on his computer stating that he had not observed anything out of the ordinary — which I took to mean no growths, cancerous or otherwise. What bothered me about the letter was it appeared to be a stock one and I wasn't absolutely sure it was generated as a result of my exam. I did not care; I wanted to go. When I asked him how much the sonogram was: $5. Oh my.

One of the first things I did when I got back to the States was go to the doctor and make sure I hadn't picked up any more bacterial diseases, had gotten rid of the original ones and that I didn't have some unnamed growth taking over my intestines. As it turned out: I was disease — and infection — free.

Once again, Afghanistan is not for the weak in mind or body!

22

Plants and Seasons and Travel

I'm staring at the middle of a cloud this morning—there is No Color anywhere—it is incredibly claustrophobic. (Email to a friend, November 24, 2009)

Plants

Along with my stuffed animals and books, I also brought some plants to Kabul. In the States I collected succulents, plants like cacti that seem to thrive with little care and less water. A couple of mine bloomed continuously throughout the year.

It crossed my mind that it might be illegal to take plants into a foreign country, but I decided to risk whatever should happen if I got caught. As they say, easier to receive forgiveness than permission. So on the last day in Charleston I took cuttings of several of my succulents, including a Crown of Thorns which was in bloom, put them in a plastic sandwich bag and packed them away in my suitcase.

As my luggage spent longer traveling than I did and ended up spending several extra days in the Kabul airport, I had little hope that the plants would survive. But they did. Hardy succulents, indeed.

Then I had the problem of pots. I found some rough clay pots behind our guesthouse and I dug up some dirt (more like clay) from the garden. The guards just watched and smiled. Crazy foreigner. I asked at school if I could have a bit of sand to mix with the dirt I had collected and the next day a cart full of sand was dumped by the front gate.

I also bought pots. On the way to and from Kabul's city center I saw vendors selling colorful pots at the foot of the hill we passed. I asked one day if we could stop so I could buy one or two. Transport did not like making unscheduled stops, but I promised I'd be quick. And I was. Got out, stumbled across the board bridging the wide drainage ditch, with escort in tow.

I'd point at a pot, *chand* (How much?). The vendor would answer in Dari and the escort would translate for me. *Bale* (Yes, I'll take it). He and the vendor kept banging the pots. Why? To show that they were good solid pots. Imagine that.

We were in and out of there in less than ten minutes.

Once again I was reminded: The problem with a foreigner going to some places and staying too long is that someone might call his friendly Taliban buddies and there might be a problem.

I stopped (never for long) along this road several times to get pots, and I also bought more than one cactus during my stay.

My room faced south and I had a nice sunny window where I placed my plant collection. They thrived and tried to bloom. In fact I brought these plants back to the States with me. Again, I knew it was probably illegal, but no one said anything. (The plants were doing fine until I gave them to my son and he stopped watering them. Oh well.)

One of my daily chores was to water everybody. Usually one doesn't need to water succulents every day since they store water, but Kabul is extremely arid and the soil dried out fast. And I liked the idea of tending my little garden. I paid Jawid, our houseman, to water the plants when I left for Christmas and spring break.

One day I made plans to visit a guesthouse down the street that had a huge garden and a greenhouse. Our gardener was "commissioned" to walk me down the street and presumably protect me from the insurgents. The gardener apparently was not pleased to have to accompany a woman down the street, as he walked ten paces in front of me. If I tried to catch up, he just walked faster.

The guesthouse's gardener greeted me and proceeded to show me his "babies." He had rosebushes, of course, but his prize plants were huge stalked flowers that I later found out were dahlias. They were deep purple and magnificent. He looked at those blooms like gardeners the world over look at their flowers: bursting with pride and a huge grin. He let me take his picture alongside his plants.

He had a few succulents in his greenhouse and agreed to let me have a cutting of one of them.

In the spring small pellets appeared around the rosebushes. Fertilizer, I thought. Thinking it was a form of Miracle-Grow or some packaged store-bought variety that we buy in the States, I went so far as to pick some up to get a better look. When I glanced up I saw the guards watching me, smiling. Probably wondering why I had picked up a handful of what turned out to be goat turds.

Another embarrassing moment in Afghanistan.

A burka-clad women makes her way home on a cold wintry eve.

The Seasons

I arrived in Kabul in August and it was hot and dry. The roses were blooming, and the air was filled with dust (and other particulate matter). The leaves on the trees were gray-green and grimy from lack of rain.

Then one day in October the leaves turned yellow, and the next day they fell to the ground. Fall was over and winter began.

By November we could see the snow on the mountains ringing Kabul. The gardeners started trimming the rosebushes to the ground. Trenches were dug to direct snow run-off.

And in our guesthouse, two diesel-fueled heaters were moved in. At school the boiler had clicked on and I "liberated" a space heater from the school storeroom.

On the street, men mixed mud and straw and added another layer to their flat roofs. Street vendors hung heavy coats on the wrought-iron fences, and folded woolen blankets were for sale along the curb.

Fuel, of all kinds, appeared along the road: wood, tires, trash and diesel. Most everything burns and most everything is used in Afghanistan — including animal poop. I was told that when it is dried, it doesn't smell. It's efficient, cheap and readily available from the herds of sheep and goats.

I had heard the stories of the terrible Kabul winters of the past. (I suspect they were particularly bad for Afghans because reliable electric power was a recent phenomenon in the city.) As it turned out, the winter I was in Kabul was quite mild. We were all issued a woolen blanket (as well as other bed linens) when we arrived. In August I found the blanket to be too heavy to sleep under, so I had it shipped to the basement, thinking I could recall it in the winter months. As it turned out I didn't need it.

It did snow that winter, but not much in Kabul. One morning from my perch on the third floor I saw nothing but a sea of white. I waved at a neighbor who was shoveling snow off the flat roof of his house. He waved back. I think he smiled.

We lived in comfort in the guesthouse. We had an air conditioner that also pumped out heat (sometimes), extra heaters and a generator as backup when the power went off. For many Afghans winter is not pleasant but just another hard time to get through. Most Afghans do not have extra heaters or generators. Power can be intermittent, and in the refugee camps, I suspect, it is nonexistent.

Spring came like gangbusters. And with a Bang. On March 16 we got this message from Kabul security forces.

> Good morning,
>   Please be advised that Security Reports indicate that ... insurgents intend to conduct rocket attacks on Afghan New Year's Day (Mar 21) targeting the ... area of central KABUL city ... and BAGRAM Airport (possibly also KABUL Airport). This department recommends no travel to these areas over the up and coming weekend.
>   Regards

And this note from our campus security.

> Restrictions on movement into the city are now in place. Your cooperation in this matter is greatly appreciated.

What fun! Rockets to celebrate the New Year! And spring break started that week as well; some of us left town. I went to India.

When I got back, Kabul had settled down — more or less. The cherry trees were blooming and then came the roses. And the neighbors bought a pair of peacocks. The flowers on the new campus were poking through the gravel, including a bright red poppy. Not the opium-producing variety, however.

Spring cleaning started. The men in the school transport office dragged their rugs outside, added soap and hosed them down. They then took off their shoes, rolled up their pant legs and jumped around on the soapy rugs, presumably helping in the cleaning process. Or they may have simply enjoyed jumping around on soapy rugs.

In our neighborhood, rugs were hauled into the yards and sprayed and hung to dry. We could see into several yards from our guesthouse, but we rarely saw any of our neighbors. But on one spring morning I saw a woman next door cleaning her rugs. She wore a head scarf. I wondered whether she always wore a scarf while doing her housework or whether she was only wearing one in that instance because she knew she could be seen by others.

Travel

Oddly enough I felt safe in Afghanistan. People asked, "Weren't you scared?" My standard reply was that I was too stupid/naive to be scared. But the reality was that in a perverse way, I felt safe in Kabul.

There were times when I ventured outside of the suggested security procedures — I took a cab or went walking about without an escort — and then there was an element of tension and anxiety, but generally I felt safe. Safe as being wrapped in a cocoon, ferried here and there and then tucked behind walls and bolted gates with armed men standing watch.

Far more terrifying than living in Kabul was trying to leave Kabul.

In addition to the winter break for Christmas, there were several other "long weekends" during the year. Most people got out of town. Six weeks was about the limit, they said, of how long we (the internationals) could go without a break from the oppressive restrictions of life in Kabul, and, of course, the chance of being in the wrong place at the wrong time and being blown up.

The city of choice to visit was Dubai in the United Arab Emirates. Actually it was one of the very few places that you could get to from Kabul. One airline flew to Frankfurt, Germany, which was a bit far for a couple of days. The other possible destination from Kabul was New Delhi, which I visited for spring break.

The first time I left Kabul was at Thanksgiving. I was recovering from a lung infection and I didn't want to be part of the Thanksgiving celebration that was being planned at one of the guesthouses. I wanted to be able to walk outside by myself without a head scarf and I wanted to breathe some clean air.

But first I had to get out of Kabul. Here's what happened that first time and it would be repeated every time I tried to take leave.

Generally there was more than one of us internationals trying to get out of town at any one time ,and we always seemed to be scheduled on the flight that left early (early!) in the morning. Transport, who always drove us to the airport, insisted on picking us up hours before and to assure that we would be beforehand "on time." (An expression that had absolutely no meaning as far as flight times were concerned, as I was soon to learn.)

Driving up to the airport we met with more and more armored vehicles and men with guns. It appeared to be heavily guarded, at least for vehicular traffic. However, it looked fairly accessible to foot traffic. Hmmmm.

First thing: pull up to the outer gate. We all get out of the van with our luggage and the van drives through the gate to wait for us, after we and our luggage had been searched. (It was unclear why a search occurred on leaving the country.) Since the whole luggage search procedure was a hassle, sometimes we wouldn't move all our bags out of the van. It was easier that way. (No one seemed to notice or care.)

Then we women would enter this shed through an opening covered by a filthy cloth hanging in shreds from the door frame. Inside were generally two women who would look in our handbags and feel our breasts and pronounce us OK.

The next stop was another shed, with long tables and two or three airport personnel opening suitcases and searching the contents. Or not, depending. That first time when I was tired and just a little sick and needed to get out of town desperately for some air, the security man kept yelling at me and I finally figured out he wanted me to put my heavy suitcase onto the table for his inspection. I snarled back (probably shouldn't have) "I can't pick the damn thing up." And right away our escort, who had been standing beside me, picked up the bag and put it on the table. They never did much of a search; I think it was a control issue.

On to the airport parking lot. Our guys could walk us up to the first building — that never seemed to be used for anything — but that's as far as they could go. Here's where it started to get expensive.

A young man would come up with a baggage cart, swing on our luggage and off we'd go: through the building-with-no-activity to a gate, where passports and tickets might be reviewed, and then to a bus. There you'd part with some money and another young man would put your bags on the bus — and he wanted money.

Then, when we arrived at the main departure building, another young man would meet us with his cart and get us through the next screening area. Our luggage would be X-rayed or whatever and Ihad to go into a closet to be searched by one or two women. Again, the breast-pawing action. (I have small breasts and I couldn't imagine what they thought I could be hiding amongst them.)

And finally our "porter" would deliver us (and our bags) to the baggage check-in counter and more money was handed over. By this time, many of us had given up hope of ever seeing an airplane.

Baggage check-in was generally easy-ish, but a feeling of dread started to creep in about this time.

After passports were checked and the baggage was weighed and whisked off, we wended our way upstairs (that's stairs, no escalator) to another area where our passports were checked — again — and then through another line where our carry-on luggage was inspected. We took off our shoes and removed our laptop from its satchel. No bottled water. And then you were free to find a seat in the waiting room and wait — unless, of course, you were called to the side for further inspection, as I was one time. I was motioned into a large closet where another woman wanted to touch my breasts. I do not know what set off the alarm, maybe my cute breasts, but it scared me witless. The feeling of dread was overpowering.

But now after all that, a chance to sit down. Or maybe try and find a bathroom. And wait.

Flights from Kabul were either by Pamir, Safi or Kam Air. And though they had a schedule of flights and you could buy a ticket on a specific flight, that flight just might not make it out of the hangar. They were never on time. Never.

There was a loudspeaker, but it was not generally in use. There was no announcement of flights, no flight arrival/departure board. Sometimes we'd hear what could have been "Pamir" or could have been "Kam Air" over the speaker. It was hard to tell, so no one paid much attention.

My first time trying to get out of town I was terrified that I had missed my flight because I was still sitting and waiting long after the scheduled time of departure. After that first attempt, I relaxed a bit — "scheduled times of departure" are a Western construct and have little meaning in Afghanistan.

So everyone sat and waited and waited. Then, suddenly, I'm not sure what happened. A whisper slightly heard or perhaps a change in air vibrations, who knows. But at some point in lemming-like fashion everyone in the room just knew — it was time.

And everyone moved to the set of doors leading to the outside. There was no other ticket check-in booth — just a set of doors where someone stood and glanced at your ticket and directed you down the stairs and onto the tarmac. Then onto another bus and finally to the line to get on the airplane.

Here's where everything speeded up. Everyone started to move faster, hurry down the stairs, run to the bus, hurry hurry. Apparently once it was decided that the plane would actually be taking off, there was the chance it would take off without you. So hurry, hurry.

Upon arrival at the plane itself, everyone was stopped again and our passports checked — again. Afghan citizens had to show a visa or some other exit papers in order to leave the country.

It was a harrowing experience. I was always scared that somehow I wouldn't be able to get out. That I wouldn't have the right paper, the right ticket or the right permit and I would not be able to leave.

And, further complicating the process: it is not in the Afghan's soul to form a queue, and so if there were Afghans waiting in what I wanted to be a line, the Afghans would be standing around and there would be a great deal of jockeying for position.

And, of course, there were always the "Very Important People" who were simply escorted to the first position.

On the other hand, there was no problem getting into Afghanistan. No baggage checks, no body checks — just come on in.

Once out of Kabul, however, Dubai was heaven. As I wrote to a friend:

I'm in Dubai — land of buildings and buildings and more buildings. But it has clean air and clean water.

I can go outside without a driver or an escort. I don't have to wear a head scarf and men don't stare at me like I'm sin incarnate. I also don't seem to be the object of any kidnapper's fantasy. There are no bombed out buildings. There are no sad blue burka-clad woman begging on the streets, no wide-eyed filthy little boys and girls with hands out. There really is a world outside Kabul, Afghanistan, and I had almost lost touch with it. They say you have to get out of Afghanistan every six weeks to get your head straight — it's been three months for me.

Dubai is a bright and clean city and not really designed for walking, but that's what I did. There was a mall not far from my hotel. I walked there and then I walked around and around and up and down and in and out of stores. It was wonderful. When I got tired, I sat at a café and ate or had a Coke and read my book and watched people. In that mall in Dubai everyone in the world seemed to pass by at some time or other: Americans in shorts and black socks, Arab men in their brilliantly white dishdasha robes followed by one, two or three wives in their black chadors. There were men and women and children and I heard English and French and German and Arabic. Everybody was there.

I also visited the *suq* (bazaar) and walked about the river park. I could even go to a bar and get a drink in Dubai. When I first asked about finding one, the receptionist told me that alcohol was forbidden in the Emirates (which I knew), but, she said, there were rumors that a certain place around the corner might serve foreigners. Okay then. Actually Dubai is the looser of the Emirates as far as acceptance of Western ways, particularly with regard to the use of alcohol.

I also felt safe on the streets of Dubai, even at night. One place I frequented was down an alley and through some back streets, but even at 10 at night people were out and about and there was no sense of danger. I was told that there is little crime in Dubai because the ex-pats there on work visas would be summarily deported if caught for wrongdoing. As far as the Emiratis themselves were concerned, the censure of the community for breaking the law apparently was enough to make them obey the law. Whatever ... it worked.

After a dose of Dubai — three days was usually plenty — I was ready to jump back into life in Kabul.

I took several other trips from Kabul during my stay there: to England and Greece at Christmas, to India during spring break, and I revisited Dubai several more times. During each excursion, the time spent in airports had scary moments and interminable stretches of mind-numbing boredom.

In some airports only my hand luggage was searched; in others I was searched. I remember standing at the luggage carousel in a foreign country where English was not the first language and watching it go round and round and not seeing my bags. And again, round and round, and still no bags. And I could feel the panic. And then on the next swing through, my luggage would appear. The relief was palpable.

I was to meet my son in Manchester at Christmas. The airport had two terminals: I walked to the other terminal to meet his plane coming in from the States. He had also walked to the "other" terminal to meet my flight from London. I stood at the wrong terminal at the right door and watched people come through, until no one else was arriving. And no Jason. I was starting to panic. Where was he and how was I going to find him? I got help from one of the attendants who could see I was near to tears and called the other terminal to see if someone was there and looking for his mother. There was. And soon here came my world-traveling son, looking as relieved as I felt.

And then on my way back to Afghanistan after Christmas there was the flight from Athens to London that was to connect to a flight to Dubai and then to Kabul. (Not the most direct of connections.) But there was a huge storm in England and all flights were cancelled. Everyone in the airport was stuck and waiting in lines and hoping to get on a flight. British Airways did a great job for everyone. When I heard I was on a direct flight from Athens to Dubai, I was elated. I did not care about the nine-hour wait that I was also promised; I was on my way. And I had books to read.

But then when I got to Dubai the scheduled plane for Kabul had sprung a gas leak or lost a wing or something. In any case — no flight.

Then it got sticky. No one seemed to know when the next flight to Kabul might be. Maybe at 11 that night —14 hours later — and maybe there would be a seat for me and the other six people who were stuck. No one had an answer for us. So I made instant friends with another woman and we spent the next many hours in Dubai, eating, walking in the park and hanging out at the airport and holding our breath. It was not a pleasant experience.

By the time I got back from that trip I was so thankful to be back in Kabul. I wrote a blog about my home there, and posted pictures of my bookcase and my stuffed animals.

Traveling out of Afghanistan was an unnerving proposition for me. I think I felt untethered when outside the country. After all, I had a place in Afghanistan, my things were there, and my job was there. Perhaps one always feels untethered when traveling, but it seemed to be worse for me because of where I was "tethered."

23

Politics

The mayor of Kabul has just been convicted of helping himself to about $16,000 and was sentenced to 4 years in jail. However, he's back at work. What I hear is that the standard procedure here—go after the little guy and ignore the fact that $10 million is moving through the Kabul airport EVERY DAY. (Email to friend, December 13, 2009)

Bureaucracy

Bureaucracy is alive and well in Kabul, with a particular Afghan twist.

In Afghanistan, I often felt I was in the midst of a Kafka novel. Things seemed to make sense to everyone but me. (I think other internationals were also "confused.")

Word went out at the university one week that we all needed to get our "permits" renewed or issued or something. The Human Resource Department at school dealt with the problems and joys of having internationals on staff: troubles with visas, work permits, passports and in Afghanistan anything else that the government chose to inflict upon the populace.

The administrator who was in charge of those issues had English skills better than mine in Dari, but he became nearly unintelligible when it came to explaining the machinations of the government. Near as I could figure out, some kind of permit was in error. I think it was the one we were supposed to hand in when we left the country and then get renewed once we were back in the country. I handed one over the first time I left. Actually "hand over" is not the right expression. I "put it in a box" on a table that appeared to be filled with other similar documents. An international told me later that I shouldn't turn in the permit, since doing so meant being without it which meant I would have to get it renewed, and that meant a trip through bureaucracy. Interesting idea!

But apparently some government person decided it was time to renew these permits. I was bundled up with an escort and a driver and off we went to the Ministry of Who Knows What. And after passing through checkpoints and guard shacks and searches, we ended up in a small room ringed by chairs filled with mostly Afghans. The escort moved me to the front of the line. There really was no line, as lines or queues are "not done" in Afghanistan; rather he moved me up to the first position. We were always shuffled to the first position by our escorts; behavior probably not appreciated by the other "customers" waiting. No wonder internationals were not always viewed in the best light.

So I was maneuvered across the room where an extremely tiny woman was sitting behind a small table that served as a desk and which was the only writing surface in the room. Her legs did not reach the floor.

She studied my passport and studied me and studied the escort and finally stamped a 3 × 5 card, which was covered with impressive writing, and handed it over.

In the corner of the room sat a box, about the size of two wastebaskets. It was filled with 3 × 5 cards with impressive writing on them. I couldn't tell if they were being filed or thrown away.

The next time I left the country, I did not turn in my permit. I didn't really know what it was about. So I kept it. It was easier that way.

Corruption

According to the 2009 report of Transparency International, a worldwide watchdog group, Somalia remains the world's most corrupt country, followed by Afghanistan.[1]

The rampant corruption in Afghanistan is one reason most everything needs work in the country — the roads, sewer system, water supply, power grids — everything. Kabul's mayor's conviction for awarding a contract without competition was only one example.[2]

An excerpt from the Al Jazeera article about this case follows:

> The mayor [Sehebi] was the first high-profile Afghan politician to be convicted since a task force was ordered by Hamid Karzai, the Afghan President, to target government officials suspected of criminal activity. The solicitor general's office is also looking into claims that Sehebi failed to account for millions of U.S. dollars that were meant to pay for reconstruction projects. Sehebi, who has appealed the conviction, is refusing government orders to give up his post and claims he is being targeted as part of a political vendetta.

The government departments involved in the case have so far **failed to agree on who should enforce the court's ruling.** [*Emphasis my own.*]

Neither the courts nor the police say they have the ability to seize Sehebi and send him to jail and he is still receiving police protection at city hall.

My comment: It is clear that few corrupt officials have been removed from office in Afghanistan, since apparently there is no established policy as to which government department is responsible for doing so.

You could not make this up.

Corruption is not just a Western construct about Afghanistan. Even the students at the university were aware of the problem. One of the English classes presented writings by the students to a general university audience one afternoon. Some read their poetry and some read from their short stories. One group put on a quick play which revolved around a young man trying to get a permit from a government employee. The transaction went through smoothly once the applicant handed over a suitcase of money.

Everyone laughed.

24

The Blame Game

I want to come home. This country is so sad—and so broken—no wonder the Afghans have this weary and resigned look about them. (Email to my son, March 22, 2010)

Most of us internationals at school tried to act as good guests in Afghanistan and kept our thoughts about the condition of the country to ourselves. It was too dreadful and too hopeless.

One member of the faculty was an Afghan whose family had left during the troubles. He had gotten his degrees in Europe and, against his mother's wishes, had returned to Afghanistan and was teaching at the university. We talked a lot about what was going on at school, but not at all about his country. Again, too hopeless.

I made a connection with one Afghan man that I worked with. I think it started with a smart remark on my part about the bureaucracy of trying to get travel papers to take a trip. And then he made a smart remark back. I started stopping in to see him regularly and would start with, "Nothing's wrong. No problems for me today."

I was in his office one day when the hopelessness of life in Afghanistan had drenched me with sadness. I could feel tears bubbling up. "Do you think anything will ever change?" I asked.

"With what?" he said. Although I think he knew what I meant. Maybe he was thinking of an answer. Maybe he was stalling.

"With everything here," was my reply.

He looked me right in my eyes and said, "We don't know who we're fighting." It was intense and heartbreaking.

I sent him an op-ed piece titled, "Why Afghanistan's Politics Are Stranger Than Fiction" (BBC News, Tuesday, November 24, 2009).[1] The last section was titled "Miserable Existence."

Children in rags tug at your coat and you fish out a battered Afghan note worth barely 50p. Then there are 10 small children grabbing at your hand and you cannot get away because the children are blocking the pavement.

And the road is a stream of rainwater, sewage and mud. A woman with a baby under her burka sees you giving money to the children and begs for some herself. And when you say you have no more one small boy persists and walks with you for 20 minutes until you relent and your reward is a genuine smile of gratitude. The daylight thickens into night and there are no street lights.

By the glow of a storm lantern, men sift through second-hand clothes on a cart and try to pick out a good winter coat. Meanwhile, a young man desperate for work weeps as he talks to me and through accusing tears says: "You've been here eight years now, and what have you done?"

"Why is my country so miserable?"

His comment was that I should try to enjoy my stay in Afghanistan as much as I could and try not to worry about what couldn't be changed. Talk about hopelessness.

He was willing to take the blame for his countrymen's failure to build their nation, but what about the rest of us?

In November, the local *Afghanistan Times*, which was printed in English, ran a picture with the following caption:

Students at ... Middle School appear in the school's annual examination in Kabul City on Monday. Lack of proper school buildings is a major problem facing the students.[2]

"Major problem," indeed. That was understatement of the highest order. The picture showed several students, all boys, writing, presumably, their test. They are dressed in winter clothes. Three of them are sitting on chairs pulled up to a long board that is serving as their desk. There is no outside wall to whatever they are sitting under. It is hard to tell if it is a real roof or simply a tarp. The outside looks gray. The children look cold.

USAID (Agency for International Development) makes its own ironic contribution to the Afghan economy. We passed one of its billboards on our way into town. It included a picture of an Afghan girl and some text in Dari, presumably about the wonderful things that USAID was doing to help Afghanistan.[3]

Part of the USAID funds are allocated for roads and other infrastructure. This particular billboard was planted on Darulaman Road, the poster child for how a road project can go so terribly wrong.

Work on the last few miles of the road, in the vicinity of the university and the guesthouses, was ongoing: widening, paving, demolishing, paving, and repaving. The story was that by the time the money filtered down to the people who actually were going to repair the bombed road in the first place, it had been depleted to the point where subgrade materials were used, subsequently requiring renovated stretches to be patched, repaired, and redone regularly. Hence the road remained a dust-strewn highway with parallel access roads complete with patchy pavement.

And then an example of a totally useless endeavor: spanning this road was a walk-over that was also in construction for the full nine months I was in Kabul. It was funded by the Turkish government, so I heard. Construction was stalled for several months — money problems, we were told — and then restarted. No one thought it would get much use. It was much easier to cross the road by crossing the road.

Once again, I thought of the many things that Afghanistan could use in the way of infrastructure, and walk-overs were not high on that list.

And then there were the Taliban — who were not just fighting NATO troops for control of Afghanistan. They were also disrupting the country's development by preventing the delivery of services to its citizens.

Here's one example: Kajaki Dam.[4] A turbine designed for a hydroelectric project in Helmand province (Taliban territory) intended to supply electricity for southern Afghanistan may never be installed. In August 2008, the turbine (220 tons) was dragged by 2,000 British troops on a five-day convoy through enemy territory. The project has been put on hold, however, since the huge amounts of cement required to install the equipment cannot be delivered safely. NATO has been unable to secure 30 miles of road against Taliban attack for the length of time needed to move the cement. The parts have been inventoried and stored away until a better time.

What was going on or not going on in Afghanistan was a sore subject amongst the internationals I knew. Some of us felt it was our (read the U.S.'s) fault in large part. The feeling was that Afghanistan had been "abandoned" in 2003 when the U.S. invaded Iraq, and that was one reason so little progress had been made in nation-building.

And there seemed to be little accountability in some areas for where and how aid money had been spent. Where was the clean water? Where were the decent roads? Where was the constant supply of electricity? Where was the money, the billions and billions of dollars that had been thrown at Afghanistan by the State Department — in particular USAID and the military? It was shameful. And once we got started moaning and groaning about the lack of progress, the deplorable conditions and the part our (U.S.) government had played — well, the conversation just spiraled into silence. Nothing to be done. So we all just did what we could — which wasn't much except to show a few Afghans that some of the guests in their country were truly sorry.

And, of course, we couldn't ignore Afghan President Karzai and his corruption-laden government's contribution to the deplorable situation in

Afghanistan. And then there were the extremists (the Taliban and their ilk) who were still wreaking their own brand of havoc on the country.

There was plenty of blame to go around.

But more importantly, not much seemed to be changing. The Afghan people are a hardy sort and will survive. I just wished their lives could be better. It all felt hopeless.

25

Stranger in a Strange Land

The Cats are here with me and we just had some cheese. (Email from my son, March 23, 2010)

Afghanistan was somewhere on the edge of the Himalayan Mountains. That's what I knew about Afghanistan before I left my safe house in Charleston, South Carolina. And I knew it was a Muslim country and women wore burkas. I tried to imagine what else and I couldn't.

I would have been better prepared for life in a grass hut in the wilds of Africa than I was for life in Kabul, Afghanistan. I would have known that there would be no TV, no roads, no air conditioning and no restaurants in a sub–Saharan village. But Kabul was a city, for heaven's sakes. It had roads, but many were impassable with rocks and pits. It had buildings, but many had been bombed and had falling roofs and holes in the walls. Animals in the street, yes, but plenty more cars. Sure there was TV, but most programs were in Dari or Hindi. And, yes, there were "D" grade movies in English but no way of knowing when they might be aired. We had electricity — most of the time.

We didn't have to pump water from a well, but we couldn't drink what came from the faucet. There was a mail service, but no one used it. Buses offered transportation, but no one other than Afghans rode on them.

I knew that Afghans were Muslims and that Islam was the state religion. But I was not prepared for how serious Afghans are about their religion and how much it permeates their lives and would touch my life in Kabul. It was hard not to be aware of the fact that we were in a Muslim country. The students were accommodated during Ramadan: they were given a break at the end of each day's fast. School was closed for the festival of Eid. The bathrooms were designed for pre-prayer ablutions. One of our Afghan faculty members was castigated by the cafeteria staff for eating lunch during Ramadan and an Afghan staff member was not allowed in a restaurant that served alcohol unless one of us signed for him.

Mosques seemed to be on every street corner. And, of course, there were the calls to prayer that we heard at school and at the guesthouse. Hotels provided prayer rugs for their guests.

Many Muslims pray wherever they happen to be when a call to prayer is heard. Some Afghans at school had prayer rugs in their offices and prayed there. The school had a prayer room and prayer rooms were available in many public facilities. I had been in a grocery store and seen someone kneeling in prayer behind a counter.

My most memorable exposure to Islam was during a dedication ceremony at school for the new gym. Benefactors had been invited and the staff and faculty were also "invited" to attend. It was an important occasion and quite solemn. In place of an invocation, common in Western society, a man took the podium and sang verses from the Holy Qur'an. It was quite beautiful. And startling. (Clapping was not appropriate at the finish.)

As Westerners, we did not, of course, generally have to observe Islamic practices. However, sometimes we were forced to because, for instance, pork products were just not sold. But that wasn't a big problem. "Pretend" pork was fine with me. And although the Qur'an forbids the use of strong drink or gambling, as Westerners we were allowed to buy alcohol and there were in fact secret gambling games, if one was interested.

One cultural difference that most of us women honored was modesty; in particular we covered ourselves up. No bare arms, no bare legs and generally we covered our hair as well. Actually this turned out to be a blessing in disguise. I got my hair cut professionally once while in Kabul, by an Afghan beautician who then left for the States. One of my housemates went to the UN compound regularly for a wash, cut and dye job. Most of the time the rest of us either scraped our hair back into a ponytail or cut it ourselves — with varying degrees of success. The head scarf covered a lot of bad hair days.

The concept of time was also different in Afghanistan. I had never considered time in either a linear or nonlinear sense, but in Afghanistan I learned the words polychronism and monochronism. In the Western world, monochronism is a way of life. Time is linear. One thing happens and then another thing happens. And in a practical sense: you take a turn and then I take a turn. It also puts Westerners in lines: queuing up for tickets and food. In traffic this translates to the car on the right having the right of way. In

Polychronism is characterized by many things happening simultaneously. In the business world the difference between monochronism and polychronism is the difference between being on time and being late. In school, my first class started at 3:00. But no one was there at that time. "Where is everyone?" I would ask. "They're coming," was the reply. And in traffic it is the difference between an orderly progression of cars and the madhouse that is traffic in Kabul.

We were all recognizable as strangers — as non–Afghans. In the United States it is hard to tell a non–American from an American — we're supposedly the melting pot: an intermarried group of clans and tribes and races and ethnicities.

In Afghanistan, as in many other countries, the difference in looks between the locals and foreigners is patently obvious. For a while after I arrived I would start a description of a student with "She has black hair..." until I realized all Afghans have black hair. Their hair is beautiful and they have mostly dark eyes. Most of us internationals had degrees of brown or blond hair and blue, green, or brown eyes. So we were easy to spot as foreigners, not even considering that many of us rode in security vans, often with UN painted on the side.

But the Afghans I met, in large part, were welcoming. I've said it before, but it bears saying again. The Afghans are incredibly hospitable people. Sometimes they acted like hosts who were not quite sure why their guests had arrived and what they wanted, but they were consistently polite.

"Good morning. How are you?"

And they smiled and nodded.

One of my favorite "gotcha" moments in Afghanistan was the first time I visited one of the grocery stores that catered to internationals. Not only were its shelves stocked with hair color kits, hand lotions, Kit Kat bars, Campbell's soups and cereals by Kellogg, but it also had a life-size Santa Claus standing at the entrance. He was holding a brass trumpet and at the flip of a switch would play a lively jazz tune and bob his head to the beat. It made me smile and I took it as a welcome to us foreigners as Santa Claus is not a visitor to Afghanistan.

And Christmas is not celebrated in Afghanistan either, but at Christmastime, several of the stores on Chicken Street had tiny pine trees outside, decorated with tinsel or plastic flowers or lights.

An unusual backdrop was available at the local photo shop. (It always seemed that we needed photos for something or other.) You could choose to have your picture taken in front of a scene of Mickey Mouse and his friends having a tea party. Another welcoming touch, I thought.

I could never have been prepared for what I found in Afghanistan. It was a strange land and we were strangers there. However, I was generally charmed by the country and welcomed by its beautiful people.

26

Lest I Forget

Well, you were looking for adventure! (Email from a friend, October 25, 2009)

Kabul was a war zone. There were armed men ... at school, at the guest-house, at the restaurants and bars and hotels. And their guns were real.

And then there were the bombings.

One morning towards the end of February there was a loud boom. I pretended for as long as possible that it was a sonic boom. That's what it would have been in South Carolina. In Kabul, however, it was not a sonic boom — it was a car bomb. And then the phone dinged and I got this message:

> There has been a large explosion and gunfire heard in the Shar-e-naw area; all International staff are restricted to their guesthouses until further notice.

and....

> Early reports suggest that at least three attackers stormed the Safi Landmark Hotel/Kabul City Center. It is understood that one BBIED [body-borne improvised explosive device] detonated near the entrance and SAF [small arms fire] is still being heard.

And that was the limit of the initial information we received in the guest-house and the limit of information that we received all day.

We had no Internet access. One of our roommates had a call from his home in Nigeria. His friend obtained the details from the Internet and passed it on to us. I heard from an escort that it was "very bad." And that "some Indians had been killed," but that was the limit of my Dari and his English.

We found out later that 18 people were killed and 36 injured, many of them Indian nationals. It was a car bomb and a suicide bomber. The Taliban claimed responsibility for the killings. Another sad, sad day for Afghanistan.

The day before was the Prophet Mohammad's birthday. I wondered about the juxtaposition of events as murder is forbidden in the Qur'an.[1]

Another really bad time occurred towards the end of the spring semester. The new president of the university had invited all faculty to his house over several mornings for coffee and sweet rolls and conversation. It was my turn that day. We were all sitting around just waiting for everyone to show when he excused himself to take a call.

When he came back, I guessed from the look on his face and asked, "How bad was it?" Then we all got messages on our phones about the attack and the advisory to stay wherever we were.

A suicide bomber had driven his explosive-laden vehicle into a convoy of American military vehicles. Eighteen people were killed and 52 injured. The blast was on Darulaman Road just down from the palace and next to the new campus area where we exercised.

I wasn't at the new campus that day; my two exercise mates were, however, and when the bomb blasted a hole in the wall they ran. One told me later that he was glad I wasn't there. (Me, too.)

We didn't dodge bullets in Kabul. We didn't dash from building to building avoiding the fighting in the streets. War zone, perhaps, but we weren't under attack. As I was told, Kabul isn't Mogadishu or Baghdad. It's just a city with people bustling here and there and cars careening around the streets and buildings. Mind you, some of the buildings have holes in them, some are falling down and there's the presence everywhere of the Afghan police in their green uniforms with their guns. But no one is shooting at anybody — usually.

There were, however, the random car bombs and suicide bombers, but the operative term is "random." If you were in the wrong place at the wrong time, you could be dead. But I couldn't think about that. And so I didn't. And neither did most other people, I suspect.

Although we were surrounded by "security," there was no way to thwart the random acts of violence. No way to protect ourselves except to leave the country. So mostly people just kept moving from point A to point B, me included.

The "war zone" nature of living in Kabul would raise its mean head now and then when a staff member had a relative or friend who was in the wrong place and died.

The extremists were out there and they were trying to make a point. What they did, however, was kill people — mostly innocent Afghans and those who had come to help.

27

And Goodbye

I'm ready for you to come home. (Email from my son, March 22, 2010)

My contract ended at the end of May, but contract renewal negotiations began in February. I had to make a decision: stay or go home.

Early in my stay in Kabul, Dee and I had a dinner together at her guest-house one night. Pizza and vodka. She lived just around the corner from me and I could simply walk to her place — with an escort. During the course of our conversation I told her that I liked being in Afghanistan. "What's there to like?" was her response.

Since I had not left the "wow" and "this sure is different" stage, I was taken aback by her reaction. How could she say that, I thought? She hadn't given the country a chance. As it turned out, she stayed on and I came home.

I did like being in Afghanistan. The people I met were kind, the students were engaged, teaching was rewarding and the mountains were breathtaking. I felt useful. And I was in Afghanistan — that faraway and fierce place of my dreams.

But Afghanistan could be a difficult place to live. It is classified as a third world and undeveloped country for good reasons. Intermittent power, undrinkable water and roads strewn with rocks and craters. But I didn't complain — that much.

And stuff broke — lots of stuff and much of the time. And things happened seemingly at the whim of the government. But generally I went with the flow: The printer's not working, oh well; school is closed, OK. No fabric softener, I can cope.

But the worst part for me was being segregated from Afghan society. It wasn't complete segregation; I did get out and about and see people and shop and go to work. But I couldn't go where I wanted when I wanted by myself without a lot of hassle.

On the most basic level, I could not open the gate and walk outside by myself without calling Transport or a taxi or arranging for an escort of some kind. We were nearly as sequestered as were many Afghan women, who could not leave home unless accompanied by a male relative. I knew the rules were designed for my protection, but believe me, the thought crossed my mind more than once: Were the guesthouse walls keeping the bad guys out, or keeping the good guys — me — in?

If I hadn't lived in a guesthouse, I would have had more freedom. I would have rented my own place, as several internationals did, if I had stayed longer. But for the duration of my stay, I lived in a guesthouse and generally abided by their rules.

But sometimes, particularly late in my stay, the living conditions overwhelmed me and I had several meltdowns. One time in particular I went berserk.

That occasion occurred because I often felt caged in, behind walls and barriers and gates and rules. From my window, however, I could see a bit of green trees, some rooftops and towering over all, the hills of Kabul. That was

Here's the final arrangement of hinged panel, green mesh and chair which allowed me to see beyond the balcony of our guesthouse.

the view I saw every time I looked up from my computer. Space. And that view made me happy and bolstered my mental health.

The wall of the balcony was part concrete topped by decorative metal latticework. In late spring the "powers" decided that since we could see out, others could see in and so it must be time to build another barrier.

A green see-through mesh was strung on a frame and attached to the latticework, obscuring the view of my mountain from my desk. AAARRRGH. I went crazy. I grabbed my handy screwdriver and unscrewed screws, cut mesh and tore open the offending curtain of green. My precious vista opened again. The guards below in the courtyard watched me with wonder, but

This young girl at Skateistan is required to wear a helmet — and a head scarf.

did not say anything. Dumbfounded, I'm sure, at the crazy American woman. I also cried.

Subsequently, the head of facilities agreed to attach the mesh in front of my window to hinged panels that I could swing open. Unfortunately, they also swung shut when the wind blew and I had to drag a chair outside to prop them open. This arrangement couldn't have been uglier, but it worked for me.

I told my students about this escapade and they remarked, "You're brave, Dr. Travis." And my reply, "Damn right, I came here, didn't I?" got a round of clapping.

But again, generally I remained calm — except when I didn't. And even though our lives were restricted — no zipping off to the movies (there were no movies) or driving a car or simply walking about — I had a somewhat satisfying social life. My contacts were expanding through the trivia games and slowly I was becoming part of the network of internationals and women in Kabul.

New opportunities presented themselves at school. As I mentioned, the university was only four years old and entering an awkward growth stage. The old guard was being reassigned or let go and the new guard, of which I was one, was working on transforming the university from a Potemkin village façade to a legitimate learning institute. I began working with institutional research data and I felt positive about my future at the university.

I went to Afghanistan to save the world. However, saving the world wasn't working out like I had hoped. I began to think it was going to take more time than I had available, but I found ways to help.

One such opportunity involved an operation I had heard about before going to Afghanistan — Skateistan. As strange as it sounds, and Afghanistan is a most strange place, Kabul has a skateboard park, a facility built by an Australian and funded by several European countries. Boys and girls skated together until they were in their teens and then at separate times, and everyone had to attend classes at the facility. The classes, however, were nontraditional and stressed communication and other social skills, rather than reading, writing and arithmetic. The management attempted to get a mix of ethnic and socioeconomic groups. Therefore, some of the children already went to school and others were street children with no schooling.

I visited the park several times and volunteered to help upgrade their operations manual. I had hopes for a continuing association with them.

A small victory for me occurred when I introduced one of our drivers, Sayed, to the world of skateboarding. He had never heard about the park and only barely knew what skateboards were. On the other hand, he was an athlete (a wrestler) and, as he said, tried to keep himself in shape. The day he drove me to the park, he watched some of the children perform and the next thing tried it himself and fell, providing a good laugh for the children.

But, being athletic he soon got the hang of it and began zipping around with some ease. He expressed an interest in the operation and wanted to come back and volunteer. I don't know if he ever did. I was invited to an opening at the park and we tried to arrange it so that he would be the driver and he'd be able to visit again on University time. Something came up and I didn't go, but I obtained an invitation for him. I don't think he went. I hope something finally came out of that introduction.

On another occasion, I tried to intervene on behalf of another Afghan employee. Emad, one of the drivers, wanted to attend the university and he wanted a job there.

His personal situation was bad: he told me that he was the head of his household and responsible for his mother and his siblings, and had been since he was nine years old when his father was killed. (This is not an unusual situation in Afghanistan; many of the fathers, older brothers and uncles of young children were killed during the troubles in the 1980s and 1990s.)

He knew he was trapped and that his life was destined to be filled with disappointments if he did not try to change his situation. His job as a driver at the university paid good money (for Afghanistan), but he wanted to go to school. He wanted to improve his English and he talked a lot with me and the other internationals, picking up new expressions and ease with the language. But if he quit the job and applied at the Kabul University where the tuition was less and English was not a requirement, then he would have no money to support his family. So his only hope was for another job at the American University that would ensure him better hours so he could go to school under their assisted tuition program.

A job became available at the time and I spoke to the school about Emad and wrote a letter of recommendation for him. But Administration told me that they wanted to hire a woman for the job. A terrific idea, of course; more women needed to be hired. On the other hand, it was sad for this young man and his future.

Trying to help wasn't always effective.

I did have some successes. I wrote a recommendation for one student of mine, who was part of the Hazara ethnic minority. Here's how he thanked me:

Having your support, I feel as I no longer belong to a minor ethnic group in Afghanistan same as my ancestors. I no longer feel to be deprived of getting educated. Your reference letter gives me a new spirit.
Once Again THANK YOU.

The decision to leave was a difficult one and perhaps the wrong one. I knew after the episode of the Green Mesh Blocking My View that I had to get out — time for a trip to Dubai or I needed to go home. I was kind of hoping that the university would let me go to the States for the summer, see my son and touch things American and then make a decision about returning. That didn't happen. So I planned to leave in May.

I never really had a chance to make a formal announcement to my students that I wouldn't be coming back in the fall — word just got around. I meant to tell my buddy Aziz separately about my decision, but during the course of a conversation about fall classes, I was forced to blurt out the news that I wouldn't be back. "You're kidding," was his response. I felt sad that he found out about my plans in what may have appeared to be in a casual and offhand manner.

And I regretted that I had contributed to the instability in many of my students' lives, including the life of Aziz. There's a tremendous attrition rate at school — not only because of the problems in Afghanistan, but also because of many problems at school.

Some students asked, "Don't you like our country, Dr. Travis?" and "Why are you leaving?" It was rough. "Yes, I love your country, but I miss my son." And, of course, they knew of my frustration at being isolated. One thing I really missed in Kabul other than the obvious (my son and pepperoni) were my cats, Mojo and Slick. Mojo is part Maine coon and has the most luxurious feel to his fur. I could almost feel it thousands of miles away.

I knew that some of my students would miss me. Some wrote me notes. One said,

> It makes me sad that you are leaving, but am happy I was your student for two semesters.

Another wrote:

> Your class increased the significant figures of my heart for chemistry.

I felt that I would be missed not just by my students, but also by some of the faculty. One professor, a repatriated Afghan, told me he was sorry I was going, "If people like you leave, what hope does the university have of improvement?"

But by the end of May I was ready to leave. I had had enough. I was safe enough at school and in the guesthouse. But after that the safety quotient went down — way down. I had gone to the City Center to shop, and it was bombed. I exercised on the property of the campus and a hole was blown in the wall. The bombing nuts seemed to be getting closer to me. It wasn't fear so much but thinking how useless it would be for me (or anybody) to get blown up and for what?

I began formulating twenty-five-words or less responses to:

"How was it?"

"What's it like?"

"Do they hate us?"

"Is the surge working?'

and

"Should we pull out?"

I didn't know if I was up to answering!!!

One more trip to campus tomorrow morning to turn in the cell phone and computer and then a wait until 1:15 when I get picked up to go to the airport for my 4:30 flight. There was a suicide bomber on that road on Saturday—luckily he just blew himself up. (Email home, May 30, 2010) Sitting here waiting for transport to take me to the airport. Said some goodbyes to my colleagues at school—a few that I will quite miss. Looking out at the wondrous mountains outside my window and thinking I'm going to see the wondrous ocean quite soon. Well, here I go. (Email home, May 31, 2010)

Epilogue

One of the pleasures I so enjoyed upon my return were showers with continuous hot running water. Sometimes I stood in my shower for a long time just because I could.

When I first returned I was overwhelmed by the differences between Kabul and Charleston, South Carolina. Driving to the grocery store on a bright morning on the smooth causeway, not having to dodge large rocks or holes, I enjoyed the golden-lit miles of water and marsh grass on both sides of the road and the bright red-pink oleanders blooming and power lines overhead zinging electricity to lights and hair dryers and and....

Being in Afghanistan was not just a move to another country or into another culture, but a tectonic shift between two states of being. More like a dream — a powerful dream that still bothers me, titillates me and makes me smile. Sometimes, now that I'm back, images from Kabul overlay whatever I'm doing. Holding my necklace of Afghan jade beads brings back the dream day I bought them from a tiny shop in the Chicken Street area. A dull green, they're the color I wish my eyes were. I went back to the same shop later for another necklace for a friend.

But when I stepped off the plane in Charleston, South Carolina, and saw my son and got in my car and drove for the first time in many months, I woke up.

Chapter Notes

Chapter 1

1. www.cia.gov/library/publications /the-world-factbook/index.html.

2. www.arzurugs.org.

3. I have changed the names in this memoir to protect everyone's privacy.

4. Islam is the state religion of Afghanistan and its holy book, the Qur'an, forbids the use of "strong drink" (Surah 5:90).

5. The people of Afghanistan are Afghans. An Afghani is the unit of currency; as of this writing it is worth about U.S. $.02. (*Afghani* can also be used as an adjective.)

Chapter 2

1. In fact, "due to the poor safety record of its civil aviation oversight system" all Afghan airlines were prohibited from flying into the European Union in 2010 (http:// www.eubusiness.com/news-eu/airline-security). When I was there Afghan airlines could fly only into Dubai, New Delhi and Frankfurt, Germany.

2. www.undemocracy.com/S-2001–11 54/page_9.

3. www.isaf.nato.int/history.html.

4. www.auaf.edu.af. Also from their website: "The idea for the American University of Afghanistan (AUAF) emerged in 2002, based on the success of other American Universities around the world." In 2005, First Lady Laura Bush visited the university site and announced a substantial grant from the United States Agency for International Development (USAID) to launch the institution. The first students enrolled in 2006. The University is "Afghanistan's only not-for-profit, non-political, nonsectarian, non-governmental, private and independent, internationally-supported university." There are several so-called American Universities around the world (e.g., Dubai, Beirut, Cairo) which are not associated with one another but which all try to use American curricula and standards. Also, classes are taught in English.

5. This is an aspect of polychronism as opposed to monochronism. Things happen when they happen not as a result of some cause. A happy outcome may be assured, but no steps are necessary to accomplish it. I found the concept intriguing, particularly as it relates to "taking turns" and forming lines.

Chapter 3

1. Surah 5:6.

Chapter 4

1. Afghanistan is not on daylight savings time. In fact it's one of the few places in the world that uses an offset time zone: offset by a half-hour from the standard time zones. September sunrise in Charleston, South Carolina, was at 7:00 A.M.; in Kabul it was at 5:30.

Chapter 5

1. Surah 2:173.

2. "T.I.A.," I was told, originated in re-

sponse to conditions in Africa: "This is Africa." A similar sentiment and expression could be applied to Afghanistan as well.

3. The Afghan Constitution has the same provision. Article 83: "At least two females shall be the elected members of the House of Peoples from each province," and Article 84: "The President shall appoint 50% [of House of Elders] from amongst women."

Chapter 6

1. Ramadan is the month of fasting which occurs in the ninth month of the Islamic calendar — it is considered one of the Five Pillars (or duties) of Islam.

2. In fact, Afghans can travel to only 26 countries without applying for a visa first. As an American I could go to 155 countries without prior permission. I could hop on a plane to England, for instance, fill out some paperwork and soon I would be walking around Trafalgar Square. (I did have to have a visa to visit India from Kabul, however.) Henley & Partners, which specializes in international immigration and citizenship law in collaboration with the International Air Transport Association, publishes a global ranking for countries based on the travel freedom their citizens enjoy. The top on the list is the U.K.; 166 countries allow British citizens to visit without first obtaining a visa.

3. In her book *The Favored Daughter,* Fawzia Koofi comments that she "battled against my brothers very hard to remain at school and be independent, and even though they didn't like it, they loved me and they let me do it." Koofi may be a candidate for president of Afghanistan in the general election of 2014.

Chapter 7

1. www.afghan-web.com/politics/current_constitution.html.

Chapter 8

1. The Qur'an enjoins women (and men) to be modest (Surah 24:31; 33:35).

Chapter 9

1. www.iec.org.af/eng/index.php.
2. www.ecc.org.af/en/images/stories/pdf/ECC%20Final%20Report%202009.pdf.

Chapter 10

1. Reuters, November 2, 2009.
2. Pigs are considered nasty creatures in Muslim countries and the Qur'an specifically forbids the eating of swine flesh (Surah 2:173).

Chapter 15

1. Sebastian Junger, "The Lion in Winter," *National Geographic Adventure,* March/April 2001.

Chapter 16

1. http://www.afghan-web.com/kabul-museum/intro.html.
2. Reuters, July 6, 2009.
3. Ibid.
4. Kabul has a yearly rainfall average of 10.7 inches; Charleston, South Carolina, 52.1 inches (http://www.weatherbase.com).

Chapter 17

1. Surah 33:53.
2. Surah 4:1, 7:189.
3. Surah 4:4, 4:11–12, 4:128.

Chapter 18

1. Surah 2:219.

Chapter 19

1. Rory McCarthy, *The Guardian,* February 27, 2001.
2. Governors are not elected in Afghanistan but appointed by the president.

Chapter 20

1. http://www.nytimes.com/2010/02/08/world/asia/08road.html.

Chapter 21

1. www.afghan-web.com/environment/kabul_air_quality.pdf

2. Oddly enough, my Ph.D. research was an epidemiological study of *H. pylori* in children. Who knew that one day I would become so intimately involved with the bacteria?

3. National Institutes of Health, 1994 "Consensus development panel on *Helicobacter pylori* in peptic ulcer disease." *JAMA* (1994) 272:1, 65–69. A. Nomura, G. N. Stemmermann, P. H. Chyou, I. Kata, G. I. Perez-Perez and M. J. Blaser, "*Helicobacter pylori* infection and gastric carcinoma among Japanese Americans in Hawaii." *New England Journal of Medicine* (1991) 325: 1132–1136.

Chapter 23

1. www.archive.transparency.org/policy_research/surveys_indices/cpi/2009/cpi_2009_table.

2. Afghanistan News Center, December 12, 2009, Aljazeera.net, Qatar Central South Asia, December 2009.

Chapter 24

1. BBC News, November 24, 2009.

2. *Afghanistan Times*, November 24, 2009.

3. USAID's 2010 budget for Afghanistan was US $2 billion (http://afghanistan.usaid.gov).

4. Jon Boone, "Taliban Stalls Key Hydroelectric Turbine Project in Afghanistan," *The Guardian*, December 13, 2009.

Chapter 26

1. Surah 5:30.

Index

Numbers in **bold italics** indicate pages with photographs.